M   S

AND EDITING

International
Ford Madox Ford
Studies
Volume 9

General Editor
Max Saunders, King's College London

For information about the Ford Madox Ford Society,
please see the website at:
http://www.open.ac.uk/Arts/fordmadoxford-society/

Or contact:
Dr Sara Haslam S.J.Haslam@open.ac.uk
Department of Literature, Open University,
Walton Hall, Milton Keynes, MK7 6AA, UK

Or:
max.saunders@kcl.ac.uk

IFMFS is a peer-reviewed annual series. See the end of this volume for a
full list of previous titles. Guidelines for contributors, including a full list of
abbreviations of Ford's titles and related works, can be found by following the
links on the Society's website. Abbreviations used in this volume are listed
from p. 281.

Ford Madox Ford, Modernist Magazines and Editing

Edited by

Jason Harding

Amsterdam - New York, NY 2010

The Ford Madox Ford Society

[Ford] should serve as a model for editors of literary periodicals; his respect for the artist, the creative being, and his determination to nourish genius made him an invaluable figure in those opening years.

Malcolm Bradbury, 'The English Review',
London Magazine, 5 (August 1958), 46-57 (p. 57).

Acknowledgements for Illustrations

Cover photograph: Ford in the 1920s. Courtesy of the Division of Manuscript Collections, Cornell University Library.

Title page illustration: Ford c.1915, pen and ink drawing.
© Alfred Cohen, 2000

Illustration on p. 5.
The cover of the first issue of the *English Review*.

Illustration on p. 6.
The cover of the April 1924 issue of the *transatlantic review*, featuring contributions from Joyce, Stein, and Hemingway.

The paper on which this book is printed meets the requirements of "ISO 9706: 1994, Information and documentation - Paper for documents - Requirements for permanence".

ISBN: 978-90-420-3055-8
E-Book ISBN: 978-90-420-3056-5
©Editions Rodopi B.V., Amsterdam - New York, NY 2010
Printed in The Netherlands

THE
ENGLISH
REVIEW

DECEMBER 1908

THOMAS HARDY : HENRY
JAMES : JOSEPH CONRAD
JOHN GALSWORTHY : W. H.
HUDSON : COUNT TOLSTOI
H. G. WELLS : THE MONTH
EDITORIAL : THE UNEM-
PLOYED : THE PERSONALITY
OF THE GERMAN EMPEROR
THE BALKAN QUESTION
REVIEWS

LONDON : DUCKWORTH & CO.

the

VOL. I. No. 4

April 1924

transatlantic

Edited in Paris
by F. M. FORD

review

CONTENTS

NEW YORK:
THOMAS SELTZER Inc., 5 West 50th St.

LONDON :
Duckworth & Co.

PARIS :
Transatlantic Review Co

CONTENTS

GENERAL EDITOR'S PREFACE

Max Saunders

Ford Madox Ford has as often been a subject of controversy as a candidate for literary canonization. He was, nonetheless, a major presence in early twentieth-century literature, and he has remained a significant figure in the history of modern English and American literature for over a century. Throughout that time he has been written about – not just by critics, but often by leading novelists and poets, such as Graham Greene, Robert Lowell, William Carlos Williams, Anthony Burgess, and A. S. Byatt. His two acknowledged master-pieces have remained in print since the 1940s. *The Good Soldier* now regularly figures in studies of Modernism and on syllabuses. *Parade's End* has been increasingly recognized as comparably important. It was described by Malcolm Bradbury as 'a central Modernist novel of the 1920s, in which it is exemplary'; and by Samuel Hynes as 'the greatest war novel ever written by an Englishman'.

During the last two decades, there has been a striking resurgence of interest in Ford and in the multifarious aspects of his work. As befits such an internationalist phenomenon as Ford himself, this critical attention has been markedly international, manifesting itself not only in the United Kingdom and the U. S. A., but in Continental Europe and elsewhere. Many of his works have not only been republished in their original language, but also translated into more than a dozen others.

The founding of the present series, International Ford Madox Ford Studies, reflected this increasing interest in Ford's writing and the wider understanding of his role in literary history. Each volume is normally based upon a particular theme or issue, and relates aspects of Ford's work, life, and contacts, to broader concerns of his time.

The theme for this ninth volume is 'editing', understood in a variety of ways; especially Ford's editing of influential modernist magazines, and the practice of editing his work. It thus also extends a larger-scale project, implicit in the conception of this series, and developed more fully in the previous three volumes, of charting Ford's engagements with other writers and artists, and with a plethora of cultural movements, forms, and media.

The main emphasis here necessarily falls on Ford's contribution to modernist magazine culture through the founding and editing of two landmark literary magazines: the *English Review* in London from 1908; and the *transatlantic review* in Paris in 1924, and the various forms of editorial friendships which resulted. These journals alone would have earned him a place in literary history, even had he not also been a prolific novelist, critic and poet. Ford had an extraordinary eye for good new writing, and though his tenure as editor was short-lived in each case, the groups of writers he gathered around his reviews helped to define Modernism in its pre-war and post-war guises. This timely volume benefits from the recent upsurge of scholarly interest in modernist magazines and periodical culture, which has given us a new understanding of the role of such publications in the production of Modernism, and of the institutions and networks that fostered it. (One manifestation of this recent attention is the excellent Modernist Journals Project, which has digitised all the issues of the *English Review* edited by Ford.)

Ford's two phases of magazine-editing coincided with upward curves of his creative and critical success. His trilogy of books about *England and the English* first got him 'boomed', and his trilogy of English historical novels, *The Fifth Queen*, about the court of Henry VIII, built on that success. But it was his work on the *English Review* which turned him into a modern novelist. While he hammered out his views on literature and culture in his editorials on 'The Critical Attitude', he was writing *A Call*: his breakthrough novel of modern passion and repression, also serialized in the *Review*, that paved the way for *The Good Soldier*.

The *transatlantic review* was launched when Ford had just written *Some Do Not . . .*, the first novel of *Parade's End*, and knew he had finally recovered his powers after his wartime 'shell-shock'. In 1924, while editing the *transatlantic*, he was producing some of his best prose – especially his tribute to his former collaborator, *Joseph Conrad: A Personal Remembrance*; and the beginning of *No More Parades* (the second volume of *Parade's End*) – as well as writing regular reviews and essays for other periodicals, especially the Paris edition of the *Chicago Tribune*.

During both his editorial phases his critical success earned him the authority to influence literary movements. And he began to earn more money from his writing as well: money he was only too happy to plough back into literature, by financing his editing; though also, in each case, he was with a companion with her own financial independence, willing to invest in Ford's literary publishing ventures.

He was perhaps too chaotic, especially where money was concerned, and too outspoken in his critical views, to be a successful long-term editor. On the other hand, the brevity of both his editorial experiments, together with his appetite for starting again despite previous losses (he was working to launch a third magazine months before his death) makes us ask whether he didn't also, at some level, need them to fail. That is, when he said he started the *English Review* with 'the definite design of giving imaginative literature a chance in England' (*LF* 39-40), didn't he imply that it had little chance; and didn't his loss of control of the review bear out that pessimism? In the case of the *transatlantic review*, Ford's 'prospectus' pitched the claim even higher. Keying into a widespread post-war internationalism, the review was not merely going to give imaginative literature a chance to exist, but to prove more effective than the League of Nations at securing lasting peace. How could that possibly go wrong? Ford was affected by the romance of lost causes, and had acquired from his grandfather Ford Madox Brown an altruistic need to help underdogs, together with a cynical expectation of getting bitten by way of thanks. The failure of his editorial plans perhaps confirmed this altruism-plus-cynicism.

The volume also gives a sense of how the story of Ford's editing ramifies beyond the covers of his reviews. His numerous editorial friendships were to prove important in other ways, and were reworked by fellow-writers such as Conrad and Wells. Some of the essays give a sense of how the concept or practice of editing also ramifies through Ford's other work. This is too vast a subject to be contained within the covers of a single volume; and, in the spirit of the whole series, it is hoped that the pioneering work here will open up new routes into Ford's less-researched writing. After all, he was a prolific contributor to periodical culture in other ways, too, as a writer for others' magazines and newspapers. He continued to write for the *English Review* under his successor, Austin Harrison, and wrote regularly for magazines such as the *Outlook*, the *Little Review*, *Poetry*, the *New York Herald Tribune Books*, and the *American Mercury*. Ford's pre-war experience of the literary world informs much of his earlier fiction, from *The Inheritors* (1901) to *Mr Apollo* (1908) and *Ladies Whose Bright Eyes* (1911). His editing of the *English Review* in particular informs novels like *Mr. Fleight* (1913), and the mostly unpublished 'Mr. Croyd'.

He also carried his editing over into his literary contacts more generally: regularly acting as an unpaid copy-editor for aspiring writers, reading their manuscripts and advising them about style, and how to make cuts. We see the effects of his editorial help on figures such as Lawrence, Pound, and Rhys here, when he was editing a review; but much the same story could be told of the longer periods when he wasn't, from his collaboration with Conrad, to his last transatlantic crossing, to France and death in 1939, with about two hundred manuscripts in his possession according to his first biographer Douglas Goldring (who had worked with him on the *English Review*).

Finally, thinking about Ford's editing touches on two aspects of his own work: his self-editing: his revising of his own work, either when drafting it, or when revising it for publication or re-publication; and the editorial questions posed by his own writing practices. These questions too are explored here; again in such a way as to open up new territory. Carcanet's 'Millennium Ford' series has already done invaluable work in giving his writing new currency; but much of it still awaits rediscovery and analysis. His books have only recently begun to benefit from scholarly editing; and far too much of his vibrant writing for periodicals remains uncollected. Many of the essays published here originated as papers given at a conference at St. John's College, Durham University, organised by Jason Harding, which also included discussion of the editing of *Parade's End*, by members of the team producing Carcanet's forthcoming critical edition of the tetralogy. The essays published here give a taste of how questions about Ford and editing will remain fruitful ones. And they also let us see ways in which his editorial principles shed light on his fiction, which attempts the same act of balancing the best traditions with avant-garde experimentation.

The series is published in association with the Ford Madox Ford Society. Forthcoming and projected volumes will be announced on the Society's website, together with details of whom to contact with suggestions about future volumes or contributions. The address is:
http://www.open.ac.uk/Arts/fordmadoxford-society/

INTRODUCTION

Jason Harding

On the launch of the *transatlantic review* in the winter of 1923, T. S. Eliot sent an open letter to Ford Madox Ford; a public salute from one great periodical editor to another. 'I welcome with extreme curiosity the appearance of the *Transatlantic Review*' Eliot began, adding 'Personally, I have always maintained what appears to be one of your capital tenets: that the standards of literature should be international.' The bantering tone of Eliot's letter – with its talk of 'antagonism' and the possibilities of future 'attack' – signalled an uneasy détente between Eliot's cosmopolitan *Criterion* and this new outlet for the best work of the international avant-garde.[1] In private, Eliot was sometimes less than flattering about Ford. However, as an elder statesman of letters in the 1950s, he came to regret the tone of his communication to the *transatlantic review*: 'I seem to have assumed an odd tone of authority in addressing a man older than myself!'[2] This comment marked a belated recognition of Ford's achievement as editor. Strikingly, Eliot's declaration in his 1954 goodwill message to John Lehmann's *London Magazine* that 'The first function of a literary magazine, surely, is to introduce the work of new or little known writers of talent'[3] echoed Ford's prospectus for the *transatlantic review* three decades earlier, where the 'first' objective of the magazine had been unambiguously stated as 'widening the field in which the younger writers of the day can find publication'.[4]

If introducing the work of young writers is the criterion for judging literary magazines, then Ford was a more successful editor than Eliot – arguably the greatest periodical editor of the twentieth century. Although 'editor' is too narrow a term to encompass the manifold ways in which Ford acted as amanuensis, collaborator, mentor – even lover, to more than one female contributor – with generations of talented writers. A measure of Ford's achievement was his success in soliciting important work from the best late-Victorian (Hardy, James, Conrad) and Edwardian (Wells, Bennett, Galsworthy, Forster) authors, as well as his remarkable 'discovery' of *les jeunes*, not only before the First World War (Lawrence, Lewis, Pound,

Douglas) but including those individuals (Bunting, Rhys) who would
carry his modernist precepts for good writing beyond the Second
World War. Pound said of Ford that 'he kept on discovering merit
with monotonous regularity';[5] praise he never bestowed on Eliot. This
editorial difference was largely a matter of temperament. Ford's
charismatic nurturing of creative rather than critical writing is evident
in the fulsome encouragement offered by his letters, a contrast to the
more businesslike editorial correspondence that a contributor might
expect to receive from Mr. Eliot, just as Ford's louche *transatlantic
review* soirées on the Quai d'Anjou were more invigorating gatherings
than *Criterion* luncheons in stolidly bourgeois Knightsbridge. Ford's
indiscretions, impetuosity and candour did not always prove as
effective as Eliot's editorial caution, leading to disagreements and
quarrels, but they ensured, as Conrad pointed out at the height of their
acrimonious split in the *English Review*, that contributions to Ford's
magazines were invariably 'for a *person* not for an *editor*'.[6]

The emphasis of this volume falls naturally and necessarily on
Ford's personal relations with his contributors. Philip Horne's richly
documented account of Henry James's appearance in the *English
Review* (drawing upon hitherto unpublished correspondence) reveals
that there was more to this connection than the 'Master' con-
descending to his 'literary flatterer'. Not only was James key to the
first issue, graced by his fine ghost story 'The Jolly Corner', but later
submissions, 'The Velvet Glove' and 'Mora Montravers', dramatised
what Horne terms a 'creative convergence' towards Ford's editorial
distaste for the commercialised vulgarity of Edwardian popular taste.
Conrad's high-minded artistic principles were also considered essential to the success of the *English Review*, albeit in this case Ford
was keen to press his claims as a collaborator (perhaps even as a secret
sharer). Alongside serialising Conrad's memoirs (initially dictated to
the editor), Ford published under the delicious nom-de-plume 'Baron
Ignatz von Aschendrof' extracts from their collaborative novel *The
Nature of a Crime* (later revived in the *transatlantic review*). Although
they fell out in the summer of 1909, Gene Moore argues that scholars
have been intent upon posthumously widening this gap by seeing
egregious portraits of Ford and Conrad in each other's fiction. On the
contrary, Moore finds a good deal of Ford in the sociable Editor of
Conrad's story 'The Planter of Malata', an indication that their work
on the *English Review* was more fruitful than partisan commentators
choose to think. Similarly, Nick Hubble strives to get back behind

Ford and Wells's lampoons of one another following their abortive negotiations to co-found the *English Review*. His chapter takes its cue from Douglas Goldring's recollections of Ford editing the magazine at the Shepherd's Bush Empire. Hubble then proceeds to consider the 'performative' nature of Ford and Wells's literary portraits. That they appear as comic turns in each other's fiction can suggest these writers were as much collaborators before a burgeoning popular audience, rather than straightforward rivals. In the first issue of the *transatlantic review*, Wells praised Ford as one 'of the greatest editors alive' (*TRev* I [Jan. 1924] 94).[7] By this time, Wells was not likely to attract great interest in avant-garde circles: he did not appear again in Ford's new Parisian review (although his wife Catherine did). Hubble reflects upon why Wells – a star performer at the *English Review* – tends to get pigeon-holed today as one of modernism's duller acts. This judgement would have surprised the literary agent J. B. Pinker: professionally speaking, Wells and Bennett were the most successful authors in his stable.

Edgar Jepson recalled that Ford's unusually exacting editorial standards emboldened him to reject submissions from some of the literary doyens of Edwardian London, making him powerful enemies.[8] In this metropolitan milieu of back-scratching, it was refreshing that Ford should recruit one of his outstanding contributors from a board school in Croydon. Jessie Chambers, who enthused that the 'coming of the *English Review* into our lives was an event, one of the few really first-rate things that happen now and again in a lifetime,'[9] sent several of D. H. Lawrence's poems to Ford and received an enthusiastic reply. Ford later claimed that he needed to read only the first paragraph of Lawrence's story 'Odour of Chrysanthemums' to appreciate the author's 'genius', however, as George Hyde's chapter explains, this touchy intellectual outsider from working-class origins soon came to resent the proprietorial claims of his editor. Goldring's story of Ford's bath-tub exposure to Wyndham Lewis is equally full of symbolism. Seamus O'Malley's chapter considers the oddity of this editorial collaboration, which nevertheless proved mutually beneficial, both in terms of Ford's introduction of Lewis's travel stories to an advanced English readership but also Lewis's mediation of *The Good Soldier*, in the pages of *Blast*, to a younger avant-garde audience. Ford occasionally received a satirical blast from the self-styled 'Enemy', but then who didn't? His friendship with Pound proved to be the most durable of his editorial relationships, founded, as Peter Robinson's subtle chapter demonstrates, upon a lifelong respect for Ford's concern that poetry be at least as well written as Flaubertian prose. Pound's memory of Ford rolling on the floor in helpless laughter doubtless impressed upon this ambitious aspirant a due regard for *le mot juste*; although, as Robinson points out, Ford himself could not always be said to substitute the sublime for the ridiculous. Nor was his selection of poetry for the *English Review*, although it showcased W. B. Yeats and most of the poets later contained in the first 'Georgian' anthology, entirely above reproach.

Richard Price's chapter shares with Robinson's a poet's fine-grained responsiveness to the nature of their craft. The necessity of using the 'living tongue' rather than an archaic 'poetical' diction was transmitted from Ford to Pound to Basil Bunting (who, on Pound's recommendation, became the *transatlantic review*'s first sub-editor). Price examines the 1971 preface to Bunting's edition of Ford's poetry alongside his own sense of these poems as living artifacts. Bunting's fondness for Ford as editor and for his poetry, particularly 'The Starling', is matched by Price's virtuoso close reading of this poem. Ford would be delighted by the line of British and American poets who continue to learn, through an exercise of tough-minded love, from the modernist apostolic succession he had prepared the ground for. Bunting recalled with affection Ford's 'kindness to young men and men in distress',[10] omitting to mention that women were also among the bohemian strays taken in by the *transatlantic review*. Elizabeth O'Connor's chapter attempts to disentangle Jean Rhys's 'entanglement' with Ford, following her first appearance in print in the *transatlantic review*. In *Quartet*, Rhys is angrily writing back to her former mentor and lover, while at the same rewriting the elliptical, adulterous complications of *The Good Soldier*. O'Connor highlights the acerbic references to 'playing the game' in *Quartet*, but whether Ford abused his editorial position, or was played by Rhys to advance her own writing career, is ultimately beside the point in assessing their literary relations. Like several contributors to this collection, O'Connor notes the tendency of commentators to sacrifice literary criticism for agenda driven biographical speculations. Such advocacy can bedevil Ford scholarship – carefully picking its way through a mined maze of fabulation, story-telling and gossip – although this aspect must inevitably be addressed in any re-evaluation of Ford's intense but sometimes fractious editorial relationships.

A sober estimate of Ford's achievement as editor entails unravelling the web of myths, many of them spun by Ford himself, that have enveloped discussion of his place in literary history. Nora Tomlinson casts a cold eye on Ford's financial mismanagement of the *English Review*. Violet Hunt has left a vivid portrait of the chaos that reigned in the editorial office at 84 Holland Park Avenue, where manuscripts were stuffed in a Spanish cabinet, but Tomlinson's careful archival research gives us a more reliable account of the facts. She reveals that a decline in circulation from a modest 2000 copies per issue (leading, in turn, to a fall in advertising revenue) was compounded by an unsustainable largesse in the payments to contributors. In little over four months, Ford and his backer Arthur Marwood had exhausted an initial capital in the region of £1000. Tomlinson shows that the journal was kept alive by injections of cash from Ford's brother-in-law David Soskice. The involvement of this exiled Russian alienated Conrad (whose serialised memoirs touched upon the family trauma behind his hostility to Russian autocracy). In fact, Soskice hated Tsarist Russia as much as Conrad and was seeking to use the *English Review* for political purposes. Rebecca Beasley has remarked that the *English Review* was 'notable for its attention to Russian politics and literature'[11]; supremely, Constance Garnett's pathbreaking English translations of Tolstoy, Dostoevsky and Chekhov, but also a series of articles on Russian domestic and foreign policy. Beasley's work provides a useful corrective to over-emphasis upon the *English Review*'s Francophile character, which is evident in Ford's editorial advocacy of Flaubertian aesthetics and French writers, notably Anatole France.

E. V. Lucas complained to Conrad that the *English Review* was 'generally too foreign for its title,'[12] missing the irony, according to Ford's recollection, that the title had been chosen by Conrad himself, who 'felt a certain sardonic pleasure in the choosing of so national a name for a periodical that promised to be singularly international in tone'.[13] But Ford's lurid description of his inner circle as a 'ring of foreign conspirators plotting against British letters' (*RY* 21) was anarchist exaggeration, downplaying the extent to which his editorials seriously engaged with Edwardian debates about the 'Condition of England'. Simon Grimble's chapter grapples with the confusing spectacle of Ford's performances in the public sphere. He argues that Ford's leading articles in the *English Review* betray an unresolved uncertainty of tone – sometimes thundering moralist, sometimes pessimistic ironist – towards his implied audience of English gentlemen. Ford's self-comforting retrospective view was that the intractable philistinism of John Bull killed the *English Review*, yet as Mark Morrisson reminds us, the bibliographical aura of the magazine – with its bulky and dignified blue cover – positioned it not as a 'little magazine' for dandies and aesthetes but as a clear successor to the great Victorian reviews of general culture, of which the *Fortnightly Review* was a prestigious twentieth-century survivor.[14] That Ford's editorials in the *English Review* hinted at connections with powerful political elites is germane to John Attridge's chapter. A series of articles by J. A. Hobson and other leading ideologues of New Liberalism, points to the review's drift away from Ford's foundational aim to exhibit 'No party bias' (*ER* I [Dec. 1908] 159). Attridge's chapter throws considerable light on Ford's complaint that Soskice was 'turning the *Review* into a Whig Socialist organ.'[15]

In December 1909, the journal was bought by the Liberal M.P. and industrialist Alfred Mond, whose first action was to replace the self-professed 'old-fashioned Tory' occupying the editorial chair with Austin Harrison. Pound's belief that by sacking Ford 'Mond killed the *English Review*' has been rightfully disputed by Martha Vogeler,[16] but it should be added that even those contributors who stayed with the journal noticed a falling off. In 1911, Conrad chafed at Harrison's proclamation of his 'Great Adult Review,'[17] while in 1913, Lawrence, who was not squeamish about adult matters, expressed regret the journal was 'so piffling now'.[18] By the time Harrison quit the period-ical in 1923, he had not published any volume that equalled the sus-tained excellence of Ford's *English Review*.

The conditions in post-war Paris in which Ford launched the *transatlantic review* were a world away from Edwardian London. However, as Stephen Rogers' chapter shows, Ford had learned little about the financing and running of a magazine in the intervening period: the editorial arrangements of this short-lived venture (it ran for only one year, perhaps illegally) were hardly less confused than the *English Review*. Ford acknowledged these difficulties in advance when he informed Eliot he was 're-starting on the weary road: founding a Review'.[19] The magazine's blue and buff cover, with the title printed in eye-catching lower-case letters, sported an emblematic small ship tossed on stormy seas beneath the motto 'Fluctuat'. Bunting soon bailed out of his duties as the magazine's accountant (and bath-time nanny to Ford and Stella Bowen's daughter Julie), perturbed by

Ford's constant editorial anxieties.[20] Yet Bernard Poli, historian of the *transatlantic review*, has calculated that the journal sold around 5000 copies of each issue in Paris, New York and London. More than that, as Andrzej Gasiorek's chapter explores, it placed Ford at the heart of the transatlantic avant-garde: significant scoops included serialising as 'Work in Progress' the first extract from James Joyce's *Finnegans Wake*, Gertrude Stein's *The Making of Americans* (and Mina Loy's letters explicating Stein), as well as publishing experimental work by Pound, E. E. Cummings, H. D., George Antheil, Mary Butts, William Carlos Williams, Tristan Tzara, Ernest Hemingway, Djuna Barnes, Jean Cocteau, Paul Valéry, Bryher, Dorothy Richardson, John Dos Passos, Nancy Cunard, and Jean Rhys. Unlike Eliot's *Criterion*, the *transatlantic* did not shy away from the radicalism of Stein and Surrealism.[21] But unlike contemporary avant-garde journals, it wasn't a coterie magazine tied to a programmatic movement. Ford's editorial tastes were always broad-minded. Gasiorek points out that the *transatlantic* encouraged transitions rather than rupture. A series of articles entitled 'Stocktaking: Towards a Re-valuation of English Literature' (which Ford published under the pseudonym 'Daniel Chaucer') were the equivalent of his earlier attempts in the *English Review* to define 'the critical attitude'. That Ford sought to undertake this 'Re-valuation' of literary tradition (a question of creative renewal) under the surname of England's first canonical poet is evidence of a post-war *rappel à l'ordre*, oddly, closer in spirit to the 'Revaluations' F. R. Leavis (a schoolboy subscriber to the *English Review*) published in *Scrutiny*, than to the extremism of the Parisian avant-garde.[22]

However, when Ford's principal backer John Quinn, New York lawyer and patron of the arts, died of cancer in the summer of 1924, Ford's editorial policy was thrown into turmoil. As Elena Lamberti's chapter stresses, this instability allowed Hemingway to strengthen the hand of American expatriates in Paris. What was conceived as the *Paris Review*, but appeared as the *transatlantic review* aimed at an American readership, shifted its editorial axis ever westward. While Ford was in New York attempting to secure the journal's future, Hemingway's stint as guest editor enabled him to drop Ford's 'Stocktaking' article and the serialisation of *Some Do Not . . .*, as well as the recently deceased octogenerian Luke Ionides's reminiscences of the Pre-Raphaelite Brotherhood – replaced by the work of Americans: Nathan Asch, Dos Passos and Williams (defending Robert McAlmon). Many of the 'lost generation' were found in the *transatlantic review*.

On his return, Ford took this affront in his stride. Although too late to alter the contents, in the editorial added to the New York edition, he noted the 'unusually large sample of the work of that young America whose claim we have so insistently – but not with such efficiency – forced upon our readers' (*TRev* II [Aug. 1924] 213). His restraint helped to keep Hemingway's new American backer, Krebs Friend, on board, but he may simply have been tolerantly bemused at the spectacle of this cuckoo in the *transatlantic review* nest.

The implacable hostility of 'that ungrateful fosterling of Ford's', (as Richard Price describes Hemingway) is not easily explained. He clearly found Ford's lordly references to 'young Hemingway' patronising and he was irritated by Ford's posturing (in Eliot's words) as 'an Officer (British) and a Gentleman'.[23] But such 'Middle Westishness' (to adopt Ford's comically ungainly coinage) was blind to the teasing ironies of Ford's *persona*. Hemingway and Eliot probably felt uncomfortable because, as Max Saunders notes, Ford's Tory ex-officer 'threw into relief' the *seriousness* of their own self-fashionings as (respectively) macho war veteran and Tory gentleman.[24] In the memorial 'Conrad Supplement' to the September issue of the *transatlantic review*, Hemingway compounded his lack of reverence towards Conrad's memory with downright insolence towards Eliot, which pained and embarrassed Ford.[25] Unable to oust Ford before the final collapse of the *transatlantic review* in December, Hemingway embellished his grievances in the libellous vignette served up in *A Moveable Feast*. Two previous sub-editors painted a very different picture. Goldring testified that: 'As an employer Ford was always characteristically and incorrigibly hospitable' (*Critical Heritage* 206). Bunting remembered Ford as 'the most friendly and tolerant boss you could possibly have'.[26]

When the *transatlantic review* was suspended, Ford initially hoped that it would be quickly revived in the spring of 1925. But the journal had inflicted heavy financial losses on him and Stella (Ford estimated they invested 120,000 francs in the review) and no wealthy patron could be found before the advent of the Wall Street Crash. Shortly before his death in 1939, he was still seeking to interest backers in relaunching the magazine. This was an indication of the importance of his role as a periodical editor, not only to his own writing career, but to the careers of those writers who depended on him providing a platform. Not that the bruised fifty-year old editor didn't sometimes look back and wonder if it had been a thankless task.

In 1924, he told Gertrude Stein that he resembled 'a sort of green baize swing door that every one kicks both on entering and on leaving'.[27] The *English Review* and *transatlantic review* had certainly witnessed a remarkable number of dramatic entrances and exits.

Given Ford's exceptional achievement as editor, it is fitting that his texts should themselves finally benefit from the care of critical editions. The challenge facing twenty-first century editors in establishing scholarly and authoritative texts of Ford's works is addressed by the final three chapters in this collection. Martin Stannard, editor of the 1995 Norton Critical Edition of *The Good Soldier*, has been tempted back into this novel's complex weave of textual uncertainties. His examination of the manuscript in the Ford archive at Cornell University, uncovers corruptions, substantive additions and deletions in the printed text which tend to work against the hesitant, conversational tone Ford aimed for in this self-reflexive narrative. The textual situation of *Parade's End*, containing numerous variants between British and American editions (both authorised by Ford), and variations between both of these and the manuscripts, is no less complicated. As Isabelle Brasme points out, this state of affairs is exacerbated further by the serialisation of *Some Do Not . . .* in the *transatlantic review*. She argues that the process of serial publication itself allows for a dynamic element of editorial revision. That is to say, Ford's ongoing self-editing of his tetralogy should not be overlooked, and can be traced in the texture of revisions and suppressions in its published volumes. Finally, Ashley Chantler addresses some of the difficulties that confront any scholarly critical edition of Ford's poetry. Taking the variegated textual history of *Antwerp* – described by Eliot as 'the only good poem I have met with on the subject of the war'[28] – as a test case, he puts forward a methodology for a new student edition of Ford's *Collected Poems*, complete with textual apparatus. Building on the critical work performed by Fordians (Wiesenfarth, Saunders, Haslam and Skinner), allied to chapters in this volume (Robinson and Price), Chantler indicates the time is ripe for a thorough re-evaluation of Ford's poetry. In this way, scholars join hands with creative writers in providing commentaries that keep the pleasures of Ford's texts alive. In 1933, Ford worried whether 150 years hence his works would be 'accepted as classics' and studied 'in, say, Durham University'.[29] The truth is: he has been canonised in half that time.

NOTES

1   *The Letters of T. S. Eliot*, vol. II, ed. Valerie Eliot and Hugh Haughton, London: Faber & Faber, 2009, p. 251.
2   Ibid., p. 251n. Written in T. S. Eliot's hand on the copy of *transatlantic review*, I (Jan. 1924) in Valerie Eliot's Kensington flat.
3   T. S. Eliot, 'A Message', *London Magazine*, I (Jan. 1954), p. 16.
4   Prospectus for the *transatlantic review* quoted in Bernard J. Poli, *Ford Madox Ford and the Transatlantic Review*, Syracuse: Syracuse University Press, 1967 – henceforth 'Poli'; p. 37.
5   *Ford Madox Ford: The Critical* Heritage, ed. Frank MacShane, London: Routledge, 1972 – henceforth *Critical Heritage*; p. 218.
6   *The Collected Letters of Joseph Conrad*, vol. IV, ed. Frederick R. Karl and Laurence Davies, Cambridge: Cambridge University Press, 1990, p. 264.
7   Throughout this volume references to Ford's magazines are given parenthetically in the text, using the standard International Ford Madox Ford Studies abbreviations – *ER* for the *English Review* and *TRev* for the *transatlantic review* – and giving just volume numbers, dates and page numbers.
8   See Edgar Jepson, *Memories of an Edwardian and Neo-Georgian*, London: Richards, 1937, p. 149.
9   Jessie Chambers, *D. H. Lawrence: A Personal Record*, by 'E. T.', London: Cape, 1935, p. 156.
10 Basil Bunting, Preface, *Ford Madox Ford: Selected Poems*, Cambridge, Mass.: Pym-Randall Press, 1971, p. ix.
11 Rebecca Beasley, 'The *English Review* and Russophile Modernism', lecture delivered at St. John's College, Durham University, 12 September 2008.
12 *The Collected Letters of Joseph Conrad*, vol. IV, p. 246.
13 Ford, *Return to Yesterday*, London: Victor Gollancz, 1931 – henceforth *RY*; p. 379.
14 See Mark Morrisson, *The Public Face of Modernism: Little Magazines, Audiences, and Reception, 1905-1920*, Madison: University of Wisconsin Press, 2001, pp. 17-53.
15 Ford to Elsie Martindale. Ford Archive 37/45, Division of Rare and Manuscript Collections, Cornell University Library. Quoted with the kind permission of the Carl A. Kroch Library, Cornell University, and Michael Schmidt.
16 See Martha Vogeler, *Austin Harrison and the English Review*, Columbia: University of Missouri Press, 2008.
17 *The Collected Letters of Joseph Conrad*, vol. IV, p. 414.
18 *The Letters of D. H. Lawrence*, ed. Aldous Huxley, London: Heinemann, 1932, p. 125.
19 *The Letters of T. S. Eliot*, vol. II, p. 239.
20 By mid-January 1924 Bunting was in Newcastle nursing his sick father.
21 Bunting recalled that he may have prevailed upon Ford to take an interest in French Surrealism. See Basil Bunting to Bernard J. Poli, 23 May 1966. Bunting Archive 160/2, Special Collections, Palace Green Library, Durham University.
22 F. R. Leavis: 'The distinction of Ford's *English Review* was that its very intelligently active defence and promotion of the finer creativity was adapted to the irreversible new conditions [....] Under Ford it was decidedly a literary

review, and he gave proof of his critical perception, and of the courage of it, in his editorial policy'. *Thought, Words and Creativity*, London: Chatto & Windus, 1976, pp. 37-8.

23 *The Letters of T. S. Eliot*, vol. II, p. 236.

24 Saunders, *Ford Madox Ford: A Dual Life*, 2 vols, Oxford: Oxford University Press, II, p. 151.

25 Hemingway wrote: 'It is agreed by most of the people I know that Conrad is a bad writer, just as it is agreed that T. S. Eliot is a good writer. If I knew that by grinding Mr. Eliot into a fine dry powder and sprinkling that powder over Mr. Conrad's grave Mr Conrad would shortly appear, looking very annoyed at the forced return and commence writing I would leave for London early tomorrow morning with a sausage grinder' (*TRev* II [Sept. 1924] 341-2).

26 Basil Bunting, 1974 radio interview with Tony Gould, Bunting Archive, Special Collections, Palace Green Library, Durham University.

27 *Letters of Ford Madox Ford*, ed. Richard M. Ludwig, Princeton, NJ: Princeton University Press, 1965 – henceforth *LF*; p. 162.

28 T. S. Eliot, 'Reflections on Contemporary Poetry', *Egoist* IV (Nov. 1917), p. 151.

29 Letter quoted by Julian Barnes in 'The Saddest Story', *Guardian Review* (7 June 2008), 3 (see *LF* 222).

HENRY JAMES AND THE *ENGLISH REVIEW*

Philip Horne

Taking up the 'Critical Attitude' in the *English Review* of November 1909, Ford Madox Ford says of Henry James and Joseph Conrad, that:

> Each takes in hand an 'affair' – a parcel of life, that is to say, in which several human beings are involved – and each having taken hold never loosens his grip until all that can possibly be extracted from the human situation is squeezed out. (*ER* III [Nov. 1909], 660)[1]

This chapter won't begin to manage such a full expression of the situation that is its subject: the relationship between Ford and James, concentrating on the period of a year and a half or so from the middle of 1908 to the end of 1909 when James contributed stories to Ford's *English Review*. But it will try to squeeze out some interest, and to make this small story somewhat novel, as well as suggestive – doing justice in Fordian fashion to what he called 'the complexity, the tantalisation, the shimmering, the haze, that life is'.[2] It will ask how seriously James engaged with the magazine's concerns, and thus how far we can think of his association with it as a collaboration. The answer will affect – and reflect – our sense of how James stands vis-à-vis modernism more largely.

First, let us review some basic, mostly familiar facts – though 'facts' is so often not the word where Ford is concerned – about the relationship between James and Ford. They first met on 14 September 1896 (Saunders I 132), through the agency of the novelist Lucy Clifford, a friend of both. Ford was a friend of Edward and Olive Garnett, who were also admirers, as well as neighbours, of James. Edward Garnett in 1899 reviewed *The Awkward Age* and Ford sent James the review. James sent a polite, complimentary, cordial reply on 7 July:

> I am not pampered by the press, I believe – but the press seems to me, in general, on literary matters, infantile. There is a figure in the carpet of *The*

A.A. which I think Mr. G. hasn't quite made out – but I am none the less yours & his most truly.[3]

James here sounds his recurrent theme – worked out in so many of his tales of the literary life in the 1890s – of the philistine press (and *The Awkward Age* wasn't warmly received). He certainly seems to suggest a mature press *would* pamper him. And by alluding to one of those 1890s tales – 'The Figure in the Carpet' – James seems to be implying that he himself is like Hugh Vereker, the enigmatic genius, so that Ford and the Garnetts resemble his close group of acolytes, admirers, interpreters. It's a joke, yet also an incitement.

Ford took the hint – but perhaps he over-took it, or at least overdid the praise in May 1901 in a now-lost letter to James – who replied that:

> I respond very gratefully to the charming things you tell me in relation to your so friendly acquaintance with things of mine. I'm delighted this sentiment & this history – which you so happily express – exist for you; & only a little alarmed – or a little depressed – as always – when my earlier perpetrations come back to me as loved or esteemed objects. I seem to see them, in that character, shrink & shrivel, rock, dangerously, in the kindly blast, & threaten to collapse altogether. (*FCJ* 37)

James seems uneasy at Ford's blast of praise; and would also prefer praise of his recent or current work to that of his 'earlier perpetrations'. In this same May of 1901, James wrote in comic-complaining vein to Lucy Clifford, who had caused Ford to call on him in 1896, about his refuge in Lamb House:

> It's only not so *much* of a retreat as it ideally might be! Joseph Conrad[,] wife, baby and trap and pony to tea all yesterday afternoon; Ford Madox Hueffer wife and guest (author of Villa Rubein [John Galsworthy]) to ditto – for hours – the day before...[4]

It sounds as if even the Conradian pony and trap demanded tea from James – and James doesn't seem adequately grateful to Ford for the chance to meet John Galsworthy – 'for hours ....'

It's perhaps as much the leakage of 'hours' as any deeper antipathy that begins to trouble James in his relations with Ford – though maybe too there's something presumptuous in Ford's manner. That's one way to read the famous episode recorded by James's typist Mary Weld, who evidently disliked Ford:

> [James] liked company on his walks. His favourite walk was the road to
> Winchelsea, but unfortunately his literary flatterer Ford Madox Hueffer who
> lived at Winchelsea used to waylay him, and this annoyed Mr James. Once we
> actually jumped a dike to avoid meeting Hueffer who was looking out for us.[5]

James remained scrupulously polite, anyway, and late in May 1906, after
Ford had dedicated *The Heart of the Country: A Survey of a Modern
Land* to James, the elder author came over to Winchelsea to pay Ford a
visit, after which both walked back together to Lamb House. After a
time, since Ford had a letter to compose and post to his wife Elsie, who
was in Florence, he was left alone in James's retreat. The letter he wrote
shows us Ford sounding a little like Prince Hal trying on the crown while
his predecessor is in decline:

> It's curious to sit at this desk & write on this [Lamb House] paper – the desk near
> the window in the little room on the l[eft]. of the hall door. The church bells are
> clamorously calling to the faithful & outside it pours. James himself has gone to
> see someone to the station – so I am sole lord of the demesne. (*FCJ* 53)

That jocular phrase, 'sole lord of the demesne', suggests a distinctly
emulous feeling – a sly fantasy of Oedipal displacement.

That same year, 1906, as Ford would record 18 years later, he
wrote *An English Girl*, one of 'two pastiches in the manner of Mr. Henry
James' (*JC* 176) – trying it on in another way. Theodora Bosanquet,
James's new secretary hired in 1907, was struck, reading it, as her diary
records: 'Read Ford Madox Hueffer's "An English Girl" which seems to
me (am I "obsessed"?) to owe a lot to Henry James's influence.'[6] 'Am I
"obsessed?"' If so, she wasn't the only one.

The *English Review* grew out of talks between Ford and other authors,
who happened also to be clients of J. B. Pinker, notably Conrad and
Wells, notably with Kent and Sussex connections – as a reaction
against what Ford would recall in 1924 as 'the crudely materialistic
atmosphere of the time' (*NC* 6). Also against an 'infantile' publishing
world. It was a chance, in fact, for Pinker's stable of writers to
establish themselves among the major authors of an uncertain day –
and to give an identity to the Edwardian period. Ford's story was
sometimes that the magazine was founded in order to publish Hardy's
poem about an abortion, which had been rejected as unsuitable by the
literary establishment. As Max Saunders puts it, 'When the first issue
appeared in December 1908, with "A Sunday Morning Tragedy" as its
vanguard, it was proclaiming the coming of age of Edwardian

literature' (Saunders I 242). Moreover, having his own organ made Ford a prominent public figure: in David Garnett's lurid account:

> For about a year or two Ford was to become an outstanding figure of literary London: he was arrayed in a magnificent fur coat; – wore a glossy topper; drove about in hired carriages; and his fresh features, the colour of raw veal, his prominent blue eyes and rabbit teeth smiled benevolently and patronisingly upon all gatherings of literary lions. (Saunders I 278)

Douglas Goldring, Ford's assistant, has described in the bitchy, impressionistic, amusing memoir *South Lodge* the bohemian chaos of the *English Review* office. It was not James's kind of place, though he did come once for tea.

The very title was a provocation. E. V. Lucas told Conrad the *English Review* was 'too foreign for its title' (Saunders I 242). But that was the point. As is now accepted, the magazine's horizons were anything but narrowly English. Eric Homberger sees the polemical thrust of this irony: '[Ford's] performance as a literary editor helped to define one of the central battlefields of "modern literature", for he sought to make an "English" review a vehicle for cultural cosmopolitanism.'[7]

Arnold Bennett, another Pinkerite, sounded a characteristic warning note to Ford: 'The chief thing that I wish you in connection with the *English Review* is plenty of capital.'[8] Ford didn't have that – or not for long; as Nora Tomlinson has made all too clear, he lacked the ability to organise, tended to quarrel with his contributors, and was monumentally inept in handling money.[9] But he did have the knack of the grand gesture. The *English Review* would pay, as Homberger says, 'one guinea per page for prose, and up to £5 per poem: [Ford's] generosity soon became proverbial [. . . .] The *English Review* sold for half a crown. It was a machine to reduce Ford to penury.'[10]

Thinking about James's relation to Ford's agenda in the *English Review*, to the cultural emphases the magazine declared itself out to promote, one perhaps shouldn't be surprised to find them in so many respects closely in tune. Its editor Ford had for a decade or more admired, and been influenced by, James, both as a writer and as a cultural critic, especially as a critic of the philistine, commercial book world.

One topic of the moment in Edwardian letters was censorship. The *English Review* had begun by printing Hardy's controversial poem, and in August 1909 attacked the notion of 'The Wholesome Play' (the essay's author being C. E. Montague).[11] In the same month, and as his third contribution to the *English Review* was appearing, James, who saw the resistance to censorship as part of the campaign for literary freedom he had been conducting as far back as 'The Art of Fiction' in 1884, wrote a wonderfully eloquent supportive letter of protest against the 'Censor's arbitrary rights' to John Galsworthy for reading to a Joint Select Committee of Lords and Commons examining the licensing of plays:

> I *do* consider that the situation made by the Englishman of letters ambitious of writing for the stage has less dignity – thanks to the Censor's arbitrary rights upon his work – than that of any other man of letters in Europe, and that this fact may well be, or rather *must* be, deterrent to men of any intellectual independence and self-respect. I think this circumstance represents according-ly an impoverishment of our theatre; that it tends to deprive it of intellectual life, of the *importance* to which a free choice of subjects and illustration directly ministers, and to confine it to the trivial and the puerile [. . . .] [The English playwright] has to reckon anxiously with an obscure and irresponsible Mr. So-and-So who may by law peremptorily demand of him that he shall make his work square, at vital points, with Mr. So-and-So's personal and, intellectually and critically speaking, wholly unauthoritative preferences prejudices and ignorances, and that the less original, the less important and the less interesting it is, and the more vulgar and superficial and futile, the more likely it is so to square [. . . .] We rub our eyes, we writers accustomed to freedom in all other walks, to think that this cause has still to be argued in England.[12]

James was also in sympathy with Ford's admiration of French literature and the sense of its more rigorous critical standards – though he was more ambivalent than Ford about Flaubert. He also believed as much as anyone in the importance of literary, and especially of fictional, technique, another of the *Review*'s announced values – and had written to Ford in 1902, as to a *confrère*, of the rationale of his procedures in *The Wings of the Dove*.[13]

As I've implied, Ford could also have taken from James – and the French – the scornful attitude to the bourgeois middlebrow novel and the whole apparatus of the literary world supporting it. As Ford wrote to R. A. Scott-James in 1910, 'I spent a great deal of money on the Review with the definite design of giving imaginative literature a chance in England. It was my own money and I was not minded to spend twopence on the dull, badly written stuff that in this country passes for "serious" work' (*LF* 40). Except in its extremism, this oppositional stance tallies, as will be seen, with James's angle of attack on the philistine world of middlebrow, middle-class art and literature in 'The Velvet Glove' and 'Mora Montravers'. And with attitudes he had been expressing for a long time – long before he met Olive Garnett in the chemist's late in 1903 and talked – as her diary records – 'of the ____ [damned?] abysmal vulgarity of the British public' (Saunders I 143).

These congruences perhaps make less striking the conspicuous part James plays in the first issue of the magazine; he's virtually a unifying theme. Ford would doubtless have been aware, incidentally, that James had been the first item – in the form of his tale 'The Death of the Lion' – in the first issue of Henry Harland's *Yellow Book* in April 1894. James's name is of course there on the front of the *English Review* lending lustre to the handsome, plain blue cover. But open that cover, and you find on page i Macmillan's advertisement for *The Novels of Henry James*, Edition de Luxe – the New York Edition. Later 'The Jolly Corner' itself occupies 30 pages. And then Ford's editorial matter brings James forward again:

> Thus to a review devoted – and let us emphasise the point – to the arts and to letters the publication of the first volume of Mr. James's collected edition is the topic of the month. (*ER* I [Dec. 1908] 158)

Ford goes on at the end of the editorial to make grand, rather cloudy claims for James's importance – claims indeed which in their heightened, excited way tend toward the avant-garde manifesto and the provocation of the bourgeois:

> And what we so very much need to-day is a picture of the life we live. It is only the imaginative writer who can supply this, because no collection of facts and no tabulation of figures can give us any sense of proportion. In England, the country of Accepted Ideas, the novelist who is intent merely to register – to *constater* – is almost unknown. Yet it is England probably that most needs him, for England, less than any of the nations, knows where it stands, or to what it trends. Flaubert said that had the French really read his 'Education Sentimentale' France would have avoided the horrors of the *Débâcle*. Mr. James might say as much for his own country and for the country he has so much benefited by making it his own. (*ER* I [Dec. 1908] 160)

James may have been a little embarrassed – indeed, puzzled – by this forceful but obscure pronouncement (Ford's reference is to Zola's novel *La Débâcle*, dealing with the Franco-Prussian War and the

Commune). It is not the kind of claim he was in the habit of making about himself.

As if this wasn't enough, Ford wrote to Pinker of James's New York Edition that 'I want to give the complete edition a long full-dress review in the second number, & as the second number is *considerably* stronger than the first, & more certain to attract attention, I think this ought to do the old man some good' (*LF* 27). Ford seems to enjoy the chance to patronise James, as (familiarly) 'the old man' – he is the sole lord of *this* demesne. However, no review of the Edition appeared in any issue of the *Review*.

Let us move back now to James's demesne, Lamb House, and try to unpick something of the tangled story of the four stories James placed in the *English Review*. Nothing was simple for James about the 'short story' – and especially that word 'short'.[14]

The tales of this period are mostly gathered in James's final collection, *The Finer Grain* (published by Methuen, 13 October 1910); the blurb on the dust-jacket suggests ways in which James has a cumulative agenda in the volume:

> 'The Finer Grain' consists of a series of five stories, the central figure in each is involved, as Mr James loves his characters to be, in one of the tangles of highly civilized existence. By the 'finer grain' the author means, in his own phrase, 'a peculiar accessibility to surprise, to curiosity, to mystification or attraction – in other words, to moving experience.' It is needless to add that the book exhibits the most delicate comedy throughout.[15]

It may be easier to follow this slightly complicated sequence with the aid of the following list:

James's last tales in order of first publication, place and date of publication, approximate length and payment (in dollars):

> 'Julia Bride' (*Harper's Magazine*, Mar-Apr 1908, 13,200 words; $450) [repr. New York Edition]

> 'The Jolly Corner' (working title 'The Second House'; *English Review* I, Dec. 1908, 12,870 words; $204) [repr. New York Edition]

> 'The Velvet Glove' (working title 'The Top of the Tree'; *English Review* IV, Mar. 1909, 10,560 words; $147)

'Mora Montravers' (*English Review* IX-X, Aug.-Sept. 1909, 21,450 words; $183)

Crapy Cornelia' (*Harper's Magazine*, Oct. 1909, 10,560 words; $450)

'The Bench of Desolation' (*Putnam's Magazine*, Oct. 1909-Jan. 1910, 18,150 words; $327)

'A Round of Visits' (*English Review* XVII-XVIII, Apr.-May 1910, 10,560 words; 40 guineas ($204) + $218 paid by *Putnam's* before folding)[16]

The Pinker archive in the Beinecke Library at Yale allows us to get at the inside story of the stories. Having seen how grandly James features in the opening number of the *Review*, one may be shocked to find James's first, private response (to Pinker alone) to Ford's solicit- ation – or solicitations, evidently – of contributions. On 16 September 1908, James wrote to Pinker, ruffled and inserting an afterthought to convey his rufflement, that '… Hueffer is <grossly> persistent in spite of a categorical refusal a month ago – but *like* the grossly persistent he seems to succeed.'[17] 'He seems to succeed': this means, of course, that James *will* give him something.

What James gave him was 'The Jolly Corner', one of his greatest and most profound ghost stories, written in 1906 and sent under the title of 'The Second House' to F. A. Duneka of *Harper's Magazine* on 28 August 1906. It had been refused by that magazine, and was now due to appear in print at last in the *New York Edition* (1907-9); but, James says to Pinker, 'I don't see that this need prevent our giving it to H. if he will publish it *immediately*'. Within ten days James received Ford's cheque for £42 for 'The Jolly Corner'. The money was the equivalent of $204 for 12,870 words; *Harper's Magazine* paid $450 for both *Julia Bride*, 13,200 words, and *Crapy Cornelia*, 10,560 words. The American journal paid, that is, at more than twice the *English Review* rate (Ford was munificent only by English standards). No wonder James preferred the U. S. option where possible.

Ford wasn't the only editor asking James for stories. On 3 December 1908, James wrote to Pinker that:

H. M. Alden has lately written to ask me for a Tale in 5000 words – one of their terrible little shortest of short stories – for Harper's Magazine, & I have answered him with a promise of the same. In fact I got, promptly, at the job – but with the usual & inevitable result that I shall have to do two or three – too irreducibly & irredeemably long, – in order to pull off the really short enough. In fact I *have* done one with infinite anguish of trying to keep it down; but the subject, the motive, has *had* to be expressed & I shall ruin it if I now attempt to mutilate it further. I shall do at least – & immediately another, in my effort to arrive at something that will *go* in 5000 words; but meanwhile I don't want to waste the thing, 'The Top of the Tree,' already, with infinite labour, produced (*reduced* from something done before & given up, but kept on hand,) & am wondering if Hueffer wouldn't care for it, yet again, for his Magazine. He is welcome to it (*cheap*, I suppose, inevitably??!!) if he would – & will you very kindly make the inquiry &c for yours very truly / *Henry James*. (Horne 469-70)

And on 4 December 1908 James sent Pinker what was to become 'The Velvet Glove' – '"The Top of the Tree", as I call the sufficiently pretty production (I think) that you will exercise your discretion about.' His attitude to the 'grossly persistent' Ford has changed – a few days after seeing the first issue of the *Review* in December. 'Other things being equal, or even a little unequal – not *too* much so! – I should rather like it, than not, to follow my fiction of this month in the blue, the *English Review*. I like the way one's stuff is presented on that rather handsome page' (Edel IV 504-5). Indeed, on 17 October James had written to Ford that 'I was very glad to see your handsome, promising page' (*FCJ* 58).

In December 1908 Bosanquet's diary records him working away at tales for Alden – not always with great relish on her part. On Thursday 17 December 1908, she records: 'Wet. Mr. James going on with "short" story for Harpers which extends mightily – & is, I think, dull.'[18] Happily, by Saturday 2 January 1909: 'Mr. James at work on another short story – which promises very well indeed…'.[19] And the following day, Sunday, she was busy again – he was a hard taskmaster at times: 'Mr. James had done a lot of his story last night & we raced along. He says he wants to do three or four – & finds his only plan is to write them himself – it keeps him more within bounds – and *then* dictate them.'[20] The constraints of length made the expansiveness of dictation – in the act of composition – prohibitive.

That same day James wrote to Pinker that:

I hope you have been able to place 'The Velvet Glove' with 'The English Review' – on possible terms! It is absurd, the labour I have incurred by trying to produce 5000 words of fiction – detestable number! – for Alden, (Harper) as I wrote you some time since I had engaged, or promised, to do. I have one consequent thing of *10 000* finished, another of about 8,000 almost finished & two others started which, or one of which, *will* be a true 5000. But all of them will be too good & too *done* to sacrifice – & the *two* shortest shall presently go to Alden; in fact all 4 ought to. It will make *five* (with the 'Velvet Glove,') started for his benefit – a most ridiculous commentary on my ruinously expensive mode of work, & the annoyance of his asking me for things of a form that I can't but

assent to for the money's sake (so pressed am I now for that article) & of which
the interrupting botherment is yet so much greater than the chance or the glory –
or the larger profit. (Horne 471)

On 19 January 1909, James told Pinker he'd been 'rather sharply unwell'
(heart trouble brought on by bad news about the likely returns from the
vast labour of the New York Edition), but that:

I have done 3 masterpieces 'for' Alden, – all of the quality of the 'Velvet
Glove', & one of which is already in his hands; but am boiling down two
more to the insufferable '5000' words ...[21]

'The Velvet Glove' was published in the March issue of the *English
Review*. It had been turned down by two U. S. magazines. Here, as with
'The Jolly Corner', despite the 'rather handsome page', the *English
Review* was not at this point for James his preferred temple of art, and
was rather a sanctuary, a decent port in a storm; it was at any rate a
second best – if mainly for financial reasons.

On 19 March 1909 James told Pinker, 'I have an all but finished short
story (as long as *The Jolly Corner*) which I intimated to you would be at
the service of the New [sic] English Review. I can't get at it again for
some two days, but then could put it through promptly, & this I mean in
fact to do.'[22] This would be 'Mora Montravers'. On 7 April 1909 James
had to apologise, characteristically: 'You must have been wondering
why you haven't received the Short Story for the New Eng: Rev: [sic]
that I have been finishing – & I am afraid my explanation falls into the
usual category of my final struggle with my precious material.'[23] It was
13 April before he posted Pinker '"Mora Montravers", for which I'm
afraid I can't hope better (though I wish I *could* – if he is brave enough,)
than that Hueffer will make two Parts.'[24] 'Mora Montravers' is thus a
tale which James had actually written for the *English Review* – unlike
'The Jolly Corner' and 'The Velvet Glove', the ones which had already
appeared.

A month later, on 13 May 1909, James writes to Pinker that
Alden has taken one of the stories he sent, 'Crapy Cornelia', but not
the other 'A Round of Visits'; so he has a copy of the latter at Pinker's
disposal.[25] By 2 July, James is writing anxiously, and hyperbolically
– that is, self-parodically – to Pinker of his 'wild dream of your having
been able to do *something* or other with the accursed two other short
stories that I did in the winter for the fond vision of immediate profit

& for the belief that the false Alden, with his complimentary letter to me, would like them.' (These are, I think, 'A Round of Visits' and 'The Bench of Desolation'.) And he asks, still suffering from the painful blow of the New York Edition, 'Do you know meanwhile when Hueffer means to publish my story in the English Review? I hoped this at least would be soon – but I have as yet no proof. If nothing better can be done financially will *he* take one of the remaining short stories? I don't want to worry you, heaven knows, but I feel rather demoralised and nervous, & if something *can* come to me of an at all substantial order, before or by the end of the month, should find it singularly sustaining & cheering.'[26]

The result of all this anxiety? On 21 July James writes to Pinker that 'clearly I have written the last short story of my life – which you will be glad to know!' (Horne 483).

'Mora Montravers' was published in the *English Review* in August and September in two parts, as foreseen. He remarked on 19 August to Pinker that, 'As I believe I have remarked before, if you can do absolutely nothing with A Round of Visits that shall be more profitable or more prompt, I should resign myself to its appearing in The English Review – shall you deem the latter's staying – & paying! – power still adequate.'[27] For already the financial difficulties of the *Review* must have been known to Pinker and James.

Pinker may have been hanging fire on that account, for on 15 October the fate of 'A Round of Visits' still seems unclear. James wrote to Pinker he was fondly hoping 'for some pecuniary news – pecuniary or other – of "A Round of Visits"'.[28]

By 4 November 1909 it was not only financial but marital difficulties that were besetting Ford, and James addressed Pinker with elaborate circumspection.

> I wrote to you some time ago that if you could do nothing more advantageous with the remaining short story of mine you have had so long in your hands – 'A Round of Visits' – I should be willing to see it in the *English Review* – if the other circumstances should be sufficiently propitious. But unless you have already put it there kindly stay your hand in that direction – I don't myself now regard circumstances as propitious: which cryptic remark I will explain when I next see you.[29]

He evidently hadn't yet seen him a week later, on the 11th, as he wrote to Pinker in a PS: 'Yes – but I wonder if you "know all" – as to the bearings of the English Review situation! I will tell you at any rate later on.'[30]

'The Bench of Desolation' appeared in *Putnam's Magazine* in America from October to December 1909, and a last instalment in January 1910. The December 1909 issue of the *English Review* was the last over which Ford had editorial control – it was sold to Alfred Mond, by Ford's own urging – and he was replaced as editor by Austin Harrison. On 9 January 1910 James wrote to Pinker that he wanted to find a place for 'A Round of Visits' 'where it will make a better figure than under Putnam's illiterate treatment of it.'[31] *Putnam's* had carried 'The Bench of Desolation' in four parts, each of under 5000 words – as James puts it, 'in deplorable little drippets of 5 or 6 pages, & never sent me any proof at all – by reason of which it bristles with gross misprints'. In the same letter James remarks that he hasn't for a long time made so little money as this last year. That is, 1909 was a very bad year for James, who was also ill. This year, of course, also ended in fairly comprehensive disaster for Ford.

On 2 February 1910 James was acknowledging a cheque for 'Putnam's payment for "A Round of Visits". This is a cheering contribution to my state', he commented; the cheque evidently softened the blow of Putnam's expected 'illiterate treatment'.[32] A week later, on 9 February, it turned out that Austin Harrison, the new editor of the *English Review*, wanted to publish 'A Round of Visits', and would do so using the Putnam proofs as his copy-text.[33] Simultaneous publication in both countries, a major support for James's career in his earlier years, but which more recently he had not managed much in a more international literary market, did not happen, however; *Putnam's* folded and was absorbed into the *Atlantic Monthly*. James at least still received double payment. James's last tale to be published in his lifetime appeared in the *English Review* in two instalments in April and May 1910.

The two stories James published in the *English Review* that I'm going to discuss are both comic, and both connect, I think, with the agenda of the magazine in suggestive ways.

The first, extraordinary tale, 'The Velvet Glove', came out in the *English Review* of March 1909. Its ironic engagement with popular fiction of the time is already suggested by the fact that it shares its title with a novel of 1901 by Henry Seton Merriman (who had died in 1903). It was inspired, famously, by an episode involving Edith Wharton; the two main characters are playfully tweaked versions of Wharton and of James himself. And this story of temptation and resistance addresses one of the dichotomies Ford signalled in the first number of the *Review*, between 'inventive literature', which tries 'to divert, to delight, to tickle, to promote appetites', and 'imaginative literature', which tries 'to record life in terms of the author – to stimulate thought' (*ER* I [Dec. 1908] 159).

'The Velvet Glove' is an ironic fantasy, an impossibly elevated phantasmagoria, set in the world of the rich and famous in Paris, and taking place all on one dreamlike evening at the studio of the artist Gloriani – who had figured in James's first acknowledged novel, *Roderick Hudson* (1876), and had reappeared in *The Ambassadors* (1903), which this tale also lightly revisits. We might read this self-reference as James involved in a retrospective taking-stock of his career, carrying a character over a 33-year span; or as a form of self-parody. The latter seems suggested by the tale's opening:

> He thought he had already, poor John Berridge, tasted in their fullness the sweets of success; but nothing yet had been more charming to him than when the young Lord, as he irresistibly and, for greater certitude, quite correctly figured him, fairly sought out, in Paris, the new literary star that had begun to hang, with a fresh red light, over the vast, even though rather confused, Anglo-Saxon horizon; positively approaching that celebrity with a shy and artless appeal. (*ER* I [March 1909] 625)

'Poor John Berridge' marks our hero as one of James's 'poor sensitive gentlemen', one of those with the 'finer grain'; but he's a younger instance than usual, and tall and reasonably good-looking, and 'poor' as he is has paradoxically here been enjoying 'the sweets of success'. Berridge is involved in Jamesian interpretative leaps from the first – 'the young Lord, as he irresistibly and, for greater certitude, quite correctly figured him' seems to mean that he guesses the approaching man is a Lord, and when the man, who seems oddly familiar, introduces himself discovers he is right. Confusion, which in various aspects is to dominate the tale, is in the air already: about the identity of 'the new literary star', for instance. As 'the sweets of success' implies, it's Berridge himself – a 'celebrity' (*OED* has the first use in this sense in 1849) who thus seems to be weirdly suspended 'over the vast, even though rather confused, Anglo-Saxon horizon'. Though this story is set in Paris, amid the French who have as Ford's *English Review* believes really demanding artistic and critical standards, its comic premise is the revelation beneath the quite blinding dazzle of a

Parisian *soirée* of the confusions and distortions of the Anglo-Saxon literary world.

Berridge has had a 'prodigious "hit"' with a novel' (625), amplified as a stage success, and 'everyone in the world (so far had the thing gone) was reading "The Heart of Gold" as just a slightly too fat volume, or sitting out the same as just a fifth-act too long play' (625); the 'fresh red light' seems to refer to the colour of the plump book. This seems a joky suggestion that *The Golden Bowl* might have had the same triumph as Du Maurier's *Trilby*, though '*Heart* of Gold' suggests an ingratiating sentimentality James himself wasn't capable of. Berridge's 'celebrity' is such that 'he found himself floated on a tide he would scarce have dared to show his favourite hero sustained by' (625). His reality has become more romantic than he feels comfortable with.

What does the young Lord want? 'He wondered, the splendid young man, he wondered awfully, he wondered (it was unmistakable) quite nervously, he wondered, to John's ardent and acute imagination, quite beautifully, if the author of "The Heart of Gold" would mind just looking at a book by a friend of his, a great friend, which he himself believed rather clever ...' (626). Berridge, who has 'the artist's real feeling for life' (627), is disappointed at the bathos of this request; the handsome Lord has inspired him with a sense of imaginative possibilities. He classes the Lord, fancifully, among 'young gods and goddesses [...] of Olympian race', the kind who 'glimmered for one, at the best, through their silver cloud, like the visiting apparitions in an epic'. The story is full of glimmering and shimmering, dazzlement and bemusement – an effect aided by the way that music now starts as 'an eminent tenor' begins a recital (629). Berridge looks round at the remarkable audience, and – perhaps because James himself had, by all accounts, a limited responsiveness to music – judges that life is better than art, that:

> It was better, in this way, than the opera – John alertly thought of that: the composition sung might be Wagnerian, but no Tristram, no Iseult, no Parsifal and no Kundry of them all could ever show, could ever 'act' to the music, as our friend had thus the power of seeing his dear contemporaries of either sex (armoured *they* so otherwise than in cheap Teutonic tinsel!) just continuously and inscrutably sit to it. (630)

For Berridge the spectacle of real life – albeit the highly artificial, super-civilised life of Gloriani's studio at its glittering best – surpasses the cultural form of Wagnerian opera. With the scene thus set, he becomes aware of the entrance of 'absolutely the most beautiful woman now present', a person 'supremely, divinely Olympian' (630).

The two Olympians, he realises, are linked – and not just by their divinity. Berridge immediately, intuitively recognises that the Olympian Lord and this Olympian Princess are together – though what prompts the connection is his sudden memory of having seen them in an Italian train in 'admirable intimacy', and not, he was sure, a 'mere blest matrimonial' one (631).

She's strangely attentive to Berridge; as the concert goes on he finds 'their eyes meeting, in deep communion, all across the great peopled room' (635) – quite as if they are falling in love. We may wonder if this is the sort of thing that happens in Berridge's own fiction – if the story is parodic in that sense of its hero's own romantic style. He's ready to believe, at any rate, that, insignificant though he thinks himself:

> what it must come to was that she liked him, and to such a tune, just for himself and quite after no other fashion than that in which every goddess in the calendar had, when you came to look, sooner or later liked some prepossessing young shepherd. (635)

In other words, Berridge harbours a romantic, indeed a sexual, fantasy that he is of interest to this 'goddess'.

He's puzzled now when the young Lord – who is the Princess's ambassador – approaches him again, now holding an object that 'could only be *his* book (it seemed also to have a tawdry red cover)'; and his heart sinks as he expects to be asked to '"signature" the ugly thing' (636). Only it's not his book, and the recognition produces 'an immediate collapse of the dream in which he had for the splendid previous space of time been living' (637). The story shifts with abrupt bathos from impossibly refined romantic stylization to grotesque comedy, the comedy of generic incongruity, of an intrusively vulgar and modern false note; Berridge is torn from his fantasy and forced to examine the red book:

> 'The Top of the Tree, by Amy Evans' – scarce credible words floating before Berridge after he had with an anguish of effort dropped his eyes on the importunate title-page – represented an object as alien to the careless grace of goddess-haunted Arcady as a washed-up 'kodak' from a wrecked ship might have been to the appreciation of some islander of wholly unvisited seas. (637)

And the young Lord in his 'glibness' clarifies: 'It's her pen-name, Amy Evans' (637). The radiant Princess, then, is also, drably, 'Amy Evans'.

Put on the spot, Berridge has no choice – and James, unusually, breaks into direct parody:

> 'Yes, I should like to look at it,' he managed, horribly grimacing now, he believed, to say; and there was in fact a strange short interlude after this in which he scarce knew what had become of any one or of anything; in which he only seemed to himself to stand alone in a desolate place where even its desolation didn't save him from having to stare at the greyest of printed pages. Nothing here helped anything else, since the stamped greyness didn't even in itself make it impossible his eye should follow such sentences as: 'The loveliness of the face, which was that of the glorious period in which Pheidias reigned supreme, and which owed its most exquisite note to that shell-like curl of the upper lip which always somehow recalls for us the smile with which wind-blown Astarte must have risen from the salt sea to which she owed her birth and her terrible moods'; or 'It was too much for all the passionate woman in her, and she let herself go, over the flowering land that had been, but was no longer their love, with an effect of blighting desolation that might have proceeded from one of the more physical, though not more awful, convulsions of nature.' (637-8)

The debased, extravagant version of literary language here, of high Edwardian tosh, pretentious and wordy and attitudinising, might remind us of *Ulysses* and Gerty MacDowell. (The second sentence, with its 'effect of blighting desolation' and the land that 'was no longer their love', of course brings us back to Berridge's own disillusion – the ghastly discovery that this beautiful woman can write so horribly.)

The princess herself – or 'Amy Evans' herself – sees he has the book, and seems aghast. 'Ah no, not that one!' she says. Berridge's ironic inner voice notes that it is a 'literary production' 'against which all the Amy Evans in her, as she would doubtless have put it, clearly wished on the spot to discriminate'. 'All the passionate woman in her'; 'all the Amy Evans in her': James pins down the affected, knowing, clichéd phrase here – and continues to play with it till the end of the story, to broad comic effect: five pages later, 'all the conscious conqueror in him, as Amy Evans would again have said ...' (642); and four pages beyond that, 'all the conscientious man of letters in him, as she might so supremely have phrased it' (646).

Berridge is simultaneously dazzled by the Princess's beauty (and her seductive interest in him), and appalled at her gratuitous involvement with debased art, her other unreal existence as 'Amy Evans'. This splitting might be understood as a mark of the falsification of modern life, of the inauthenticity of experience modern culture fosters. The Princess is double: she has a gift for life, for the art of life, despite her engagement in bad, commercially driven, print. He understands from her actions that she is humanly open to romantic experience, isn't only a churner-out of cheap romances, and he understands it:

> in spite of books and publics and pen-names, in spite of the really 'decadent' perversity, recalling that of the most irresponsibly insolent of the old Romans and Byzantines, that could lead a creature so formed for living and breathing her Romance, and so committed, up to the eyes, to the constant fact of her personal immersion in it and genius for it, the dreadful amateurish dance of ungrammatically scribbling it, with editions and advertisements and reviews and royalties and every other futile item: since what was more of the deep essence of throbbing intercourse itself than this very act of her having broken away from people, in the other room, to whom he was as nought, of her having, with her *crânerie* of audacity and indifference, just turned her back on them all as soon as she had begun to miss him? (640)

It seems to be proof of her generosity of spirit, her spontaneous responsiveness to the moment – and to him – and to what James calls suggestively 'the deep essence of throbbing intercourse itself' – that she now gives Berridge:

> a tremendous further throb, from what she had gone on to say to him in so many words – though indeed the words were nothing and it was all a matter but of the implication that glimmered through them: 'Do you *want* very much your supper here?' (640-1)

'The implication that glimmered through them', one takes it, is that they'll leave together in pursuit of 'the deep essence of throbbing intercourse itself'. And in fact they do go – leaving Gloriani and a great dramatist who is also charmed by the Princess cross and jealous, but the young Lord oddly indulgent.

In the intimate space of her car, her 'chariot of fire' (642), with the backs of the chauffeur and *valet-de-pied* against the glass like 'a protecting wall', Berridge has 'a vision of tall guards erect round eastern seraglios' (643). Dazed by the Princess's physical proximity, he forgets that he's also with 'Amy Evans' – until she starts saying, 'it's a compliment a clever man is always so glad to pay a literary friend' (644). 'Clever' as he's supposed to be, he's 'really [...] quite at sea as to what she was talking about'. "'A 'literary friend'?" he echoed' (644).

She wants him to write a Preface. This realization is where 'all the conscientious man of letters in him, as she might so supremely have phrased it, struggled with the more peccable, the more muddled and "squared" [...] comrade' (646). Perhaps he's so 'muddled and "squared"' because of the high, intimate price, the *quid pro quo*, she seems to be prepared to pay for it. He's overcome, though, by 'the really affecting folly of her attempt to become a mere magazine mortal' (646), her debasement or profanation of herself in her dedication to what, in Fordian terms, is mere 'inventive literature' – for Berridge, even if *The Heart of Gold* has failings, is a devotee of 'imaginative literature'. There is indeed a pathos in her absolute failure to imagine him.

In the very striking, even shocking last scene, as the car approaches her house in 'her great smooth empty, costly street', she kisses his hand, and he 'took in with a smothered sound of pain that this was the conferred bounty by which Amy Evans sought most expressively to encourage, to sustain and to reward' (647). It is hard to say if his pain is at the crudity of her bribe, his understanding that his romantic, sexual desire can be fulfilled only at the price of a bargain his integrity despises; or at the implication that this hand-kissing will be the *only* 'conferred bounty'. Now, at any rate, after being so dazed and passive throughout the story, he finally takes action – takes possession of *her* hand and returns the kiss – 'and with an intention the straighter that her glove had by this time somehow come off' (647).

So here is the titular moment of 'The Velvet Glove', beautifully overdetermined. She is seemingly – 'somehow' is always a highly charged word in James – beginning to undress. But in the common phrase, when the gloves are off, the fight becomes really dirty: in another sense, we see how forcefully she desires his Preface, how crude the world of 'editions and advertisements and reviews and royalties and every other futile item' can get. The attempt at seduction reveals the iron fist in the velvet glove the title has implied from the start.

At which he signals to the footman 'his view of their stopping short' – stopping short, presumably, of going all the way – and gets out before it pulls into her house. He says, causing her unprecedented confusion, as if she's never been refused before, 'Good-night,

Princess. I sha'n't see you again' (647). She's puzzled. 'And you won't do my Preface? [...] Then you don't like me–?' (648). Berridge replies, 'Princess, I adore you. But I'm ashamed for you [...] You *are* Romance [...] You don't need to understand. Don't attempt such base things. Leave those to us. Only live. Only be. *We*'ll do the rest' (648).

His 'Only live. Only be' recalls Lambert Strether's famous 'Live all you can. It's a mistake not to' in *The Ambassadors* – and this twist on that instruction-cum-warning indeed occurs not so far from Gloriani's garden.[34] He is pained by her 'dire non-intelligence', and fears she will continue to plead, stupidly, as she cries with disappointment. To prevent her saying something even worse:

> he uttered, in a deep-drawn final groan, an irrepressible echo of his pang for what might have been, the muffled cry of his insistence. 'You *are* Romance!' – he drove it intimately, inordinately home, his lips, for a long moment, sealing it, with the fullest force of authority, on her own [...] (649)

The passive imaginative writer may not get physically to consummate his attraction to the Olympian being, the goddess – but 'he drove it intimately, inordinately home' implies that there's a displaced sexual energy in his words, if not actual 'throbbing intercourse' then a 'pang for what might have been'. After this he breaks away and the car sweeps her into her gateway. It's a disturbing ending in its invocation of sexual violence, and also of masculine dominance in 'the fullest force of authority'; but it strongly implies the strength of the passions that underlie and exceed the banality of the literary marketplace.

'Mora Montravers' appeared in the *English Review* in August and September 1909. It's an amazing, very funny story, to the details of which this essay can't do as much justice as Neil Reeve's brilliant, subtle, penetrating essay on it, 'Living Up to the Name: "Mora Montravers"'.[35] It's a parodic suburban awakening narrative, comparable with – though very different from – Wells's *Ann Veronica*; and again an ironic revisiting of *The Ambassadors*, as well as of *The Wings of the Dove* (there's a scene in the Dutch room in the National Gallery). But it's also – which is germane to the *English Review* agenda – an engagement with middle-class values, with the sexual hypocrisy that had prevented publication of Hardy's poem 'A Sunday Morning Tragedy' till Ford took it on.

The hero of the story, Sidney Traffle, and his wife Jane are a childless couple living in genteel Wimbledon; they have living with them – or have had – Jane's niece, whose name is Mora Montravers. Mora is under twenty, but as the story starts she's already shockingly, scandalously left the Traffles and is living in London, under the protection of a talented young artist called Walter Puddick with whom she's been taking lessons. The question, as in *The Ambassadors*, is what to do about it. Sidney is the Lambert Strether of Wimbledon, a timid and unsatisfied painter with a spotless but barren studio, but peculiarly accessible to curiosity and mystification, who admires Puddick's chaotic creativity – and he is sympathetic to the beautiful Mora's announcement (when she reappears) that 'I want to be free' (*ER* III [Sept. 1909] 223). But Jane, his wife, on whom the comedy of the story mostly hangs, is an embodiment of convention, a Mrs. Newsome who is mostly all too present, not conveniently away in New England. Pleading to her that Mora 'has tremendously the sense of life' (*ER* III [Aug. 1909] 32) is useless; for Jane, 'Mora was a monster' (35). Jane embodies a passive-aggressive repression: Sidney suffers from:

> Jane's damp severity; *she* never ceased crying, but her tears froze as they fell – though not, unfortunately, to firm ice, any surface that would bear the weight of large argument. (31)

Throughout, Jane inspires James to metaphorical extravagance and this kind of pointed wit. In evoking, for instance, Sidney's sense of her physical appearance:

> He had felt how more than ever her 'done' yellow hair – done only in the sense of an elaborately unbecoming conformity to the spasmodic prescriptions, undulations and inflations of the day, not in that of any departure from its pale straw-coloured truth – was helped by her white invalidical shawl to intensify those reminders of their thin ideals, their bloodless immunity, their generally compromised and missed and forfeited frankness, that every other feature of their domestic scene had just been projecting for him. (31)

James's assault on the bourgeois here takes the form of a devastating portrayal of the grotesque consequences of the blinkered life with its 'bloodless immunity'. The picture of Sidney and Jane is a great, bleak, comic portrait of a sterile marriage.

She is 'plain' Jane in more than just her 'elaborately unbecoming conformity' – she's plain-spoken in good *Daily Mail* fashion. When Walter Puddick, the painter, has been summoned to

Wimbledon for a talking-to, Sidney is appalled at her bluntness. 'What I want to know in plain terms, if you please, is whether or no you're Mora's lover?' she says (42-3). Marital loyalty – all on the surface – prevents Sidney's saying what he thinks: 'It was a fool's question' (43).

Jane insists Mora should conform to society's rules and marry Puddick, even offering a bribe. And Mora does marry him. However, Jane's managing, moralistic pressure is entirely counterproductive – she drives her niece into the moral wilderness. The goaded Mora is by the story's end poised to leave her husband Puddick and become an aristocrat's mistress. Sidney sees this happening, but in his weakness can do nothing: 'it was in fact with fatal Jane tied as a millstone round his neck that he at present knew himself sinking' (*ER* III [Sept. 1909] 220). James finds pathos as well as humour in this portrayal of a passive, intelligent man shackled to a millstone by which he is – like Isabel Archer – being ground in the very mill of the conventional.

The twist is that when Jane discovers Mora is leaving her husband Puddick, she seems not aghast but positively pleased, feels no compunction about having precipitated this disaster. Puddick has become a pure victim, available for Jane's sentimental appropriation. The interest at the end is 'Jane's own evolution' (230) – the formerly abominated Puddick becomes a romantic, quasi-sexual object for her. Traffle calls it 'the extraordinary somersault you appear to have turned' (232) – her capacity for acting in her own narrow interest without minding the inconsistency, which she refuses to acknowledge. In this, James's imagery says, she is like the popular press: 'she was as stuffed with supersessive answers as if she were the latest number of a penny periodical: it was only a matter still of his continuing to pay his penny' (228). Her unblinking complacency here – and the suggestion that she is bulging with the 'Accepted Ideas' of the age – makes a link to Ford's editorial on 'The Two Shilling Novel' and the cheapening of literature, further on in the same issue of the *Review* – where it might seem as if Ford were drawing on James's contribution.

> But complacently the public continues to steal the bread from the mouths of the heirs of men of letters, and to read the halfpenny papers. In these islands literature has never come into its own; perhaps never will, perhaps never can. (318)

Real 'literature' in this sense entails what Traffle calls 'the sense of life'. In the brave speech he makes to the implacable Jane early on in defence of Mora, his reduced ironic equivalent of Strether's 'Live all you can' in Gloriani's Parisian garden, he recognises that the starved suburb of Wimbledon is deathly. He asks despairingly:

> 'What do we know about the sense of life – when it breaks out with real freedom? It has never broken out here, my dear, for long enough to leave its breath on the window-pane.' (*ER* III [Aug. 1909] 32)

And as he reflects later, 'one couldn't be a *raffiné* at Wimbledon – no, not with any comfort [...]' (*ER* III [Sept. 1909] 216). At the end of the story Traffle is dispossessed and lonely – Jane has claimed Puddick for her own, and he asks himself the question asked by so many of the heroes of *The Finer Grain* in their tangles:

> what would have been the use, after all, of so much imagination as constantly worked in him. Didn't it let him into more deep holes than it pulled him out of? Didn't it make for him more tight places than it saw him through? Or didn't it at the same time, not less, give him all to himself a life, exquisite, occult, dangerous and sacred, to which everything ministered and which nothing could take away? (238)

This question of the 'use' of the imagination too connects directly with the editorial already quoted from the same number of the *English Review*, which goes on from saying that 'In these islands literature has never come into its own' to declare gloomily and satirically that:

> Probably it never can, since, our public being strictly utilitarian, it cannot be proved that reading imaginative literature ever led to the invention of the steamboat, the gaining of a new colony for the British Crown, the improvement of the morals of Society, or the extension of the Franchise. (318)

The imagination is, with such a utilitarian public, without a recognised use. It's driven into the sacred space of the private mind – the only place where poor Traffle can have 'all to himself a life'.

How then should we 'read' this 'affair', this 'parcel of life'? This chapter offers only some suggestions. It should be remembered that 1909 was an unusually traumatic year for both Ford and James. Ford's marriage finally broke up, his affair with Violet Hunt began, he went from triumph as a London literary impresario to the loss of his creation, the *English Review*, quarrels with many of his friends, and suicidal despair. James was ill, nervous, thought of himself as short of money and as losing ground in the literary marketplace.

The 'affair' can be read, from both sides, in terms of status, tensions and pragmatic self-interest. Both Ford and James had their own careers to pursue, their own literary interests to protect – had something to gain from this unstable alliance. Ford's bitter remark in his 1913 legal deposition that 'owing to [the *Review*'s] obvious non-success I had lost nearly all my friends of the world of letters, who are mostly gentry looking out for what they can get' (Saunders I 290), which may well include James in its denunciation, seems coloured by sour grapes, and may not be reliable in its implication that he himself was driven by pure disinterestedness in his conduct of the *Review*. His boosting of James was, perhaps, commercially speaking, ill-advised, but it did give the magazine an unmistakeably high tone and a famous name – and a direct line of inheritance from his hero Flaubert, with whom James had been friendly. On James's side, not being 'pampered by the press' meant that it was to his advantage to have his status as Master cemented by Ford, even if at a lower rate of pay than an American magazine could muster, and at the cost of having his name attached to what by his standards might seem some rather dubiously extreme editorialising. As James's correspondence with Pinker shows, there was a measure of desperation in the Master's dealings with the literary market, and Ford was certainly here a friend in need.

Some will see James's participation in the *English Review* as the culmination of a process in which Ford was his persistent 'literary flatterer', in Miss Weld's term, with James as the at first tolerant, but finally impatient, Master. Ford's emulousness towards James – his vision of himself as 'sole lord of the demesne' at Lamb House, his sedulous cultivation of certain Jamesian tics, his hyperbolic public proclamations of James's importance, his repeated pastiches in his fiction of Jamesian themes and manner of treatment – could be seen as a form of sycophantic-rivalrous aggression. The *English Review* could be seen as giving him the chance to dispense some patronage to James, to show who holds the purse-strings. After all, he ends in 1934 by admitting (to Janet Adam Smith) that 'as the years have gone on I have grown more and more antipathetic to the Master of Rye'.[36]

Others will view Ford as more innocent in the 'affair', a sincere admirer of James's work and what he stood for, and simply led on by the more established writer's invitations, visits, cultivation of the mystique of the 'Master', allusions to 'The Figure in the Carpet' and enjoyment of the notion of a small élite of admirers or disciples. James's magisterial 1902 letter to Ford about the technical difficulties of *The Wings of the Dove* treats him as a serious writer, a *confrère*; but mostly he fends him off, playing, one might say, hard to get. James's initial response to the privileged place Ford awarded him in the *Review* looks from such an angle somewhat churlish. 'Grossly persistent' might in a pro-Fordian reading represent Jamesian egotism and stiffness, a refusal to help with an idealistic, worthy enterprise when greater pecuniary advantage is to be got in American magazines. And James's cutting of ties with Ford and Violet Hunt in November 1909, and temporary termination of his relationship with the *Review*, would in such a reading represent a cowardly fear of scandal and a betrayal of friendship (rather than for instance a mark of friendship towards Ford's wife).

But to be pro-Ford or pro-James in these ways is probably not, here, to be fully Fordian or Jamesian. While such considerations of self-interest are inevitable – writers have to play the public literary game – we perhaps can't afford not to be more generous, more James-ian, *and* more Fordian, in our recognition of the subtlety of human relations here, 'the complexity, the tantalisation, the shimmering, the haze' – and in particular of the happy conjunction between gener-ations and what it represents.

Though James was ill and preoccupied in 1908-9, and his creative energies were moving powerfully towards retrospective and autobiographical experiments, he recognised after initial distrust the handsomeness of Ford's enterprise. Ford's admiration for James's achievement is indubitable – and honourable. Ford was perhaps inspired in his impractically high-minded conduct of the *Review* by his reading of James, by the values in James's works, with their 'poor sensitive gentlemen' and variously baffled and defeated heroes and heroines too fine for an ugly, greedy world. The Jamesian equations of tales like 'The Lesson of the Master' or 'The Next Time' see the great public as always stupid, vulgar and arbitrary; popular success can never guarantee artistic value. The temptation of this perspective is to regard defeat as a mark of superiority; the energising force of it is the stimulus it gives towards a noble independence of majority tastes and opinions.

We should close, then, by emphasising the creative conver-gence of Ford and James in the *Review*. They came together in their vision of the literary mass-market and their sense of it as a symptom of a debased culture in contrast to the true values of artistic ambition and artistic freedom. Ford wrote of 'the crudely materialistic atmosphere of the time [...] when the *English Review* was founded'. The *Review*'s (Quixotic) opposition to the cheapening of literature by the forces of the book industry and modern capitalism as they adapted to the conditions of a new democratic, literate mass-society – in the 'Two Shilling Novel' for example – in its way shares the thrust of James's 'Velvet Glove'. Above all, perhaps, it is to 'Mora Montravers', the last tale James wrote and the one most likely to have been conceived *for* the *English Review*, at a time when he had seen and been won over to the magazine, that we should look for his most direct involvement with the Fordian agenda. 'The Jolly Corner' and 'A Round of Visits' take place in New York, 'The Velvet Glove' in Paris. 'Mora Montravers' is set in Wimbledon. What could be more 'English', and where could the battle for the freedom to feel and say – the battle for art – need to be more fiercely waged?[37]

NOTES

I would like to thank Bay James for her kind permission to quote from unpublished Henry James letters; also the Beinecke Rare Book and Manuscript Library at Yale and the Houghton Library, Harvard, which hold the original documents. I am very grateful for advice and encouragement to Jason Harding; and to Matthew Beaumont, Oliver Herford, Richard Price and Peter Robinson.

1   This chapter began as the Annual Ford Madox Ford Lecture, delivered at St. John's College, Durham University, 12 September 2008.
2   Max Saunders, *Ford Madox Ford: A Dual Life*, 2 vols, Oxford: Oxford University Press, 1996 – henceforth 'Saunders'; I, p. 455.
3   Brita Lindberg-Seyersted, *Ford Madox Ford and His Relationship to Stephen Crane and Henry James*, New Jersey: Humanities Press International, 1987 – henceforth *FCJ*; p. 35.
4   *'Bravest of Women and finest of friends': Henry James's Letters to Lucy Clifford*, ed. Marysa Demoor & Monty Chisholm, English Literary Studies Monograph Series No. 80,Victoria, BC, 1999, p. 37.
5   H. Montgomery Hyde, *Henry James at Home*, London: Methuen, 1969, p. 154.
6   Theodora Bosanquet diary, MS, Houghton Library, Harvard: bMS Eng 1213.1 box 1, Tuesday 5 November 1907. On the same day, she records that 'As he let me out I restored "An English Girl" & "Kipps"[.] He says Hueffer *ought* to be pronounced in the German way but round here people called him "Hufer." He also asked me what I thought of "Kipps." He thinks himself it's the cleverest & most wonderful novel that's been published for several years!'

7   Eric Homberger, 'Ford's *English Review*: Englishness and its Discontents', *Agenda*, 27/28 (Winter 1989/Spring 1990), 66.
8   *Ibid.*, p. 61.
9   See Nora Tomlinson '"An Old Man Mad About Writing" but Hopeless with Money: Ford Madox Ford and the Finances of the *English Review*' in this volume.
10 Homberger, p. 61.
11 Even James fell victim to the word 'wholesome': his travel book *Italian Hours*, published on 28 October 1909 by Heinemann, was reported in an anonymous letter to *The Times* to have been censored by the manager of one of the circulating libraries on the grounds that carrying the book 'would be detrimental to the good name our library holds for the circulation of thoroughly wholesome literature' (Samuel Hynes, *The Edwardian Turn of Mind*, London: Pimlico, 1991; 1st pub. 1968, p. 302.)
12 *Henry James Letters*, ed. Leon Edel, 4 vols, Cambridge, Mass. and London: Harvard University Press, 1974-84 – henceforth 'Edel'; IV, pp. 532-3.
13 James to Ford, 9 September 1902: 'The book had of course, to my sense, to be composed in a certain way, in order to come into being at all, & the lines of composition, so to speak, determined & controlled its parts & account for what is & what isn't there; what isn't, e. g., like the "last interview" (Hall Caine wd. have made it large as life, & magnificent, wouldn't he?) of Densher & Milly. I had to make up my mind as to what was my subject & what wasn't, & then to illustrate & embody the same logically.' (*Henry James: A Life in Letters*, ed. Philip Horne, London: Penguin, 1999 – henceforth 'Horne'; p. 371.) Ford would later make a target of the vulgar Caine.
14 I have written before about the long, comic, perverse, admirable history of James's persistent problems with length, in a piece called 'Henry James and the Economy of the Short Story', in *Modernist Writers and the Marketplace*, ed. Ian Willison, Warwick Gould and Warren Chernaik, London: Macmillan, 1996, pp. 1-35.
15 Leon Edel and Dan H. Laurence, *A Bibliography of Henry James*, The Soho Bibliographies, viii, Third Edition, revised with the assistance of James Rambeau, Oxford: Clarendon Press, 1982, p. 146.
16 I have drawn here on the data assembled in Michael Anesko's 'Appendix B: Henry James's Literary Income', in his invaluable *'Friction with the Market': Henry James and the Profession of Authorship*, New York: Oxford University Press, 1986, 167-97.
17 James's 'grossly' is an inserted afterthought; unpublished letter, Beinecke Library, Yale; Za James 1 Vol. 2.
18 Theodora Bosanquet diary, MS, Houghton Library, Harvard: bMS Eng 1213.1 box 1, Tuesday 17 December 1908. Just after this she is cross at being given a glove box for Christmas by her employer – 'just the sort of thing one would give an illiterate housekeeper'. The story is probably 'Crapy Cornelia'.
19 Theodora Bosanquet diary, MS, Houghton Library, Harvard: bMS Eng 1213.1 box 1, Saturday 2 January 1909.
20 Theodora Bosanquet diary, MS, Houghton Library, Harvard: bMS Eng 1213.1 box 1, Sunday 3 January 1909.
21 James to Pinker, 19 January 1909, unpublished letter, Beinecke Library, Yale; Za James 1 Vol. 2.

22 James to Pinker, 19 March 1909, unpublished letter, Beinecke Library, Yale; Za James 1 Vol. 2.

23 James to Pinker, 7 April 1909, unpublished letter, Beinecke Library, Yale; Za James 1 Vol. 2.

24 James to Pinker, 13 April 1909, unpublished letter, Beinecke Library, Yale; Za James 1 Vol. 2.

25 James to Pinker, 13 May 1909, unpublished letter, Beinecke Library, Yale; Za James 1 Vol. 2.

26 James to Pinker, 2 July 1909, unpublished letter, Beinecke Library, Yale; Za James 1 Vol. 2.

27 James to Pinker, 19 August 1909, unpublished letter, Beinecke Library, Yale; Za James 1 Vol. 2.

28 James to Pinker, 15 October 1909, unpublished letter, Beinecke Library, Yale; Za James 1 Vol. 2.

29 James to Pinker, 4 November 1909, unpublished letter, Beinecke Library, Yale; Za James 1 Vol. 2.

30 James to Pinker, 11 November 1909, unpublished letter, Beinecke Library, Yale; Za James 1 Vol. 2.

31 James to Pinker, 9 January 1909, unpublished letter, Beinecke Library, Yale; Za James 1 Vol. 2.

32 James to Pinker, 2 February 1910, unpublished letter, Beinecke Library, Yale; Za James 1 Vol. 2.

33 James to Pinker, 9 February 1910, unpublished letter, Beinecke Library, Yale; Za James 1 Vol. 2.

34 Henry James, *The Ambassadors*, ed. Adrian Poole, London: Penguin Classics, 2008, p. 176.

35 See N. H. Reeve, 'Living Up to the Name: "Mora Montravers"', in *Henry James: The Shorter Fiction: Reassessments*, ed. N. H. Reeve, Basingstoke: Macmillan, 1997, pp. 138-155.

36 *LF* 232. This is not, as Max Saunders has helpfully pointed out to me, what Ford writes publicly on James in the piece he writes for Janet Adam Smith, which presents his ambivalence more judiciously: 'He was the greatest novelist – perhaps after Turgenev – that the world has ever seen, the most consummate artist, the most contagious figure. But that alone made him dangerous – infinitely dangerous. For if a figure is so great that you have no hopes of surpassing him you are in terrible peril of imitating his tricks and having one more shy at solving his social problems [. . . .]' ('Writers of America – VIII: An Author Both Sides of the Atlantic,' *Listener*, 12 (19 September 1934), 500-1).

37 'The freedom to feel and say' comes from James's 1884 essay 'The Art of Fiction': Henry James, *Literary Criticism: Essays on Literature, American Writers, English Writers,* edited by Leon Edel and Mark Wilson, New York: Library of America, 1984, pp. 44-65 (p. 50).

FORD AS EDITOR IN JOSEPH CONRAD'S 'THE PLANTER OF MALATA'

Gene M. Moore

The relation between an author's life and his works is one of the main-stays of literary criticism, but the expression of the 'life' in the fiction is anything but simple. To suggest that every novel is ultimately a *roman à clef*, an artistic assemblage of biographical elements, seems as obvious as the notion that every living body is an assemblage of chemicals; but it is far less obvious that one can presume in either case to break the code or find the right 'key' to explain the text or the body in question. How could an author possibly produce a work that is unlike himself? Biographical explanations have played a major role in Conrad and Ford criticism; yet when critics have taken up the game of decoding fictional characters for biographical evidence, the complex relations between Conrad and Ford have all too often been understood in terms of a kind of soap-opera psychology that fails to do justice either to the works in question or to their authors.

Joseph Conrad and Ford Madox Ford both acknowledged that they found their characters in real life, drawing inspiration from friends or acquaintances or from the sight of total strangers glimpsed only in passing. Conrad often took his 'Author's Notes' as occasions for recalling the real-world origins of his characters; in a memorable passage in *A Personal Record*, he confronts the pathetic shade of Almayer and attempts to justify his appropriation of the trader's identity for artistic purposes. In *It Was the Nightingale*, Ford recalls how the characters of *Parade's End* came to him in the course of a train journey from England to France: Christopher Tietjens would be based on Arthur Marwood, who had described himself as 'an elephant built out of meal sacks';[1] Valentine Wannop would be modelled after the actress Dorothy Minto, 'small and blonde and light on her feet'; and the unforgiving Sylvia was derived from a golden-haired woman 'in a golden sheath-gown' glimpsed in the waiting crowd at Amiens station. But having thus presented his cast of characters, Ford then issues a surprising disclaimer: 'I may make the note that I never in my life, as far as I can remember, used a character from actual life for purposes of fiction – or never without concealing their attributes very carefully' (*IWN* 210-11). An unkind stickler for consistency – or a Conrad scholar – might regard this as yet another sign of Ford's deplorable 'unreliability,' of his trying to have his cake and eat it too; but I suspect there is more to it than that. I would like in what follows first to challenge the most notorious case of satirical portraiture in the Conrad/Ford canon, and then to propose a new instance of 'borrowing' from life that has hitherto failed to receive sufficient attention.

Although both Ford and Conrad often mentioned the real-world models on which their fictional characters were based, neither of them ever spoke of using the other as the model for a fictional character. Ford recorded his artistic debts to Conrad on many occasions, and Conrad acknowledged Ford as the anonymous 'omniscient friend' who provided the first hint for what became *The Secret Agent*, but both were reticent about identifying their models too closely, especially when these were known literary figures or personal friends. Scholars have shown far less reticence. In particular, the critical reception of Ford's *The Simple Life Limited* has been determined almost entirely by its notoriety as a vicious caricature of Conrad in the character of Simeon Brandetski, who left his Slavic homeland to seek his fortune in South Africa before anglicizing his name to Simon Bransdon and becoming an author in English (the title of whose most celebrated work, *Clotted Vapours*, echoes early criticism of the exoticism of Conrad's style). Thomas C. Moser argues that Ford 'must have written the book [...] to avenge himself on Conrad, who had rejected him,' and sees it as fulfilling 'a need beyond revenge, Ford's need to express his profound self-loathing, the inevitable counterpart of his boundless vanity'.[2] The novel is understood as an elaborate *roman à clef* in which Ford sought to pillory all those who had let him down, and until recently, criticism of the novel has been limited almost exclusively to speculation about the identities of the encoded characters.[3]

What is perhaps most curious about this critical tradition is that it has gone unchallenged even though the surviving letters and memoirs provide no corroborating evidence of vengeful intent; to the contrary, the extant documents from this period and afterwards show little sign of irritation on Conrad's part, and betray no awareness on his part that Ford had attempted to insult him. This absence of any hard evidence of malicious intent has led the major biographers of both authors to adopt an argument of last resort (italics added):

> Conrad never spoke on the subject, although *it is hard to imagine* that he never read *The Simple Life Limited.*[4]

> *It is hard to imagine* Conrad forgiving Ford for putting so much of him into Brandson [*sic*].[5]

Maybe; but it strikes me as much harder to imagine that a man who considered himself deeply offended, especially someone as sensitive as Conrad, could maintain utter silence on a matter affecting his personal honour. Not only did he keep silence forever, but he wrote to Ford in Giessen, Germany, on 29 March 1911, six weeks after the novel was published, in exceedingly warm and complimentary terms. The letter, to 'My dear Ford,' opens with 'I can't tell you how happy we are to know you are at peace at last,' perhaps in reference to the German divorce Ford was seeking to obtain. Conrad then told Ford he had ordered his 'latest' – not *The Simple Life Limited*, but *Ancient Lights*, published just five days earlier[6] – and spoke of the anticipated joy of reading it in terms impossible to imagine as those of an offended man: 'I am confident of finding in your pages a delicate flavour of feeling, a wishfulness which is the charm of things remembered and a perfectly worthy, human appreciation of a phase of art untainted by self-seeking – as pre-raphaelism of the early time has always seemed to me.' The letter was signed with 'Our love.'[7]

   It is really *not* very hard to imagine that Conrad never read a first novel by an unknown author calling himself 'Daniel Chaucer,'[8] especially given that the book disappeared almost without a trace upon publication. It left no traces in the memoirs of Violet Hunt, who was involved with Ford at the time the novel was written (or dictated).[9] Nor is it mentioned by Douglas Goldring – no great admirer of Conrad – in his recollections of Ford's involvement with the *English Review* and its aftermath. Stranger still, if Jessie Conrad were aware that Ford had caricatured her husband, it is very hard indeed to imagine that she would not have added this charge to the long list of grievances she levelled at Ford in her two volumes of memoirs.[10] *The Simple Life Limited* contains coy references to the *English Review* and even to Ford himself, yet the reviewer for the real *English Review* thought for some reason that the author was a woman.[11] According to Moser, an entry in Olive Garnett's diary dated 10 April 1911 reads 'Julius West

asked me if I had written the "Simple Life"'; with a later marginal
scrawl she identified the author as Ford and called the novel 'a pot
boiler and scandalous'. Hardly an impartial observer, Olive Garnett
was close to Ford's wife, and 'as Elsie became further estranged from
Ford, so did she'.[12] Her use of the word 'scandalous' suggests wider
social consequences, but no further traces of scandal have been recorded in the available documents. Not until 8 July, nearly six months
after the novel was published, did Garnett note that 'the cat is now
completely out of the bag'.[13] It seems that the secret of the book's
authorship was sufficiently kept until after the wave of reviews had
passed and the novel itself was consigned to oblivion. Although Olive
Garnett might well have shared her indignation with Elsie Hueffer and
with her older brother, there is no hard evidence that Edward Garnett
was ever aware of Ford's satire, which is all the more surprising since
the colony of Russian émigrés and Simple-Lifers at Coombe Luscombe is based on Garnett's circle at the Cearne in Limpsfield. In
sum, given his solitary habits and the aversion to gossip shown in his
letters, it is *not* hard to imagine that Conrad might well have remained
forever unaware of the existence of *The Simple Life Limited*, or, if he
were aware of it, unwilling to look into the matter further. Disparage-
ment of the novel as a thing that 'smells of malicious gossip' (Najder
218) cannot be sustained on the basis of documentary evidence; if
there was any offence in it, it was taken not by Conrad, but later, by
Conrad scholars on his behalf.[14] It is time for *The Simple Life Limited*
to be reassessed more positively (and more in the spirit of the first
reviews) not as a malicious gesture but as an expression of Ford's
lifelong, bohemian interest in The Simple Life with all its Limitations,
and as a fictional testimony to his experience of kitchen-gardening,
ecological living, and the age-old problem of how to make the Simple
Life 'pay'.

The Simple Life Limited is not the only case in which Ford is
alleged to have 'borrowed' Conrad as a character,[15] but it is the most
egregious. Ford is also thought to appear in several of Conrad's works,
though the attributions are based not on physical characteristics or
biographical details but on verbal similarities. There is general agreement that Ford is the 'omniscient friend' who supplied Conrad with
information about anarchists for *The Secret Agent*. As a cousin and
neighbour of the Rossettis, Ford grew up in relatively close contact
with anarchist circles, as recorded in *A Girl among the Anarchists*
(1903), published by Helen and Olivia Rossetti under the pseudonym

Isabel Meredith, or in Ford's sister Juliet Soskice's memoir *Chapters from Childhood* (1921), or in the 'Farthest Left' chapter of Ford's own *Return to Yesterday* (1931).

Taking his cue from Conrad's description of this 'omniscient friend' who 'liked to talk to all sorts of people and [...] may have gathered those illuminating facts at second or third hand, from a crossing-sweeper, from a retired police officer, from some vague man in his club, or even perhaps from a Minister of State',[16] Norman Sherry has suggested that Ford served as the primary model for Mr. X in Conrad's story 'The Informer,' who 'collects acquaintances' and 'has met with and talked to everyone worth knowing on any conceivable ground'.[17] There is of course a difference between collecting 'illuminating facts' and collecting 'acquaintances,' but Sherry notes that the 'collector' in Conrad's story 'performs precisely the same function in the story as did Ford in real life'[18] by introducing the narrator to a famous anarchist.

Moser has also argued that after the publication of *The Simple Life Limited*, Conrad retaliated by using Ford as a model for the villainous financier De Barral in *Chance*.[19] It must be said that De Barral bears no striking physical resemblance to Ford: he is 'old,'[20] 'stiff as a ramrod' and ghostly in appearance (245), with 'a thin, somewhat sunken face, with a tightly closed mouth' (285), 'lank and angular' (365), 'with a rigidly carried head' (356), 'grey hairs' (367), and 'thin obstinate lips' (368) that twitch and writhe uncontrollably (357, 363). The only thing he seems to share with Ford is his 'faded blue eyes' (363). Yet despite the evidence, Moser insists that like De Barral, Ford was a 'cold, vain, self-deluded charlatan' and that 'De Barral looks, talks, and acts like Ford.'[21] The clincher for Moser is a letter to Galsworthy from the end of March 1912 in which Conrad mentioned a New Year's visit from the 'great F.M.H.' accompanied by 'the somewhat less great V. H[unt]' (Conrad V 37), applying the same epithet to Ford (albeit without capital G) as to De Barral. The adjective 'great' appears a total of 72 times in the text of *Chance*, seven times in reference to De Barral, who proclaims himself 'the Great Mr. de Barral' three times.[22] He is dubbed 'the Great de Barral' three more times by Marlow (372, 384, 436), and 'The Great de Barral' is also the title of the penultimate chapter.

If the case for Ford as a model for Mr. X or 'the Great de Barral' is tenuous at best, a much stronger case can be made for Ford's appearance in another Conrad story where a character not only resembles him both physically and temperamentally, but indeed 'performs precisely the same function in the story as did Ford in real life,' namely as the Editor in Conrad's story 'The Planter of Malata.' It is remarkable that this connection has never been fully explored, although at least three critics have noticed it. The first to suggest that Conrad's Editor is based on Ford may have been R. J. Herndon, in his unpublished Ph.D. thesis on 'The Collaboration of Joseph Conrad and Ford Madox Ford' (Stanford University, 1957). Bernard C. Meyer complimented Herndon for the 'considerable plausibility' of the idea;[23] Meyer cites it twice in his 'psychoanalytic biography' of Conrad, but fails to follow up on its implications. In his own psycho-biography of Ford, Moser briefly mentions 'the Conradian hero' and 'the Fordian "Editor"' but takes no further interest in what this double portrait could tell us about the relationship between the two authors; instead, he abruptly dismisses the ending of the story as 'nonsense': 'In [...] "The Planter of Malata," the Conradian hero's assistant and then the hero die, leaving to the Fordian "Editor" only a grave and deserted beach. What nonsense.'[24] In general, critics have paid far more attention to the romance between Geoffrey Renouard and Felicia Moorsom than to the relationship between Renouard and his 'only friend and crony' (84), a character who is never named but identified only as 'the editor and part-owner' of an 'important newspaper' (3).

When *Within the Tides* was published in February 1915, the review on the 'Red Page' of the Sydney *Bulletin* called attention to local Australian references in two of Conrad's tales, including the incident in 'The Planter of Malata' where 'a poet from the bush, the latest discovery of the editor,' falls asleep 'on the hearthrug of the editorial room' (49). 'Do editors really do such things in Sydney?'[25] asked the reviewer. In a reply published in the *Bulletin* on 23 March, Conrad affirmed that:

> the episode of the poet on the hearthrug which seems to have shocked my good reviewer on the Red Page is a fact! I don't know if such things happen in Sydney. They do happen in London though, where – as you know – everything happens. And the office was the office of a still rather young review. I mustn't tell you its name, but you know it well. (Conrad V 555)

Annotating 'a still rather young review,' the editors of the *Collected Letters* add a footnote that hesitantly connects the Sydney newspaper with the *English Review* but fails to mention any link with Ford: 'The *English Review*? The weekly in Conrad's story bears a suspicious resemblance to the *Bulletin* itself' (Conrad V 555n4). Preoccupied with the Sydney newspaper, the editors make no mention of the striking similarities between Ford and the Editor in Conrad's tale. Given the many accounts of Ford's editorial discoveries (including his own account, in *Portraits from Life*, of his discovery of D. H. Lawrence), it is entirely plausible that a poet from the English 'bush' might well have slept on the hearthrug of the *English Review*, all the more given that Ford's sub-editor Douglas Goldring described him as 'the most incorrigibly hospitable man I have ever met' (*South Lodge* 32).

Ford's urban sociability, and his ability to enter into conversation with different types and conditions of people, stand in marked contrast to Conrad's more aloof and solitary temperament. This contrast also plays an important role in 'The Planter of Malata' from the very beginning. The Editor and his visitor, the planter Renouard, are immediately introduced as opposing types: the Editor is '[t]he stouter of the two, fair, and with more of an urban look about him,' while Renouard is a 'lean, lounging, active man' with 'a fine bronzed face.'[26] The Editor is repeatedly described as 'all-knowing' and at ease in society, 'a man whose business or at least whose profession was to know everything that went on in this part of the globe' (8). In contrast, Renouard speaks of his own 'solitary manner of life away there' (4) on the remote island of Malata.[27] He has come to the Editor for information about a strange social encounter the previous evening because, as the narrator explains: 'Solitary life makes a man reticent in respect of anything in the nature of gossip, which those to whom chatting about their kind is an everyday exercise regard as the commonest use of speech' (5).

This contrast between Renouard's social shyness and the Editor's fondness for gossip is remarkably similar to the temperamental difference that biographers have often noted between the reclusive Conrad and the gregarious Ford. Najder, for example, states that 'Conrad did not live within a community. He was not a member of a group or coterie; he lived in the country, led an unusually isolated life, until his last years without a stable social environment'; Conrad was, in Najder's words, 'a stranger from an unfamiliar country, a recluse, a social oddity' (viii-ix). In nearly identical terms, Renouard tells the Editor: 'Everybody knows I am not a society man' (7). The Editor, on the other hand, is described as 'an experienced man of the world' (17), the very terms in which Najder describes Ford as editor of the *English*

Review: 'Now Ford, as editor, was a man of the world, perambulating in a horse cab all over London and patronizing young writers; he became the self-appointed hub of a large circle of people, and Conrad felt himself being drawn into a web of multiple interrelationships' (398). Like Ford, the Editor can speak to anyone, and has learned the story of the Moorsoms for example from young Willie Dunster, whom Renouard dismisses with the remark (in free indirect discourse): 'Of course the proper person to go to would have been young Dunster, but he couldn't stand Willie Dunster – not at any price' (12).

The Editor shares not only Ford's notoriety and social energy but also the omniscient and patronizing manner that irritated so many of Ford's acquaintances. In the 'Author's Note' to *The Secret Agent*, Conrad had acknowledged Ford's help (without naming him) as that of an 'omniscient friend' (8.6) with a 'characteristically casual and omniscient manner' (5.18-19); with similar insistence, the Editor is repeatedly characterized as 'the all-knowing journalist' (10), '[t]he all-knowing man' (11), 'the all-knowing one' (55, 56), 'the all-knowing Editor' (13, 84), and '[Renouard's] patronising friend' (23).

What the narrator of 'The Planter' describes as the Editor's 'professional vanity [...] well known to Renouard' (13) has also been richly documented in Ford's own case. Like Ford, the Editor sees himself as the guardian of art and culture in a land of philistines, whose greatest happiness is in discovering and promoting new literary talent: 'Such discoveries were the business, the vocation, the pride and delight of the only apostle of letters in the hemisphere, the solitary patron of culture, the Slave of the Lamp – as he subscribed himself at the bottom of the weekly literary page of his paper' (49). This high calling also authorizes him to behave imperiously, as when he effect-ively commandeers Renouard's schooner for a voyage to Malata to find the missing Arthur. The Editor is accustomed to 'managing' people, as Renouard acknowledges with a wry compliment: 'You are a heaven-born discoverer and a first-rate manager' (53); but in his own mind Renouard curses the Editor as a 'confounded busybody arrang-ing everything' (56). At the time of their row about Conrad's contribu-tions to the *English Review*, Conrad complained to his friends about Ford in similar terms, explaining to his fellow contributor Norman Douglas that 'The fact is that H. loves to manage people. No doubt he helps too but his assistance has an obverse side' (Conrad IV 205). To Dr. R. D. Mackintosh, who treated Conrad's gout and whose plans to visit Conrad were suddenly pre-empted by Ford, he complained of

Ford's 'mania for managing the universe, worse even in form than in substance' (Conrad IV 214-15). To his agent J. B. Pinker he described Ford as 'a megalomaniac who imagines that he is managing the Universe and that everybody treats him with the blackest ingratitude' (Conrad IV 265).

If the Editor shares many of Ford's characteristics, Renouard also has much in common with Conrad. As he tells Felicia Moorsom, 'I came out to wander at large in the world when I was nineteen, almost directly after I left school' (10-11); by the age of nineteen Conrad had made three voyages to the Caribbean, and he celebrated his 21st birthday on his first outbound voyage to Australia. It was as true of Conrad as of Renouard that '[h]e had not seen a single human being to whom he was related for many years' (26). Renouard also has a stubborn streak in which he takes pride: he is even 'almost ill-famed for his ruthless daring' (43). The Editor shares with him the local gossip about himself: 'You know what has been said of you? That you couldn't get on with anybody you couldn't kick,' adding that 'when your heart is set on some object you are a man that doesn't count the cost to yourself or others' (28); and he repeats this gossip to the Moorsoms (43). In his 'Author's Note' to *Within the Tides*, Conrad acknowledged this aspect of his resemblance to his protagonist: 'I resemble Geoffrey Renouard in so far that when once engaged in an adventure I cannot bear the idea of turning back' (viii). The 'Author's Note' for *The Secret Agent* records a similar expression of pride in his perseverance: 'It is one of the minor satisfactions of my writing life that having taken that resolve [i.e., to apply an ironic method] I did manage, it seems to me, to carry it right through to the end' (7.29-32).

Renouard also shares Conrad's familiarity with things French. Felicia Moorsom's first question to him is 'Are you French, Mr. Renouard?' (10). Professor Moorsom, who has been likened to both William James and Bertrand Russell as someone who 'has made philosophy pay' (16),[28] is scheduled to deliver lectures in Paris, and presumes a sufficient familiarity with French culture on Renouard's part to warrant a conversational allusion to Charles Perrault's 'Blue-beard' (70). Renouard's name – 'Mr. Geoffrey Renouard' (15) – phonically anticipates the 'Monsieur George' who narrates *The Arrow of Gold*, and Renouard's spellbound attendance on Felicia Moorsom can be seen as a sketch for Monsieur George's idolatrous infatuation with Rita de Lastaola. There are perhaps even more interesting parallels between Renouard's mountaintop confession to Felicia Moorsom and the closing scene of *Heart of Darkness*. Like Marlow, the Planter of Malata also tells a lie to another man's Intended; but while Marlow claims to have 'laid the ghost of [Kurtz's] gifts at last with a lie,'[29] Renouard's lie raises a ghost that haunts him to his death; and when Renouard finally confesses his lie and declares his own 'true love,' Arthur's Intended responds – in French – with Kurtzian horror: '*Assez! J'ai horreur de tout cela*' (78).

One must be wary of drawing inferences about an author's life from the way his characters behave in the world of fiction, but the fictional portraits in 'The Planter of Malata' call for a reconsideration of the extent to which the relationship between Conrad and Ford can be understood by reading *The Simple Life Limited* and other works as exercises in 'malicious gossip' or expressions of revenge and 'self-loathing'. The portraits of Renouard and the Editor are not simple and not unmixed: Renouard is a confirmed sociopath who doesn't 'count the cost', and the Editor's skills as a 'manager' end by costing Renouard his life. Moreover, fictional portraits are always necessarily inexact: we are told for example that Renouard's 'intercourse with the meddlesome journalist was that merely outward intimacy without sympathy some young men get drawn into easily' (55), a description fully at odds with the sympathy that Conrad and Ford continued to express for each other both as authors and as human beings. In his last letters to Ford, although he was irritated by details concerning the French royalties on their collaborations, Conrad remembered their *English Review* days fondly and without rancour: 'The mere fact that it was the occasion of you putting on me that gentle but persistent pressure which extracted from the depths of my then despondency the stuff of the "Personal Record" would be enough to make its memory dear'; he spoke of Ford's bullying as a 'marvellously successful in-stance of editorial tyranny!' and added, 'I have forgiven you long ago' (Conrad VIII 205). In a letter written six weeks before his death, Conrad praised Ford's latest work, *Some Do Not ...*, as 'tout à fait chic' (Conrad VIII 361). In December 1911, at the very time Conrad was completing 'The Planter of Malata,' Ford published in the December issue of the *English Review* a long and laudatory essay about Conrad that celebrated not only his skills as a writer but especially the moral effect of his works on his English readership. Ford claimed not only that Conrad was 'without an equal for getting an atmosphere' and for 'describing an action',[30] but that *Lord Jim* 'has made many men better Englishmen' because Conrad 'has given us a sense of responsibilities. He has made us desire more sedulously to do our duties. He has taught us above all to desire to be shipshape – to be shipshape on our decks, on our drawing-room carpets, and in the thoughts that we think in our minds' (*CE* 85).

In general, Conrad and Ford were far more tolerant of each other's faults than critics and biographers have been willing to recognize. There is no hard evidence that Ford intended Simeon Brandetski to be seen as a Frankenstein monster composed of Conrad's parts or a Dorian Gray portrait of Conrad's soul. Instead, the well-documented silence maintained by Conrad and Ford makes it 'hard to imagine' that offense was taken. If 'The Planter of Malata' can be seen as a fictional representation of the relations between the two authors, it does not follow from this that Conrad was consciously or deliberately trying to send a message to Ford (who, as far as I am aware, never singled out the story for comment, nor the volume in which it appeared). In a letter to Conrad from the front, Ford recorded his notes on the specific sights and sounds of war, and offered them to Conrad on the grounds that 'a pocketful of coins of a foreign country may sometimes come in handy. You might want to put a phrase into the mouth of someone in Bangkok who had been, say, to Bécourt. There you wd. be! And I, to that extent, shd. once more have collaborated' (*Presence* 177). In the same spirit, future scholars may well find it 'handier' to consider the ways that Conrad and Ford are represented in each other's works not as acts of revenge, but as forms of collaboration.

NOTES

1   Ford, *It Was the Nightingale*, London: William Heinemann, 1934 – henceforth *IWN*; p. 208.
2   Thomas C. Moser, *The Life in the Fiction of Ford Madox Ford*, Princeton: Princeton University Press, 1980 – henceforth 'Moser'; pp. 91-2.
3   This approach is complicated because Brandetski begins as a grotesquely reclusive sea-creature but emerges at the end of the novel as an energetic hero who organizes the rescue of the 'Simple Lifers' from a mad arsonist. The decoding of fictional characters is an inexact science: Ford is thought to have insulted himself in the person of Horatio Gubb, and some characters lack real-world referents while others are thought to be amalgamations based on more than one model.
4   Zdzisław Najder, *Joseph Conrad: A Life*, tr. Halina Najder, Rochester: Camden House, 2007 – henceforth 'Najder'; p. 424.

5   Max Saunders, *Ford Madox Ford: A Dual Life*, 2 vols (Oxford: Oxford University Press, 1996) – henceforth 'Saunders'; I, p. 324.

6   David Dow Harvey, *Ford Madox Ford, 1873-1939: A Bibliography of Works and Criticism*, Princeton: Princeton University Press, 1962, p. 33.

7   Laurence Davies *et al.*, eds., *The Collected Letters of Joseph Conrad*, Cambridge: Cambridge University Press, 1983-2007 – henceforth 'Conrad'; vol. 4, pp. 433-4.

8   Ford recycled the pseudonym for *The New Humpty-Dumpty*, published in July the following year, and used it again in the *transatlantic review* after the war.

9   A letter from Ford to J. B. Pinker indicates that the manuscript was apparently completed by the end of March 1910. See *Letters of Ford Madox Ford*, ed. Richard M. Ludwig, Princeton, NJ: Princeton University Press, 1965, pp. 41-2.

10 Her enmity may have had chiefly to do with the differences between Ford's bohemian habits and her own bourgeois upbringing: whenever Ford would arrive unannounced, she felt herself obliged suddenly and without forewarning to abandon her domestic plans for the day in order to receive her husband's friend in proper style, in a proper dress and with her hair done up properly. She hated him all the more because he remained utterly oblivious to all the ways in which he was constantly – if inadvertently – inconveniencing her.

11 Saunders I 570n3. *The Simple Life Limited* is not included in Frank MacShane's *Critical Heritage* volume, London: Routledge, 1972, but the brief excerpts from three other reviews between February and May 1911 reprinted by David Dow Harvey (pp. 304-7) do not identify Ford as the author and show little interest in the identities of his models.

12 Saunders I 237.

13 Cited in Moser, p. 91.

14 What 'smells of malicious gossip' is not Ford's work but the long habit in Conrad studies of disparaging Ford at every opportunity, which sadly shows no sign of abating in the latest biographies by Zdzisław Najder and John Stape, both published in 2007. Najder characterizes Ford only by his weaknesses, depicting him as essentially snobbish and unreliable, as if he were most himself when most obnoxious. He is almost never mentioned without gratuitous abuse: as 'the volatile, bragging Ford' (416) with his 'snobbery' (277), his 'haughty manner and absurd naiveté in business matters' (398), the author of 'half-baked stuff' (284) and of memoirs which 'contain an overwhelming amount of bunk' and 'have practically no documentary value' (278). In the same hard-to-imagine vein, Najder speculates that 'It is difficult to rid oneself of the suspicion that [Conrad] considered Ford a likeable, extremely gifted but somewhat superficial featherbrain' (278). Stape sees Ford as 'a drawing-room autocrat' (*The Several Lives of Joseph Conrad*, London: William Heinemann, 2007, p. 167) who 'enjoyed playing the bull in the English china shop, burnishing his German credentials when it suited him' (109); Ford's *Joseph Conrad: A Personal Remembrance* is dismissed as 'typically Fordian – unbalanced, insouciant as to facts, and extravagantly creative' (265).

15 Moser, in particular, reads Conrad and Marwood into many of Ford's novels.

16 Joseph Conrad, *The Secret Agent: A Simple Tale*, ed. Bruce Harkness and S. W. Reid, The Cambridge Edition of the Works of Joseph Conrad, Cambridge: Cambridge University Press, 1990, p. 5.27-30.

17 Joseph Conrad, *A Set of Six*, Dent's Collected Edition, London: J. M. Dent & Sons, 1954, p. 73.
18 Norman Sherry, *Conrad's Western World*, Cambridge: Cambridge University Press, 1971, p. 209.
19 Thomas C. Moser, 'Conrad, Ford, and the Sources of *Chance*,' *Conradiana*, 7 (1976), 207-24, esp. pp. 214-19.
20 Joseph Conrad, *Chance: A Tale in two parts*, Dent's Collected Edition, London: J. M. Dent & Sons, 1949, p. 355. Subsequent page references are to this edition.
21 Moser, p. 98. Ford read *Chance* while recovering from gas attacks in a hospital in Rouen, but failed to see the resemblance. He told Conrad, 'The end is odd, you know, old boy. It's like a bit of Maupassant tacked onto a Flaubert façade': *The Presence of Ford Madox Ford*, ed. Sondra J. Stang, Philadelphia: University of Pennsylvania Press, 1981 – henceforth *Presence*; p. 176.
22 With a curious change of verb tense each time (italics added): 'I *am* the great Mr. de Barral (yes, yes, some of them twisted their mouths at it, but I *was* the great Mr. de Barral)' (362), 'But have you a notion who I am? Listen! I *have been* the Great Mr. de Barral' (432).
23 Bernard C. Meyer, *Joseph Conrad: A Psychoanalytic Biography*, Princeton: Princeton University Press, 1967, p. 80.
24 Moser, p. 111. Moser overlooks the possibility of a psychological reading of the story as a *nouvelle à clef* in which Renouard and the Editor act out the parts of Conrad and Ford, with young 'Master Arthur' (20) – who, like his namesake, 'ailed and ailed' (74) – representing a wrongly accused and subsequently exonerated Arthur Marwood.
25 The name of Sydney appears in the manuscript (now in the Berg Collection, New York Public Library) but is not mentioned in the story as published.
26 Joseph Conrad, *Within the Tides: Tales*, Dent's Collected Edition, London: J. M. Dent & Sons, 1950, p. 3. Subsequent page references are to this edition.
27 Florence Clemens identified Conrad's 'Malata' as Malaita in the Solomon Islands, which were declared a British protectorate in 1893; see 'Conrad's Malaysian Fiction,' Diss. Ohio State University, 1937, p. [288].
28 For the similarities with William James, see Stanisław Modrzewski, 'The Consciousness of Cultural Models in "The Planter of Malata,"' *The Conradian*, 13 (December 1988), 174; for Russell, see Stape, pp. 192-3.
29 Joseph Conrad, *Youth – Heart of Darkness – The End of the Tether*, Dent's Collected Edition, J. M. Dent & Sons, 1946, p. 115.
30 Ford, *Critical Essays*, ed. Max Saunders and Richard Stang, Manchester: Carcanet Press, 2002 – henceforth *CE*; p. 83.

A MUSIC-HALL DOUBLE ACT:
FORDIE AND WELLS'S *ENGLISH REVIEW*

Nick Hubble

Max Saunders argues that the *English Review* 'signalled the presence of English modernism' not only by publishing Lawrence, Lewis, Pound, Conrad, James and Ford but also by publishing these writers alongside Wells, Galsworthy and Bennett.[1] Clearly, this is not modernism as it was primarily conceived until recently within the Academy; it doesn't reflect the division Virginia Woolf subsequently made in which modernism is defined precisely against Wells, Galsworthy and Bennett.[2] Therefore, thinking of the *English Review* as modernist – as the first moment of English modernism – actually requires a leap beyond our usual intellectual habits. Rather than view this moment as one of pre-lapsarian utopian wholeness, I want to draw an analogy deriving from Ford's tendency to edit the manuscripts for the *English Review* while 'sitting in a box or the stalls of the local music-hall' (Saunders I 247). This form of modernism, I would suggest, operates as a series of theatrical turns in which the complex performative interactions, both with mass audiences and fellow modernists, are integral elements of the overall experience. In other words, the works of these writers endlessly dramatize their relationship with other writers in what would be a completely ridiculous manner if it wasn't for the fact that they are also performances intended to satisfy the demand of mass audiences for entertainment. This can be seen clearly in the case of Wells and Ford where the story of their interaction over the *English Review* was to be competitively retold by each of them in increasingly bizarre forms: in Wells's *Tono-Bungay* (serialized from the first issue of the *English Review* in 1908) the story becomes that of the mass marketing of the eponymous quack medicine, whereas in Ford's two books written as Daniel Chaucer, *The Simple Life Limited* (1911) and *The New Humpty-Dumpty* (1912), it is retold respectively as the setting up of a colony of simple lifers and as the struggles of a group of conspirators plotting a counter-revolution in a small foreign country.

I would suggest that these frenzied reworkings actually express something about the modernism of the *English Review* that was not expressed elsewhere – and indeed that they are a symptom of the failure of this type of modernism to establish itself. In that sense these fictional accounts are the nearest we get to an account of the rise and fall of the *English Review* and an indication of what was actually lost in that process. While Ford's reputation has fluctuated ever since, arguably it was Wells who suffered most from this loss as is witnessed by the amount of effort he expended in replaying the arguments for years afterwards, notably in *Boon* (1915) and *The Bulpington of Blup* (1932). Nevertheless, Wells's caricatures of Ford are on the whole kinder than Ford's of Wells; although both must be considered relatively considerate to each other when compared, for instance, with the nastiness both display in portraits of Conrad.[3]

The first place to look for the modernism of the *English Review* is in *Tono-Bungay*, often considered Wells's best book and wryly acknowledged by Wells himself as perhaps the nearest he came to 'a deliberate attempt upon The Novel'.[4] Indeed, Max Saunders points out that 'Wells's bravura performance' in the first person mode was a possible influence on Ford's *The Good Soldier* (Saunders I 454). The reason why the serialization of *Tono-Bungay* from the eighty-first page of the first number of the *English Review* is absolutely fitting and integral to that journal's modernist project is because it is simply the best fictional account – probably the best sociological account as well[5] – of what happened to England in the closing decades of the nineteenth century:

> The great house, the church, the village, and the labourers and the servants in their stations and degrees, seemed to me, I say, to be a closed and complete social system. About us were other villages and great estates, and from house to house, interlacing, correlated, the Gentry, the fine Olympians, came and went. The country towns seemed mere collections of shops, marketing places for the tenantry, centres for such education as they needed, as entirely dependent on the gentry as the village and scarcely less directly so. I thought this was the order of the whole world. I thought London was only a greater country town where the gentlefolk kept town-houses and did their greater shopping under the magnificent shadow of the greatest of all fine gentlewomen, the Queen. It seemed to be in the divine order. That all this fine appearance was already sapped, that there were forces at work that might presently carry all this elaborate social system in which my mother instructed me so carefully that I might understand my 'place,' to Limbo, had scarcely dawned upon me even by the time that Tono-Bungay was fairly launched upon the world.[6]

Tono-Bungay describes the unprecedented social change that resulted in the emergence of twentieth-century mass society: the historical condition from and against which all versions of modernism arose. More than anyone else, Wells, the son of a shop-keeper and a domestic servant, embodied that social change by becoming one of the major writers of the age. Wells sometimes comes across as conceited but it needs to be remembered that he was exceptional: very few people ever underwent a comparable career path simply because of the difficulty of overcoming the attendant mental frameworks. Much of the thrust of *Tono-Bungay* stems from Wells's attempt to analyze how he himself broke free from those mental frameworks and yet still maintained sanity. Ultimately, the narrator, George Ponderevo, defines himself as an escaper from a decaying society – defined by his mental purpose and symbolically represented in the closing passages of the novel as he cuts through the Thames and out into open waters in a destroyer of his own design. It is actually a high modernist moment, as Jason Harding points out: 'The novel closes with a journey down the Thames in which the ancient river is contrasted with the ugliness and vulgarity of modern London. Wells's lyrical description of this oily, polluted river-front anticipates the "sandwich papers" and "cigarette ends" drifting towards Greenwich in T. S. Eliot's *The Waste Land* (1922), as well as evoking Conradian allusions'.[7] Indeed fog pervades *Tono-Bungay*, as it does Conrad's *The Secret Agent* (1907), and Ponderevo's departure at the close of the novel might be interpreted as Wells's rejection of the muddled moral and political uncertainty that characterized Edwardian England.

But, of course, that is not the whole story of the novel. Much of the enjoyment and interest is generated from the middle sections in which the fog is penetrated by the amazing powers of Tono-Bungay, as depicted in one of the sketches for advertising posters Wells inserts into the body of the text.[8] Tono-Bungay is the dream child of George's uncle Edward, who is presented as a caricature of Ford, or at least Wells's impression of Ford as someone out of touch with moral and factual reality, shamelessly drawing other people into their unsound financial schemes:

> 'I want to get you into this' – puff – 'George,' said my uncle round the end of his cigar. 'For many reasons.'
> His voice grew louder and more cunning. He made explanations that to my inexperience did not completely explain. I retain an impression of a long credit and a share with a firm of wholesale chemists, of a credit and a

prospective share with some pirate printers, of a third share for a leading
magazine and newspaper proprietor.
    'I played 'em off one against the other,' said my uncle. I took his point in
an instant. He had gone to each of them in turn and said the others had come
in.
    'I put up four hundred pounds,' said my uncle, 'myself and my all. And
you know—'
He assumed a brisk confidence. 'I hadn't five hundred pence. At least—'[9]

This is clearly a fictional version of the profit-sharing scheme Ford
employed to secure friends as contributors for the *English Review*.
Certain writers including Wells waived their normal fees and
contributed work to the journal on the basis that they would share in
the profits.[10] The irony in this case is that Wells was satirizing the
arrangement in the piece of work he was contributing under its
conditions. However, the potential negativity of this caricature of Ford
is leavened by Wells, at the outset of the novel, describing Edward
Ponderevo as the 'Napoleon of domestic conveniences'[11] and thus
invoking Ford's own description of the 'Napoleons' of business in *The
Soul of London* (1905), the first volume of *England and the English*
(1907): 'It would be fanciful to make Buonaparte too responsible for
the Modern Type; but he, upon the whole, was the discoverer of the
principle: apply yourself to gain the affection of the immense
crowd'.[12] Edward Ponderevo is a character to whom the novel's
readers, and presumably its author, feel affection. The personal satire
is therefore less important than Wells's understanding of Ford's idea
that the attempt to meet mass desires is potentially utopian. This
potentially utopian outcome is the dream behind a high-concept
product like Tono-Bungay or the *English Review* – or as George
Ponderevo's bohemian artist friend, Ewart, puts it, the 'poetry' of such
an undertaking:

And it's not your poetry only. It's the poetry of the customer, too. Poet
answering to poet – soul to soul. Health, strength, beauty in a bottle – the
magic philtre like a fairy tale [....]
    Think of the little clerks and jaded workers and overworked people.
People overstrained with wanting to do, people overstrained with wanting to
be.... People, in fact, overstrained.... The real trouble of life, Ponderevo, isn't
that we exist – that's a vulgar error; the real trouble is that we *don't* really
exist and we want to. That's what this – in the highest sense – much stands
for! The hunger to be – for once – really alive – to the fingertips![13]

The narrative struggle in *Tono-Bungay* is between a higher mode of active existence – the life of the Wellsian mind – symbolized by the destroyer leaving the Thames and the kind of mental adjustment to actually existing modern society – the utopian pursuit Ford advocated in *England and the English*[14] – symbolized by the quack medicine pushed by the Fordian Edward Ponderevo. Wells's choice of symbolism and the way he ends the novel appear to indicate a conscious decision to reject the Fordian position, but the whole feel of the book – the actual pace and wit and enjoyment of it – tends in the other direction.[15] One explanation for this inconsistency is that what Wells actually rejects is his own desire to side with Ford, which would contradict his status as a dynamic man of science. This explanation is supported by the early passage in his autobiography in which Wells describes the construction of his own scientific persona as a conscious and ongoing process of lonely struggle against 'the life of every day' in which he has been 'too preoccupied and too experimental to give [himself] freely and honestly to other people'.[16] In an editorial in the *English Review*, after the serialization of *Tono-Bungay* had been completed, Ford analyzes this tendency of Wells, whom he implies is not the prophet he likes to believe himself but a fine imaginative writer. In developing this critique into a general argument, Ford expresses what must be considered a core value of the type of modernism represented by the *English Review*:

> It is perhaps foolish – it is certainly perilous for the imaginative writer to attempt to occupy the position of a man of intellect. The imaginative writer, in fact, has practically never any intellectual power whatever except in one or other department of life. His business is to register a truth as he sees it, and no more than Pilate can he, as a rule, see the truth as it is. Moreover, in all intellectual subjects the accepted truth of to-day is the proven lie of to-morrow, and it is only the specialist who can discern in any given realm of human knowledge what is the fashion of to-day and what is permanent. The main energies of the imaginative writer must always be directed to voicing the desires and the aspirations of his day. And this occupying so much of his energies he has not the time that the specialist has at his disposal – he has not the power, the energy or the austerity to state what will be good for to-morrow. And this last is the business of the prophet. (*ER* III [Nov. 1909] 667)

It is the failure to follow this advice that characterizes the difference between Ford and the subsequent generation of modernist writers; Lawrence, Lewis and Pound in particular.

While Wells is carefully delineated in Ford's editorial as the most important contemporary novelist 'outside the circle of those who work consciously at a conscious art' (666), he is clearly marked as 'valuable', in a similar sense to that expressed by *Tono-Bungay*'s Ewart, as 'a poet fascinated by the aspects, borne away by the emotions of the moment' (668). As if to prove this performatively, Ford goes off into a fictional thought experiment:

> We imagine that, supposing him to discover by accident in an old furniture-shop a piece of Venetian embroidery sufficiently beautiful to arouse his enthusiasm he might end as a Mediaevalist. In that case he would begin to weave beautiful theories as to the Communism of City Guilds before the thirteenth century and he would discover once more that life fell hopelessly to pieces at the introduction of machinery. (668)

The inherent unlikeliness of this possibility might indicate naïveté on Ford's behalf if it were not for the fact that he did fictionalize Wells as such a 'Communist Mediaevalist' in *The Simple Life Limited* and thereby reveal his dialectical power as an imaginative writer.

Horatio Gubb is described unflatteringly as 'a close disciple and friend of the late Mr. William Morris, a parasitic gentleman, who fattened entirely upon the associations and upon the ideas of such distinguished people as would permit him to enter their houses'.[17] The complicated plot of the novel turns on Gubb's realization, stemming from his relationship with the novelist Simon Bransdon, that 'the Simple Life paid' (*SLL* 92) and his consequent efforts to acquire land and buildings and let them out to simple lifers at sufficient rent to cover communal necessities. His desire is not to make a profit but to become 'the actual organizer, the dictator of a prosperous "going" concern along lines of sufficient idealism to gain for himself a certain sphere of influence' (*SLL* 93). However, his attempts to treat Tory landowner Gerald Luscombe as a 'milch cow' (*SLL* 262) founder as it becomes apparent that Luscombe has always been in control of the situation and is merely letting things happen for his own ends, leaving Gubb looking as grubby and stupid as his name suggests. All of this would be no more than heavy-handed satire if Ford was simply portraying himself as Luscombe to Gubb's Wells, but the complexity of the novel lies in the fact that Ford is also satirising himself as Gubb in relation to Bransdon's Conrad. This allows him to examine the potential accusations that he built his reputation through a parasitical relationship with Conrad and that his founding of the *English Review* was an attempt to set himself up as the dictator of a going concern of sufficient idealism to gain himself a certain sphere of influence. In this latter context, Ford includes the amusing detail that Gubb's preparation for his enterprise includes reading 'with attention all the periodical literature of an idealistic nature or of a hygienic materialism ranging from the leaflets of Mr C. B. Fry to *The English Review*' (*SLL* 94). Gubb's overdetermination seems both an acknowledgement that the *English Review* was the product of a collaboration with Wells which failed and a hint of a suggestion that the collaboration might have succeeded if Wells had been purely the kind of imaginative writer that Ford valued. Thus the presence of the perverse narrative twists in *The Simple Life Limited* which function, in the face of seemingly overwhelming evidence, to hold open the question of whether Gubb is 'right or wrong' (*SLL* 249). It is as though Ford wants to keep alive the possibility of an *English Review* modernism that he knows is already doomed. This possibility is further expressed in Gubb's son, Hamnet, who embodies a particularly purist form of *English Review* modernism: 'He says that every word that the Fabians ever uttered is perfectly true and perfectly valid as applying to a state of society such as ours is. But he says that it simply doesn't interest *him*' (*SLL* 213). In some ways, Hamnet is reminiscent of Lawrence and suggests a symbolic relationship in which Lawrence, or a purer imaginative Lawrence, represents the legacy of *English Review* modernism. Indeed, the most tangible real-world legacy might well be F. R. Leavis's conception of the 'Great Tradition' which, as Saunders observes, was sharpened by first reading Lawrence, alongside James and Conrad, 'between the blue wrappers of the *English Review*' (Saunders I 249). However, the net effect of Ford's imagination of Wells as a 'Communist Mediaevalist' is surely not the rejection of sociology in the name of a Leavisite notion of 'Life' but an attempt to move, beyond both positivist and puritanical approaches to social problems, towards a poetic sociology such as that promoted in the *English Review* and found in imaginative writing like *Tono-Bungay*.

While Wells's fictional attitude to Ford is unconsciously doubled – overtly a rejection but actually an expression of affinity – Ford's attitude to Wells in *The Simple Life Limited* is consciously doubled and the penetrating satire squarely directed as much at himself. Therefore, rather than struggling to construct a rigid persona by projecting his unwanted tendencies on to a caricature of his 'double', as Wells does with Ford, Ford is forced to contend not only with his own unwanted tendencies but also with the tendencies of his 'double'. As a consequence, on a fictional level at least, Ford was able to work through his internal divisions more successfully than Wells because he was forced beyond them into a wider acceptance of intersubjectivity. The defence of Gubb as 'just a theatrical manager in a small way' (*SLL* 347) is almost postmodern in its self-reflexive acknowledgement of the value Ford places on the way that both he and Wells dramatized their relationships with each other. On a more practical level, although Gubb is portrayed in a unflattering light in comparison with Luscombe, the overdetermined construction of the relationship allowed Ford to overcome his fury at what he perceived as Wells's personal betrayal concerning the *English Review*[18] and achieve a more measured view:

> 'Chaps who haven't had a sound classical education are always sketchy in their moral senses. And Gubb probably thinks that an undertaking can only be really sound if it really pays. He'd say that was a cursed commercialism if it were uttered by Everard or Lady Croydon or me. But if *he* said it, it would be principle. And mind you,' Gerald continued, 'I don't know that the chap isn't perfectly right – from his own point of view.' (*SLL* 279)

However, the greater logic of this argument, in the context of the novel trying to find a way of allowing Gubb to be right, is that one needs to adopt Gubb's point of view and not that of Luscombe or Bransdon. Indeed, Bransdon's complaint after Gubb having proved a practical hero at a moment of crisis is particularly wide of the mark: 'The commonplace psychologist would say that because you'd showed spunk at the fire you wouldn't behave like a shopkeeper after it' (*SLL* 369). Gubb's 'rightness' is ultimately dependent on his ability to behave like a hero and a shopkeeper simultaneously.

I've argued elsewhere that this desire to be simultaneously shopkeeper and hero features in a number of Ford's other novels such as *A Call* (1910), *The New Humpty-Dumpty* and *Parade's End* (1924-28), in which 'Tietjens escapes the last post and the parades and is finally seen in the guise of the Wellsian (antiques) shopkeeper hero, bicycling off into the sunset to support his new family'.[19] The fictional expression and resolution of this desire was a crucial dimension of Ford, the everyday dreamer, emerging as a creative force from the aftermath of the war to the incredulity of Wells, the prophet and dynamic man of science, who clearly expected a new social order to

arise which would value him greatly over those 'who work consciously at a conscious art'.

   Wells's anticipation of post-war triumph was already evident in
Boon (1915). This book is mainly known for its attack on Henry
James: 'The thing his novel is *about* is always there. It is like a church
lit but without a congregation to distract you, with every light and line
focused on the high altar. And on the altar, very reverently placed,
intensely there, is a dead kitten, an egg-shell, a bit of string [. . . .]'[20]
Of course, what this pointed attack foregrounds is exactly the
difference between the hushed reverence of James's writing and the
boisterous music-hall atmosphere shared by the fiction of Ford and
Wells. However, this attack is actually only a relatively minor section
– eleven pages – of a sustained satirical work whose main target, the
eponymous Boon, is very much a caricature of Ford. As in Ford's
Daniel Chaucer books, the effect is complicated by Wells putting his
name only to the introduction and purporting the book to be the work
of Reginald Bliss. This allows him to indulge in his own self-reflexive
fun in the introduction: 'Bliss is Bliss and Wells is Wells. And Bliss
can write all sorts of things that Wells could not do' (*Boon* 6). One
thing that Bliss can do is be omnisciently judgmental about
Boon/Ford, as though writing an epitaph:

> His was indeed essentially one of these suspended minds that float above the
> will and action; when at last reality could be evaded no longer it killed him; he
> never really believed nor felt the urgent need that goads my more accurate
> nature to believe and do. Always when I think of us together, I feel that I am
> on my legs and that he sits about. And yet he could tell me things I sought to
> know, prove what I sought to believe, shape beliefs to a conviction in me that
> I alone could never attain. (*Boon* 15)

As can be seen from this passage, the attitude to Ford is much more
generous than that displayed to James. Indeed the whole book is in
some ways a very fond account of the literary politics of the pre-war
period and the shared endeavour by which Boon and the Wellsian
Bliss were engaged in a greater *English Review* type project to realize
'the mind of the Race' or, in other words, in the attempt to catalyze
England's development into an utopian civilization in which everyone
achieved full intellectual development. The gist of the argument is that
Boon's attempt to achieve this had been by illusion – analogous to the
snake-oil of *Tono-Bungay* – and consequently the war (inevitable of
course to someone of a proper scientific intellect) necessarily

destroyed his faith in the triumph of universal intellect. The twist in
the tale is that the war inverts the relationship between Boon and the
other main Wellsian character, Wilkins, who has hitherto been the
scientific sceptic. Boon's crisis of confidence clears the way for
Wilkins to advance a properly scientific road to the universal intellect
and thus the only possible salvation of the human race.

But of course this no more represents the simple triumph of
Wells over Ford than *The Simple Life Limited* represents the simple
triumph of Ford over Wells; it is the anticipated triumph of one
version of Wells over a Wells-Ford composite figure. However, far
from being the straw man in the argument, the character of Boon
demonstrates great textual investment on Wells's behalf: for example,
the sketches, purported to be Boon's, which copiously illustrate the
text and add considerably to its charm are Wells's sketches. The
everyday utopian dreams here associated with Ford attracted Wells in
spite of himself, as we have seen in respect to *Tono-Bungay*. So
Ford's apparent imminent demise along with the rest of the Edwardian
world-order presented the opportunity to finally rid himself of all
those aspects of himself which stood in the way of his properly
scientific unity of purpose. *Boon* is not just the epitaph for Ford, it is
also the epitaph for the old Wells.

Therefore, once Wells's incredulity at Ford's survival as a
going concern after the war had worn off, he must have perceived it at
a symbolic level as a return of his own old identity which he had
repressed in order to fully embrace a new scientific identity. It is this
threat posed by the return of his old identity which eventually led to
Wells's late novel, *The Bulpington of Blup*, as he implicitly
acknowledges in his autobiography:

> Throughout my life, a main strand of interest has been the endeavour to
> anchor *personas* to a common conception of reality [. . . .] But this theme of
> the floating *persona*, the dramatized self, returns at various levels of
> complexity and self-deception, in Mr. Hoopdriver in *The Wheels of Chance*, in
> the dreams of Mr. Parham, in *Christina Alberta's Father*, and most
> elaborately of all, in *The Bulpington of Blup*. This last is a very direct
> caricature study of the irresponsible disconnected aesthetic mentality. It is
> friendship's offering to the world of letters from the scientific side.[21]

Theodore Bulpington is, of course, ostensibly modeled on Ford and, in
particular, Wells's conception of the transition from his more rational
Edwardian persona which became conspicuous after the war: 'his

extraordinary drift towards self-dramatization – when he even changed his name to Captain Ford'.[22] The novel culminates in a post-war evening during which Bulpington, now referred to by the text as 'the Captain', tells ever greater lies about the war – including single-handedly capturing the Kaiser – before launching into a theatrical soliloquy:

> I am a liar in a world of lies. Lies? Dreams! World of dreams. Hidden world [. . . .] World of self-delusion. But most of us never find out it is self-delusion. I happen to know. And because I know it, I shape my life as I like, past and future, just as I please. What wasn't true is true now. See? I *make* it true. I enlisted by a trick when the doctors had rejected me. Yes, I did, I tell you. I led that rally before Amiens. I – your humble servant. I took the Kaiser prisoner. I talked to him for hours. And so forth and so on. If I wish it, it has to be so. From now henceforth. Lie for lie. Who believes my lie is my friend. It's a fair trade, and plenty doing. I shall find plenty of friends. Was friendship ever anything but a lie-exchange? Corroboration. Love me, love my lie. And who will object?[23]

But is this self-dramatization simply a bravura act of ventriloquism on Wells's behalf or a more complex self-reflexive passage of displaced reflection about his own construction of a scientific persona?

Wells seemingly accounts for Ford's duality – fictionally represented by Theodore Bulpington and his fantasy alter-ego the Bulpington of Blup – as an act of self-deception that enables him to love two women, Margaret and Rachel, simultaneously. Of course, real life examples of Ford loving two women simultaneously are too numerous to list and nor was Wells entirely immune to the same phenomenon. As I have argued elsewhere, Ford simultaneously wanting two women was a way of hiding his duality from himself and actually affecting a notional unity of purpose.[24] However, it never became a way of life for him in the way that maintaining unity at all cost was for Wells. Wells transfers his own fault on to the Ford character in this novel and that is what gives the book both its intensity – which is that of unconscious autobiography and, of course, it really becomes all lies then because Wells was certainly not in the war, let alone at the front – and its poignancy. Because in the end the book is a lament for a lost time and place – the radical milieu of London circa 1909, just before the world changed according to Virginia Woolf – when the main protagonists Theodore, Teddy and Margaret seem on the cusp of a shared transformative vision. It is this overwhelming sense of loss that dominates the novel but in the process of retelling the story once again, Wells comes his closest to recapturing the poetic sociology which characterized the modernism of the *English Review*.

In the end it remains the case that Ford almost always comes across in Wells's fiction as an object of affection whatever Wells's intentions might have been. The use of the friendly nickname 'Bulpy' for the hero, or perhaps anti-hero, of *The Bulpington of Blup*, makes him impossible to dislike and undermines the attempt at sustained satire. The fact that Wells linked the novel with *Kipps* (1905) and *The History of Mr Polly* (1910) as all containing 'caricature-individualities of which I am not ashamed' suggests that it was, after all, more labour of love than hatchet job: 'Theodore Bulpington is as good as Kipps'.[25] Through his compulsive caricaturing of Ford, Wells kept himself in touch with the everyday dreamer in himself that he consciously sought to transcend. It was a friendly gesture to the scientific side from the world of letters.

NOTES

1   Max Saunders, *Ford Madox Ford: A Dual Life*, 2 vols, Oxford: Oxford University Press, 1996 – henceforth 'Saunders'; I 248-9.

2   Virginia Woolf, 'Modern Fiction', *The Crowded Dance of Modern Life*, ed., Rachel Bowlby, Harmondsworth: Penguin, 1993, pp. 5-12.

3   For example, the brig captain in Wells's *Tono-Bungay* and Bransdon in Ford's *The Simple Life Limited*.

4   H. G. Wells, *Experiment in Autobiography: Discoveries and Conclusions of a Very Ordinary Brain (Since 1866)*, vol. II, London: Gollancz and the Cresset Press, 1934, p. 503.

5   As Saunders notes, the writing of Charles Masterman's influential *The Condition of England* (1909) was partly inspired by reading instalments of *Tono-Bungay* in the *English Review*. See Saunders I 252.

6   H. G. Wells, *Tono-Bungay*, London, Pan, 1972, p. 8.

7   Jason Harding, 'The Englishness of the *English Review*', *Ford Madox Ford and Englishness*, ed. Dennis Brown and Jenny Plastow, Amsterdam: Rodopi, 2006, pp. 137-45 (p. 143).

8   Wells, *Tono-Bungay*, p. 122.

9   *Ibid.*, p. 107.

10   See Saunders I 243.

11   Wells, *Tono-Bungay*, p. 4.

12   Ford, *England and the English*, ed. Sara Haslam, Manchester: Carcanet, 2003, p. 50.

13   Wells, *Tono-Bungay*, p. 130.

14 See Nick Hubble, 'Beyond Mimetic Englishness: Ford's English Trilogy and *The Good Soldier*', *Ford Madox Ford and Englishness*, ed. Dennis Brown and Jenny Plastow, Amsterdam: Rodopi, 2006, pp. 147-62 (pp. 151-2).

15 The fact that he wrote *The History of Mr Polly* (1910) soon afterwards, a novel which expresses very different everyday tendencies, suggests that his mind was not fully made up at this time.

16 Wells, *Experiment in Autobiography*, vol. I, p. 23.

17 Ford, *The Simple Life Limited*, London: John Lane, 1911 – henceforth *SLL*; p. 7

18 Wells, *Experiment in Autobiography*, vol. I, pp. 256-7.

19 See Hubble, 'The Origins of Intermodernism in Ford Madox Ford's Parallax View', *Ford Madox Ford: Literary Networks and Cultural Transformations*, ed. Andrzej Gasiorek and Daniel Moore, Amsterdam: Rodopi, 2008, pp. 167-88 (pp. 182-6).

20 Wells, *Boon, The Mind of the Race, The Wild Asses of the Devil, and The Last Trump: Being a First Selection from the Literary Remains of George Boon, Appropriate to the Times*, London: T. Fisher Unwin, 1915 – henceforth *Boon*; pp. 106-7.

21 Wells, *Experiment in Autobiography*, vol. II, p. 624.

22 *Ibid.*, p. 622.

23 Wells, *The Bulpington of Blup: Adventures, Poses, Stresses, Conflicts, and Disaster in a Contemporary Brain*, London: Hutchinson & Co., 1932, p. 403.

24 Hubble, 'The Origins of Intermodernism', pp. 176-7.

25 Wells, *Experiment in Autobiography*, vol. II, p. 499.

LAWRENCE, FORD, STRONG READINGS, AND WEAK NERVES

George Hyde

In *Dying Game*, David Ellis's final volume of the Cambridge Biography of D. H. Lawrence, Ford Madox Ford, rather surprisingly, still figures. It is 1925, in Mexico, and Ford is just over 50, but he has lingered in the memory of Lawrence and his wife, when he was still a significant, though fading, presence ten years earlier in Lawrence's literary life. Frieda, as reported by a visiting writer named Kyle Crichton, prompts Lawrence 'in a strong German accent' as he does one of his dreaded satirical impersonations – of Ford Madox Ford – but not altogether unkindly.[1] She, on the other hand, is still resentful of Ford's comments about Germany in 1915, in connection with the Prussian treatment of Belgium, when Ford, like some other eminent men of letters, was working for Charles Masterman's War Propaganda department, and his own German ancestry was in the process of being discarded in favour of what many saw as a new, and somewhat French, persona. It was more than Frieda, a Prussian Baroness, could stomach, and the animosity lingered on, perhaps augmented by the fact that it was Jessie Chambers who had first sent Lawrence's poems to Ford and urged him to cultivate the editor of the *English Review*. Ford's literary interventions in Lawrence's life were nothing if not tendentious.

The man whom Pound styled simply 'The stylist'[2] exerted, for a number of years, a considerable influence on London literary life, as the author of *The Good Soldier*, called by John Rodker 'the finest French novel in the English language',[3] and even more as the editor of the *English Review*, which he founded in December 1908. In his autobiographcal work *Return to Yesterday* (1931), published a year after Lawrence's death, Ford looks back in a colourful sketch of Eastwood, at the time when Lawrence was submitting some of his earliest writings to the *English Review* and deferring to Ford's well-meant criticisms; that is, from 1909. The gushy (but also ironic?) description of the little Midlands mining town has been much quoted:

All the while the young people were talking about Nietzsche and Wagner and Leopardi and Flaubert and Karl Marx and Darwin [...] the French Impressionists and the Primitive Italians and [they would] play Chopin or Debussy on the piano.[4]

One can't help wondering how many of the 'young people' were involved in all this artistic activity, and at what level, but it is certainly the case that Lawrence, to impress his group of friends, and especially Jessie, could be (as he later called himself) a young prig capable of turning on quite a flow of high culture, embracing all the arts. The names cited are perhaps not random: a passionate engagement with Nietzsche and Wagner colours Lawrence's early fiction, especially *The Trespasser* (1912), written to a sort of steamy Wagnerian subtext, as it does in *The Rainbow* (1915), with its elaborate music-drama construction. Perhaps more to our immediate purpose, though, is the powerful presence in the *English Review* of Flaubert, and the closely related question of Impressionism.

Lawrence commended the *English Review* to Louie Burrows, the girl he almost married, rather pompously, as 'the best possible way to get into touch with the new young school of realism'.[5] Ford's choice of authors set the tone of the journal, which Lawrence was evidently aiming to be consonant with in the two early stories he submitted, 'Goose Fair' and 'Odour of Chrysanthemums', the latter of which might serve to epitomise the best of his early manner, and the kind of writing that many early admirers later condemned him for turning his back on. Ford's comments on 'Odour of Chrysanthemums' are worth quoting for their Olympian tone and the appreciation of the deliberate Maupassant-esque or Flaubertian realism of the tale:

The very title makes an impact on the mind. You get at once the knowledge that this is not, whatever else it may turn out, either a frivolous or even a gay springtime story. Chrysanthemums are not only flowers of the Autumn, they are the Autumn itself [...] This man knows what he wants. He sees the scene of his story exactly. He has an authoritative mind.[6]

Ford liked to call Lawrence a 'genius', as we shall see, and kept congratulating himself for having discovered him, although these comments are strangely without any apparent sense of Lawrence's complex sense of form and the 'Wagnerian' musical structure in which the crucial image of the flowers is embedded. The second issue of the *English Review* prints Anatole France in French, which may well have been the prelude for the *Spectator* complaining later that the

Review was 'dumping garbage on the nation's doorstep'[7] (the sort of objection that Lawrence himself was soon to incur). In addition to the French, especially Flaubert and Maupassant, Ford's interest in the Russians left a significant mark on Lawrence. Through Ford, Lawrence met Edward and his wife Constance Garnett, the most important contemporary translator from Russian, an event which changed his life and his writing.

Lawrence's personal relationship with Ford mutated rapidly and bewilderingly. He responded early on to Ford's professional openness: 'he is a really fine man, in that he is so generous, so understanding, and in that he keeps the doors of his soul open, and you may walk in' (Lawrence I 141). But within three years he was less enthusiastic: 'I suffered badly from Hueffer re Flaubert and perfection' (Lawrence I 417), he said, wounded by Ford's well-meaning efforts to help the young provincial conform to a more disciplined and detached style of writing. And Lawrence simply did not take kindly to being surrounded by successful professional writers; he was always to some degree the outsider by choice. After Ford had recommended *The White Peacock*, Lawrence's first novel, to Heinemann, publisher of Constance Garnett's Russian translations, and persuaded Harley Granville Barker to read Lawrence's first two plays (to no avail), we have Lawrence writing ungratefully 'Last night I dined with celebrities [...] but I'd give it all up for one of our old evenings in the Haggs [Farm] parlour' (Lawrence I 138), looking back nostalgically to the meetings with Jessie and her family where he commonly held court.

Very soon Lawrence was complaining that Ford's own writing had 'more art than life' (Lawrence I 141). By 1910, he is already referring sardonically to 'those who belong to the accurate-impersonal school of Flaubert' (Lawrence I 169). Ford had now taken to criticising Lawrence for being too like the Russians, whom Henry James labelled formless. *The Trespasser* was an instance: 'Hueffer abused me for it roundly' said Lawrence, and 'Mr. Hueffer accuses me of Dostoieffskyism [...] the dear cranky Russian's stuff is as insane as it can be' (Lawrence I 199). Dostoevsky had still not been assimilated by the English, an event that had to wait for John Middleton Murry's intervention in the role of prophet and populariser. Lawrence was later to call *The Trespasser* a 'decorated idyll running to seed in realism',[8] and the seedy realism of it is certainly of the Russian school: there are distinct echoes of *The Possessed* in the events surrounding Siegmund's suicide. In fact there are many signs that Dostoevsky is no longer the 'dear cranky Russian' that Lawrence had once thought him but an original, very modern force to reckon with. When Ford managed to lose the manuscripts of Lawrence's first two plays he got cross. He told Edward Garnett that Ford had called *The Trespasser* a 'rotten work of genius', and went on to defend its 'true form' against Ford's complaint that 'it has no construction or form'. Actually, *The Trespasser*, with its insistent Wagnerianism, is all too consciously 'formed', and if it is a pre-echo of the musicality of *The Rainbow* and *Women in Love*, being (as Ford indeed says of it) 'all variations on a theme', it is infinitely cruder. But why 'variations' should be, as Ford apparently told Lawrence, 'execrably bad art' (Lawrence I 399) is a great mystery: Elgar's masterpiece had been written not long since, and Schoenberg's *Variations for Orchestra* would follow in 1928; indeed a chain of unending metamorphoses was beginning to look like the only modern way of writing music, and perhaps literature too.

The word 'genius', which (as I've said) Ford liked to bandy about regarding Lawrence, rankled for several reasons. As Lawrence himself said, people used it as if to console him for 'lacking their own incomparable advantages'. Short of money most of his life, Lawrence could not help being sensitive to the opulent and self-indulgent lifestyle of writers who had inherited it, or made lots of it. To be patronised as a 'genius' instead of properly appreciated for the great writer he was could be upsetting. As he said himself:

> I wish Hueffer wouldn't introduce me as a genius. When a fellow hasn't enough money to buy a decent pair of boots and not enough sense to borrow or steal a pair he's ticketed 'genius' as a last resource: just as they call things 'very desirable' when nobody on earth wants them. (Lawrence I 170)

But the thorn in the flesh called Hueffer goaded Lawrence into more than just disgruntled outbursts. Ford's 'rotten work of genius' remark was followed by the phrase 'one fourth of which is the stuff of masterpiece', and although Ford didn't say which fourth that was, Lawrence endorsed Ford's view that the novel did not cohere, beginning as 'decorated idyll' before 'running to seed in realism'. Ford's comments, as reported to Louie Burrows, went on:

> He belongs to the opposite school of novelists to me: he says prose must be impersonal, like Turgenuev or Flaubert. I say 'no'. (Lawrence I 178)

The assertion that there is a diametrical opposition between 'impersonality' and 'me' is at least interesting, and Lawrence went on to develop it more subtly in different contexts. Very soon 'impersonality' spelt 'classicism' and was 'bunkum' (Lawrence IV 500); and the argument about 'form' became very intense in Lawrence's correspondence with Edward Garnett (his editor at Heinemann) in connection with *Sons and Lovers*, his third novel.

A lot of this had to do with sex, which is a bit ironic if one thinks of Ford in terms of his best-known novel, that 'French' masterpiece *The Good Soldier,* a classic of the new 'sexual' writing. Lawrence's early work was perhaps steamy in a rather adolescent way, but the steaminess accompanied a Puritan quest for truth, which is an uncommon combination, and one which proved quite disconcerting to many readers, amongst whom was Ford. *The White Peacock* had been trimmed of its mildly naughty homoerotic passages for publication; but *The Trespasser*, in Ford's words, was originally 'much more phallic than the book as it stands' as well as 'much more moral in the inverted-puritanic sense'. These comments are ultimately misleading. What actually happened was that a lot of very personal material was subjected to the quasi-mythological, Wagnerian reworking that characterises the novel as it stands, with the Dostoevskian realism of the ending jarring more than a little. Ford's observation that 'the whole effect' (of the original manuscript) 'was the rather dreary one of a schoolboy larking among placket-holes, dialoguing with a Wesleyan minister who has been converted to Ibsen' (*MS* 121) is amusing but very wide of the mark. 'Larking' is precisely what the novel is not: if the novel makes the reader laugh, it is not a laughter under its author's control. Moreover, Lawrence was brought up a Congregationalist, not a Wesleyan, and there is no trace of Wesleyanism in his work: in fact he often expressed a real dislike of the Methodists, and says why. Ibsen may have left his mark here, but it is not very apparent, compared with the influence of Nietzsche and Wagner. Of course the novel is indeed personal, as it is the work of a relatively inexperienced young man; but so (according to Lawrence) was (for example) that classic of well-formed French realism *Le Rouge et le Noir*: 'I often think Stendhal must have writhed in torture every time he remembered *Le Rouge et le Noir* was public property' (Lawrence I 353). Anyway, Ford expressed his approval when Lawrence declared at one point that he had decided not to publish it, a decision he quickly went back on.

Soon the Lawrentian account of Ford was changing radically. He wrote to J. B. Pinker: 'Tell Arnold Bennett that all rules of construction hold good only for novels which are copies of other novels' (Lawrence II 479). Lawrence was arriving at his doctrine of Art for My Sake (as against Art for Art's Sake, or 'style' as such). *Sons and Lovers* saw him painfully finding his true voice: and he remarked laconically that it was 'not so strongly concentric as the fashionable folk under French influence' in the same letter that goes on to complain that he suffered from Ford 're Flaubert and perfection' (Lawrence I 417). Edward Garnett, reader for Heinemann, the husband of Dostoevsky's marvellous English translator, had many problems with *Sons and Lovers*, but he was much less doctrinaire than Ford, who had retrospectively become the enemy. '[Hueffer] sent me to W[illia]m Heinemann with *The White Peacock* and left me to paddle my own canoe. I very nearly wrecked it and did for myself. Edward Garnett, like a good angel, fished me out' (Lawrence I 471). This sounds, at last, like Lawrence's authentic voice. The times were, in any case, changing. With the traumatic experience of the First World War, Lawrence was of course scapegoated rather as Ford himself had been. With a divorced Prussian aristocrat for a wife (a von Richthofen no less) and a reputation for immorality, he found that his masterpiece *The Rainbow* (1915) was so totally unacceptable to the authorities that the first edition was confiscated by the police and publicly burnt. This, in turn, held up the publication of *Women in Love* for many years. But Ford could not be blamed for that.

NOTES

1   David Ellis, *D. H. Lawrence: Dying Game, 1922-1930*, Cambridge: Cambridge University Press, 1998, pp. 261-2.
2   Ezra Pound, *Personae: Collected Shorter Poems*, New York: New Directions, 1990, p. 192.
3   Max Saunders, *Ford Madox Ford: A Dual Life*, 2 vols (Oxford: Oxford University Press, 1996, I 428.
4   Ford, *Return to Yesterday*, London: Gollancz, 1931, p. 392. John Worthen, *D. H. Lawrence: The Early Years*, Cambridge: Cambridge University Press, 1991, p. 171, calls the story 'a finely-crafted imaginative account of the group's behaviour', and assumes that the visit never took place.

5   *The Letters of D. H. Lawrence*, 8 vols, ed. James T. Boulton et al., Cambridge: Cambridge University Press, 1979-2001 – henceforth 'Lawrence'; I 139.
6   Ford, *Mightier Than the Sword*, London: George Allen & Unwin, 1938 – henceforth *MS*; pp. 100-3.
7   See 'The Great Adult Review', *The Spectator*, 10 June 1911, pp. 875-6.
8   See G. M. Hyde, *D. H. Lawrence*, London: Macmillan, 1990, pp. 25-30.

THE FEROCIOUSLY ODD, MUTUALLY BENEFICIAL EDITORIAL RELATIONSHIP OF FORD AND WYNDHAM LEWIS

Seamus O'Malley

Ford Madox Ford and Wyndham Lewis had an oddly symmetrical relationship. Although Ford was a few years older, both were active in the pre-war literary scene; both fought in the Great War; and both now occupy the outskirts of the English modernist canon.[1] Both associates of Ezra Pound, they traveled in similar circles and were well acquainted with each other's work. Although not close emotionally, they were beneficial to each other throughout their careers, providing important publishing opportunities and enabling each other to reach previously untapped audiences.

The specific symmetry that I want to explore is their mutual editorship: Ford gave Lewis his literary start, publishing his first three pieces in the *English Review* in 1909. Lewis returned the favour five years later, publishing the first few chapters of *The Good Soldier* in his groundbreaking avant-garde journal *Blast*.

But before getting into the details of editing, however, I would like quickly to survey what they have written about each other, and note some of the recurring themes that we can trace back to their editing. Both use each other as generational foils, Ford using Lewis to represent *les jeunes* – the younger avant-garde – and Lewis casting Ford as the professional man of letters whose time had passed. More interestingly, both seem to see the other as some sort of fictional character or constructed persona. Whenever they interacted in print, the result was a striking meditation on narrative and how we construct stories, the intertextuality of their memoirs echoing their early mutual editorship.

In *Rude Assignment: An Intellectual Autobiography* (1950), Lewis describes Ford:

> This ex-collaborator with Joseph Conrad was himself, it always occurred to me, a typical figure out of a Conrad book – a caterer, or corn-factor, coming on board – blowing like a porpoise with the exertion – at some Eastern port.

> What he *thought* he was, was one of those military *sahibs* who used to sit on
> the balcony of a club in Hindustan with two or three other *sahibs*, *stingahs* at
> their sides, and who, between meditative puffs at a cheroot, begins to tell one
> of Conrad's tales.[2]

Lewis here stages the double role that they each played in their
memoirs: he depicts Ford as believing that he is a teller of Conradian
tales, whereas actually, for Lewis, Ford is a character in the tale itself,
the product, not producer, of the narrative. At the same time Ford is a
'character' in Lewis's own 'story' of his life. Of course every memoir-
ist borrows from the techniques of fiction to tell one's life story, but
the depiction of Ford here seems strikingly self-conscious.

In the same piece Lewis then turns himself into a character:

> So I was for some years spiritually a Russian – a character in some Russian
> novel. As such I made my bow in London – to the deeply astonished Ford
> Madox Hueffer – which lemonish pink giant, it is true, in his quilted dressing-
> gown, with his mouth hanging open like a big silly fish, surprised *me*. (*RA*
> 161)

Lewis here depicts himself as a fictional character as much as he does
Ford. But Lewis seeing himself as Russian is borrowing from the elder
writer, who in *Return to Yesterday* (1931), referring to Lewis as 'D.
Z.', says that:

> He seemed to be Russian. He was very dark in the shadows of the staircase.
> He wore an immense steeple-crowned hat long black locks fell from it. His
> coat was one of those Russian looking coats that have no revers. He had also
> an ample black cape of the type that villains in transpontine melodrama throw
> over their shoulders when they say 'Ha-ha!'[3]

The Lewis of *Rude Assignment* playfully borrows from Ford's earlier
depiction of him, in a dizzying doubling of intertextual characteriz-
ation. The two memoirs engage with each other, each writer casting
the other as someone not real but rather fictional and textual – Ford's
Lewis wears clothes only worn by villains from fiction – and Lewis
carries Ford's notion of his Russianness over from *Return to
Yesterday* into his own reminiscences, recycling the Russianness and
fictionality of his persona.[4]

They also appear as foreigners in each others' work: Ford
becomes an international trader; Lewis, because of his continental
garb, a Russian. They may possibly be commenting on how they were
both outsiders viewed from mainstream English life, Ford because of

his then-German name and German roots, and Lewis because of his aesthetic (and sartorial) affinities with the continent. This projection of foreignness may also have been due to their shared sense of alienation from their English milieu (Lewis was born in Canada but was raised in England).

Despite their similarities, the two writers saw each other as foils rather than as doubles. Lewis noted of Violet Hunt that 'her spirit dwelt with the pre-Raphaelites, as did half of her husband's' (*RA* 131). The 'half' – a reference to Ford's descending from the Pre-Raphaelite painter Ford Madox Brown and his many pieces of writing on the Pre-Raphaelites – is a canny judgment on how Ford's writing crosses over from Victorian to modern modes, embodying an older tradition while also championing more experimental work. Ford in turn often used Lewis as shorthand for the younger avant-garde. Looking back at his tenure as editor, he wrote that '*The English Review* seemed then profoundly to have done its work. Ezra and his gang of young lions raged through London. They were producing an organ of their own. It was to be called – prophetically – *Blast*' (*RY* 399). Ford uses their two journals, each including the other, as markers in the history of English literature before the war: each writer edited a magazine that was the foil of the other. Ford's review had 'done its work' by allowing a space for more experimental work to be produced. Of course, Ford stresses that he never receives credit for this clearing of aesthetic ground, and throughout his career he seems to enjoy playing the unappreciated elder statesman: 'As far as I can remember, except for Ezra, not one of the writers whose first manuscripts I printed or whose second efforts I tried to give lifts to – not one of them did not in the end kick me in the face' (*RY* 391). And in his memoirs, no one underappreciates Ford more than Wyndham Lewis. Whenever Lewis appears in Ford's memoirs he is either mysteriously silent or hectoringly loud. In one scene Lewis explains how Ford and his generation are through: '*Tu sais, tu es foûtu! Foûtu!* Finished! Exploded! Done for! Blasted in fact. Your generation has gone [. . . .] This is the day of Cubism, Futurism, Vorticism. What people want is me, not you. They want to see me. A Vortex'. Lewis then explains the difference between these movements and Ford's impressionism: 'You and Conrad had the idea of concealing yourself when you wrote. I display myself all over the page. In every word. I ... I ... I ...' (*RY* 400). Against the Flaubertian code of impersonality that guided Conrad and Ford, Lewis here flaunts his personality as much as possible. (The fact that Lewis was not known for this kind of conversation suggests that Ford is responding more to Lewis's writing persona than to his social personality.)

While Ford depicts Lewis as his aesthetic nemesis, he simultaneously suggests that it is through the *English Review* that the movements Lewis is shouting about are able to exist in the first place. Max Saunders writes that Ford is:

> seeing Lewis as a kind of double of his artistic self, someone who is continuing his lifelong campaigns for new forms, only by other, more belligerent, means; and, most importantly, recognizing that the kind of art Lewis is advocating should not be seen as in uncompromising opposition to his own work, since he has been practicing something like it all along, perhaps without realizing it.[5]

If they are on opposite sides it is still the same coin, and this may be why they were so drawn to each other in their memoirs. They may also have seen that as interdependent foils they explored the seemingly contradictory nature of modernism, which always vacillated between impersonal and subjective, exterior and interior.

Ford saw that every revolution must turn on its founders, and offers himself up in his memoirs as fodder for future writers. It is hard being continually kicked in the face, but one must not protest: 'That is Nature asserting itself. In the end the young cockerels must bring down the father of their barnyard. Without that the arts must stand still' (*RY* 391). (Lewis never literally kicked Ford in his face, except by artistic proxy: while lecturing at Lewis's Rebel Art Centre in 1914, Lewis's painting *Plan of War* fell on Ford's head.) Ford, in accepting his role as punch-bag for the avant-garde, also signals his importance to these movements, positioning Impressionism as the movement that precedes theirs, just as theirs would precede the high modernism of the twenties.[6] Notably, the above passages from *Return to Yesterday* were adapted from their original appearance in *The Outlook* in 1914, and one section that Ford cut for his later memoir read:

> Mr Lewis presents you with a story that is to other stories what a piece of abstract music by Bach is to a piece of programme-music. I don't just figure out what it means, but I get from it ferociously odd sensations – but then I do not understand what Bach meant by the Fourth Fugue, and I don't want to.[7]

The 1914 version is more cynical and bemused at *les jeunes*, openly professing his lack of comprehension as to their projects. By 1930,

Ford presents a more principled defence of the avant-garde. It may be that by the later text he had formulated his tradition of literary history, seeing the rise and fall of movements as essential to what he would soon term *The March of Literature*.[8]

The initial meeting between Ford and Lewis, in which Ford accepts Lewis's manuscripts for the *English Review*, has been recounted by Ford several times. He kept returning to this episode because it casts him again as benefactor to *les jeunes*, but also because he recognized one of the seminal moments in what we now call literary modernism. In *Return to Yesterday* he begins by recounting how disappointed he was in that month's issue, and implores his assistant to say a prayer to St. Anthony. Lewis then arrives, 'extraordinary in appearance'. Ford explains how he does not want any more 'Russian revelations', having already rejected several Slavic contributions.

> All the while I was pushing him down the stairs. He said nothing. His dark eyes rolled. He established himself immovably against the banisters and began fumbling in the pockets of his cape. He produced crumpled papers in rolls [. . . .] He produced them from all over his person – from inside his waistcoat, from against his skin beneath his brown jersey. (*RY* 390)

Lewis is literally bursting with manuscripts, a fictional character come to life, seemingly made out of texts. In this version, Ford shows the manuscripts to Arthur Marwood, who reads them 'for no more than a second' and responds 'We are saved. St. Anthony has answered our prayer'. The version of this encounter that appeared in *The Outlook* in 1914 is similar, but Douglas Goldring's account of Ford's anecdote eliminates Marwood from the scene and has Ford in the bath when Lewis approaches.[9] Like many of Ford's anecdotes, there are multiple versions, none of which are likely to be factually accurate, but they point to something vital about the issues involved. This story dramatizes the role that Lewis would play in the *English Review*, arriving like a thunderbolt, writing in a style immediately recognizable as distinct and new. Ford originally said that he started the *Review* to provide a place to publish Thomas Hardy, but by including figures like Lewis and D. H. Lawrence it soon became clear that Ford wanted to showcase younger, more experimental work as well. Lewis, in an unsent letter to T. Sturge Moore, wrote that 'I hope Hueffer will keep to his promise of taking me on as a regular hand. Troublesome as the monthly article would be, it would be nothing compared to the

uncertainties of other work'.[10] If Lewis is correct about Ford's intentions (there is no other record of this job offer), it may be that Lewis
was destined to act as the young buck in the room – Basquiat to Ford's
Warhol – much like Ernest Hemingway would for the *transatlantic
review*.[11]

The three pieces that Ford published following this dramatic
initial meeting were 'The "Pole"', 'Some Innkeepers and Bestre', and
'Les Saltimbanques'. The stories were eventually rewritten for
Lewis's short story collection *The Wild Body*, but reading them in
their original context in the *English Review* helps us to appreciate their
revolutionary style, as Lewis's pieces appear just after work by such a
writer as W. H. Hudson. It is hard to believe that Hudson and Lewis
are from the same era, let alone published in the same journal. Beyond
the linguistic aggression of Lewis's pieces is their desire to break the
mould of genre, especially that of the travel piece.[12] All three essays
depict travelling in Brittany but in Lewis's hands they are much more
(and possibly much less, as they are not very reliable as travelogues of
the region). 'The "Pole"' is ostensibly about a Polish or Slavic community in Brittany. It soon becomes clear that the term 'Pole' (always
in quotation marks) is used to refer not to an ethnic group so much as
a social class. The 'Poles' are poor, proud, and dramatic. Lewis
describes the antics of one of them: 'And when he is offering one of
the most heroic spectacles imaginable of force of character, he is
regarded by the exasperated reader, entirely misapprehending the
situation, as a monster of indecision'.[13] What is notable here is that the
'exasperated reader' is not the reader of Lewis's piece, but rather the
characters in the story who are witnessing this Pole's actions. The
Pole's theatrics transform him into a text which other characters
'read', just as Lewis and Ford would later transform each other into
textual characters. Lewis is using the travel genre to explore the idea
of narrative itself.

'Some Innkeepers and Bestre' is another study in narratology. It
describes how innkeepers use their inns as places to tell stories: their
public space becomes a site in which to weave stories and narratives.
But first he describes how:

> To those inns scattered up and down through fiction and history all men have
> taken either their dreams, their indigestions, their passions, or the thread of
> their stories – the latter principally occupied with their hero or heroine, who
> happened to be sojourning there, and chiefly concerned with using them as a

> trysting-place of alarms, surprises, misadventures, brawls, and flight. (*CWB* 221)

Writers have used inns as fictional sites for their characters for centuries, but Lewis stresses that in fact real inns are locations of narrative themselves, just as later he would describe Ford as a character in a Conradian tale, not the teller of it. Lewis then selects a group of storytellers whom he sees as a kind of innkeeping avant-garde:

> It has its brilliant and eccentric exponents, who live not only unrecognized, but scorned. So subtle is their method and manner of charming the public that it has an opposite effect; the latter becomes furious, thinking that it is being trifled with. It needs a public as imaginative as the landlord to appreciate what is often the most bold and revolutionary scheme of hospitality. (*CWB* 221)

We might read passages like this as an early anticipation of the reaction to his brand of modernism – as one of the 'Men of 1914' he would later be prepared to face public scorn as he attempted to create an aesthetic that did not pay tribute to the average reader.

The final piece, 'Les Saltimbanques', concerns clowns in small Breton villages, but the focal point of the essay is how the Breton peasants see the clowns as people and not actors.

> They [the peasants] do not readily dissociate reality from appearance. Why primitive people are more imaginative is because everything for their mind retains its apparent diversity. However well they got to know the clown they would always think of him the wrong way up, or on all-fours. (*CWB* 241)

The clowns exist only as clowns, never as actors playing roles. In Lewis's account the peasants have no ability to distinguish between what Russian Formalist theory terms the *fabula* (the basic story material) and *sjuzet* (the arrangement of incidents as the plot) of narrative. This, we may see, is in contrast to the story itself, which is keenly aware of the distance between the two semiotic levels of narrative, as Lewis's already-signature style of striking images and violent syntax do not seek 'faithfully' to reproduce the real in the style of nineteenth-century realism or naturalism, but rather widen as far as possible the gap between his language and the supposed referent of the Breton peasants.

Fittingly, the stories by Lewis that Ford published were as much about the process of travel narratives and creating fictional characters as they were about Brittany itself. Ford's own musing on the problematics of any narration was *The Good Soldier*, a portion of which Lewis published in the first issue of *Blast* in 1914 under Ford's original title, 'The Saddest Story'. The novel was actually meant to be serialized in its entirety; but, like Lewis's sub-editorship, the full serialization never came to fruition, the war interrupting it after only one installment.[14] Lewis's decision to have Ford appear with writers and artists like Pound and Gaudier-Brzeska seems like the reverse of Ford's inclusion of Lewis in the *English Review*. Ford clearly stands out as the most established contributor, having already published over thirty books by this point. The section of Ford's novel is interspersed with illustrations by Frederick Etchells and William Roberts, producing a striking juxtaposition between Ford's stately prose and the artists' angular, fragmented images. Ford immediately noted this contrast in styles, writing that in *Blast* is 'a portion of a novel by myself which appears unexciting when I see it in print' (*Reader* 177). The modernism of *The Good Soldier* has a hard time being heard over the aggressive post-Cubist images and the stridency of Lewis's play *Enemy of the Stars*. But of course *The Good Soldier* is a masterpiece of fragmentation and nonlinear narrative, which is why Ford may be using his words precisely when he says that the section of the novel '*appears* unexciting' next to the other works in *Blast*. If read beyond the opening chapters, *The Good Soldier* launches an experiment just as radical as anything that Lewis printed in 1914, and Lewis may have keenly appreciated this aspect of Ford's work.

We may wonder, however, how much Lewis had read of it, and what his motivations were for including *The Good Soldier* in *Blast*. It may be that, just as Ford used Lewis as his younger, more avant-garde counterpart, Lewis may have wanted Ford included in *Blast* to lend an air of legitimacy and professionalism to his project. Ford, ex-collaborator with Conrad, friend of Henry James and publisher of Thomas Hardy, provided a link to those previous generations of English literature towards which Vorticism and other movements were mostly hostile, although *Blast* does 'Bless' Jonathan Swift 'for his solemn bleak wisdom of laughter' and Shakespeare 'for his bitter Northern Rhetoric of humour'. (The inclusion of Ford may also be due to Pound's continual championing of Ford's work to young writers.)

Lewis's editing of the sections of *The Good Soldier* that appear in *Blast* may have made their way into the book version of the novel published the following year. Martin Stannard, in his 'Note on the

Text' to the Norton Critical edition of the novel, writes that 'It is impossible at this distance to disentangle Lewis's editorial interference from Ford's corrections [. . . .] But we cannot be sure, and collation raises the interesting notion that some of Lewis's corrections might have found their way into the final text'.[15] This textual mystery is appropriately unsolvable, falling into Fordian uncertainty. But it is tempting to assume that two important modernist figures, who liked to make each other characters in their memoirs, would collaborate on this modernist masterpiece of narratological self-reflexivity.

After Ford died in 1939, Lewis wrote to Pound that he was not a 'Fordie-fan' and had never been able to read more than a few lines of his fiction.[16] He may be forgetting, or choosing to forget, his inclusion of *The Good Soldier* in *Blast*. But Lewis continued to praise Ford's gifts as an editor, in a rare instance of the young cockerel praising the old father:

> Hueffer was probably as good an editor as could be found for an English literary review. – He had by birth artistic associations and could write himself much better than most editors. His literary standards were too exacting for latter-day England. Such productions as he was peculiarly fitted to edit are expensive to run and the circulation insignificant today. He was denied in his milieu the possibility of exerting an influence which would have been productive of more vigorous literary standards. Then his vanity never interfered in the least with his appreciation of books by other writers. (*RA* 131)

NOTES

1 For more parallels and connections between the two authors, see Alan Munton, 'The Insane Subject: Ford and Wyndham Lewis in the War and Post-War', and David Trotter, 'Ford Against Lewis and Joyce', in *Ford Madox Ford: Literary Networks and Cultural Transformations*, ed. Andrzej Gasiorek and Daniel Moore, Amsterdam: Rodopi, 2008, pp. 81-104 and pp. 105-131.

2 Lewis, *Rude Assignment: An Intellectual Autobiography*, Santa Barbara: Black Sparrow Press, 1984 [1950] – henceforth *RA*; p. 13.

3 Ford, *Return to Yesterday,* London: Victor Gollancz, 1931 – henceforth *RY;* p. 389.

4 Lewis's first novel *Tarr* (1918) was heavily influenced by Dostoyevsky, as he was well aware: see Paul O'Keeffe's Afterword to the 1990 Black Sparrow edition of the novel, pp. 379-80.

5 Max Saunders, *Ford Madox Ford: A Dual Life*, 2 vols, Oxford: Oxford University Press, 1996 – henceforth 'Saunders'; II, p. 190.

6   Ford included *Tarr* in his list of 'second flight' novels (and also works by Joyce, Lawrence, and Richardson) in 'A Haughty and Proud Generation' in the *Yale Review*, July 1922. See *Critical Essays*, ed. Max Saunders and Richard Stang, Manchester: Carcanet Press, 2002, p. 208.

7   *The Outlook*, 14 July 1914. Reprinted in *The Ford Madox Ford Reader*, Sondra Stang ed., New York: The Ecco Press, 1986 – henceforth *Reader*; pp. 173-7.

8   Ford's history of literature, published in 1938. Lewis and Vorticism make only a brief appearance, as 'August 1914 blew all that out of existence'. *The March of Literature*, New York: Dalkey Archive Press, 1998, p. 828.

9   See Saunders I 246. In *It Was the Nightingale*, London: William Heinemann, 1934, p. 299, Ford takes credit for the hasty acceptance, saying that 'I have accepted manuscripts by unknown writers after reading the first three lines. This was the case with D. H. Lawrence, Norman Douglas, (Percy) Wyndham Lewis, and H. M. Tomlinson'.

10 *The Letters of Wyndham Lewis*, ed. W. K. Rose, Norfolk: New Directions, 1963, pp. 39-40.

11 See Elena Lamberti's chapter, '"Wandering Yankees": The *transatlantic review* or how the Americans came to Europe' in this volume.

12 Paul Peppis writes that Ford's *English Review* 'articulate[s] the paradoxes of Edwardian liberalism': 'Lewis's travel stories fitfully imitate, attack, affirm and revise the literary modes and political ideals being celebrated in Ford's journal as cosmopolitan, civilized, and modern'. *Literature, Politics, and the English Avant-Garde: Nation and Empire, 1901-1918*, Cambridge: Cambridge University Press, 2000, p. 22.

13 Lewis, *The Complete Wild Body*, ed. Bernard Lafourcade, Santa Barbara: Black Sparrow Press, 1982 – henceforth *CWB*; p. 212. This edition includes the versions published in the English Review as well as Lewis' later revised versions.

14 Only one more issue of *Blast* appeared, the July 1915 'War Number', in which Lewis printed Ford's poem 'The Old Houses of Flanders'.

15 Ford, *The Good Soldier*, ed. Martin Stannard, Norton Critical Edition, New York and London: W. W. Norton & Company, 1995, p. 186.

16 Jeffrey Meyers, *The Enemy: A Biography of Wyndham Lewis*, London: Routledge and Kegan Paul, 1980, p. 29. Meyers believes that 'Lewis [...] appears as George Heimann in Ford's first postwar novel, *The Mardsen Case* (1923)', although offers no evidence for this supposition (p. 30).

'WRITTEN AT LEAST AS WELL AS PROSE': FORD, POUND, AND POETRY

Peter Robinson

Ford Madox Ford may be credited with the invention of practical criticism when he fell off his chair and rolled on the floor clutching his head in helpless laughter – or so we are told. Ezra Pound related the story against himself in his 'Ford Madox (Hueffer) Ford; Obit' of August 1939:

> he felt the errors of contemporary style to the point of rolling (physically, and if you look at it as mere snob, ridiculously) on the floor of his temporary quarters in Giessen when my third volume displayed me trapped, fly-papered, gummed and strapped down in a jejune provincial effort to learn, *mehercule*, the stilted language that then passed for 'good English' in the arthritic milieu that held control of the respected British critical circles, Newbolt, the backwash of Lionel Johnson, Fred Manning, the Quarterlies and the rest of 'em.
>
> And that roll saved me at least two years, perhaps more. It sent me back to my own proper effort, namely, toward using the living tongue (with younger men after me), though none of us has found a more natural language than Ford did.[1]

The list of names and institutions isn't merely a roll call of Pound's objects of contempt. Thirty years earlier, Henry Newbolt had written an appreciative note to Pound on the publication of *A Quinzaine for This Yule*, while in November 1909 Pound wrote to Ford that 'Manning has just written this quite beautiful "Persephone" which I can praise without reservation. I think you will thank me for getting it sent to you'. David Moody comments: 'Manning's "Koré" appeared at once' in the December issue of the *English Review*. The first poem in Pound's third book, *Canzoni*, is subtitled 'Written in reply to Manning's "Korè"'.[2] In 1915, Pound published a Preface to the *Poetical Works of Lionel Johnson* for Elkin Matthews. Less than a month before Germany's September 1939 attack on Poland, Pound's elegiac evocation has stiffened into a dismissal of English poetry circa 1910, using Newbolt, the derogatory 'backwash', and the ambiguously intimate 'Fred' to signal that this literary ambience and its persecution of Ford, against which he is presented as being in editorial revolt, was compounded of national prejudice and imperial hauteur. It exemplifies the retrospective blight of Pound's soured relations with literary London during the First World War, a world that he and Ford could appear allied against. Yet Pound's list also hints at some nostalgia for his youth that would come flooding to the surface in *The Pisan Cantos*. Pound's self-presentation in the obituary is as the 'E. P.' of the opening 'Ode' in *Mauberley*, the man who 'strove to resuscitate the dead art / Of poetry; to maintain "the sublime" / in the old sense'.[3] Equally, Ford's help is misleadingly expressed. The older man didn't so much send 'me back to my own proper effort' as to laugh him into taking a better direction, the one implied in 1914 when Pound praised T. S. Eliot for having 'modernizing himself *on his own*'.[4]

Implausibly but loyally comparing Ford's poetry with Homer's, Pound notes that 'never can you read half a page without finding melodic invention, still fresh, and [...] hear the actual voices, as of the old men speaking in the course of their phrases'; and it 'is for this latter quality that Ford's poetry is of high importance, both in itself and for its subsequent effect on all the best subsequent work of his time. Let no young snob forget this' (*P/F* 172). That last phrase exemplifies the combative attitude-mongering that would incline young snobs to do more than forget. Nevertheless, poets such as Basil Bunting, Robert Lowell, and Kenneth Rexroth have echoed Pound's praise. Yet Bunting also bluntly notes in his Preface to *Selected Poems* (1971) a limit to this 'quality' in Ford's poetry: 'I dare not maintain that Ford Madox Ford was a great poet or even a very good one; nevertheless in a few years before and after the first German war he did write some excellent poems which had a wider influence than anybody has acknowledged except Ezra Pound, and which might have more.'[5] Ford's poetry has its unequivocal admirers,[6] but the views of the hedging poets are what concern me here.

Such limiting judgments might equally be applied to his editorial example, at least as far as poetry is concerned. This can be sensed by the alacrity with which he responded to the directing of Manning's poem to him for the *English Review*. Moody observes:

> As Pound told it, what actually saved him was Hueffer's feeling the errors of style in Pound's *Canzoni* (1911) to the point of falling over and rolling about on the floor. That gives a dramatic impression of the master making his point to the 'jejune provincial'; yet one just wonders, if the master felt the errors so strongly, why had he published four of those 'canzoni' in his review?[7]

The following poems by Pound had appeared in the *English Review* before his third book was published: 'Sestina: Altaforte' (*ER* II [June 1909]); 'Ballad of the Goodly Fere', 'Nils Lykke', 'Un retrato [sic]' (*ER* III [Oct. 1909]); 'Canzon: The Yearly Slain', 'Canzon: The Spear', 'Canzon: To Be Sung beneath a Window' (*ER* IV [Jan. 1910]); 'Canzon: Of Incense', and 'Thersites; on the Surviving Zeus' (*ER* V [April 1910]).[8] Ford had thus featured the first four poems that appeared in *Canzoni*. But what does Moody doubt here? It could be Pound's story, and his 'As Pound told it' introduces a qualm. Equally, it could be that the story of the roll on the floor is true, but then Pound has exaggerated the single-minded significance of the physical action, dramatizing it for his readers not as a comic interlude effected by 'the Master', but as a message to the aspirant genius about where his work must improve if it is to achieve anything of lasting value. Or could Moody doubt the single-mindedness and purity of Ford's motives? Might he be suggesting that, as editor of the *English Review*, his standards were less stringent than as friend of a poet whose recent work, he thought, had mistaken its best direction?

One answer may be in 'Canzone à la Sonata', dedicated by Ford to 'E. P.' and collected in *High Germany*, which, although dated 1911, appears to have been published by Duckworth in February 1912.[9] The poem may, then, have been written in the aftermath of Pound's August visit to Ford in Giessen, and since it is called a 'Canzone', a genially mocking imitation cannot be ruled out:

> What do you find to boast of in our age,
> To boast of now, my friendly sonneteer,
> And not to blush for, later? By what line
> Do you entrain from Mainz to Regions saner?
> Count our achievements and uplift my heart;
> Blazon our fineness, Optimist, I toil
> Whilst you crow cocklike. But I cannot see
>
> What's left behind us for a heritage
> For our young children? What but nameless fear?[10]

Compared with E. P.'s canzoni, this is downbeat and plain spoken. Pound's 'Canzon: To be sung beneath a Window', for example, begins: 'Heart mine, art mine, whose embraces / Clasp but wind that past thee bloweth?'[11] What might have made Ford roll on the floor was not only the inept style of lines such as these, but their youthful enthusiasm, their etherealized sexual longing, their deafness to the

European political situation – in the light both of Ford's personal predicament, his being a father attempting to get a divorce by taking German nationality, and of the rivalries in Europe in 1911, which Ford had noticed. His poem isn't suffering from the faults of Pound's *Canzoni* not least because written as pastiche. That Ford was worried about war (his own nationality) and children is evident. Both he and Pound signed a card to Ford's daughter Christina, and 'He could not have been reassured by the children who set off percussion caps outside his window and shouted "Tag! Engländer"'.[12] Pound's explanation of the roll is that it criticized his 'style', but if '*le style c'est l'homme même*' then it wasn't just their style that Ford had in mind. It is as if this scene in Giessen were a try-out for the transatlantic misunderstandings of *The Good Soldier*, with Pound as the optimist, blithely unaware of what was going on around him. Oddly enough, this is the note Henry James had struck to describe Ford's response to *The Wings of the Dove* in a letter of 9 September 1902: 'Such is the contagion of your charming optimism.'[13]

In discussing the Pound poems Ford had published in the *English Review*, Moody is not considering the pressures of magazine editing, or of the nature of the publication, a regular book-sized volume. Ford had to publish the best he could find, even if it didn't quite fit either his aesthetic principles, or those of, say, five years later. Pound's retrospective propagandizing set a standard of modern poetry that in the 1909-11 period did not exist in London – and while Ford's roll might have helped to bring it into being, his own poetry only occasionally exemplified it. Pound's ambivalence about Ford's published poetry can be heard in 'A Retrospect' where under the heading 'Language' he writes: 'Don't use such an expression as "dim lands *of peace*". It dulls the image. It mixes an abstraction with the concrete. It comes from the writer's not realizing that the natural object is always the *adequate* symbol.'[14] The phrase 'dim lands of peace' is from Ford's own 'On a March Road (Winter Nightfall)' in the 1904 collection *The Face of the Night*.[15] Later Pound writes: 'Since March 1913, Ford Madox Hueffer has pointed out that Wordsworth was so intent on the ordinary or plain word that he never thought of hunting for *le mot juste*.'[16] This Flaubertian analogy for Ford's critical efforts is another instance of Pound not quite grasping the nature of the older man's art either in poetry or prose.

Ford's practical criticism of Pound's *Canzoni* was not the only instance of doubt regarding a misjudged volume. On 30 May 1916 its author wrote to the publisher Elkin Matthews: 'It is *not* so good as the others. I was affected by hyper-aesthesia or over-squeamishness and cut out the rougher poems. I don't know that I regret it in that case for the poems weren't good enough, but even so the book would have been better if they had been left in, or if something like them had been put in their place.'[17] James G. Nelson in his book on Elkin Matthews notes that reviews of *Canzoni* were 'mixed' and adds:

> The declining enthusiasm in England for Pound's poetry which was registered in the reviews of *Canzoni* was reflected in the disappointing sales of the book. That out of 1,000 sheets, only 250 were bound, indicates Matthews' rather pessimistic assessment of the book's chances, and assessment borne out by the fact that only 134 copies had sold some year and a half later, when the publisher's account of sales showed that of the almost £31 he had invested in *Canzoni*, only £11.13.9 had been recouped.[18]

These figures derive from a letter Matthews sent to Pound in November 1912, and are not given by Pound as any explanation for his sense of the need to modernize his style. In the light of the mediocre reviews and poor sales, the elevation of Ford's roll on the floor to the level of a mythical road to Damascus moment has the benefit of creating a history of endeavour and of apostolic succession, one to which Ford would also contribute in memoirs that assume a march of modern literature.

Pound generalized Ford's practical critical roll into the slogan that 'Poetry must be *as well written as prose*'[19] and in 'Mr Hueffer and the Prose Tradition in Verse' that it should be 'written at least as well as prose' (*P/F* 17). Pound could have drawn his idea from the introduction to Ford's first *Collected Poems* (1913). Its argument by no means promising for the idea of himself as a poet, there Ford admits to an amateur attitude to the art, and contrasts it with his professionalism about prose:

> But the writing of verse hardly appears to me to be a matter of work: it is a process, as far as I am concerned, too uncontrollable. From time to time words in verse form have come into my head and I have written them down, quite powerlessly and without much interest, under the stress of certain emotions. And, as for knowing whether one or the other is good, bad or indifferent, I simply cannot begin to trust myself to make a selection. And, as for trusting any friend to make a selection, one cannot bring oneself to do it either. (*CP1* 9)

However, a murmur of commentary by poets down the years has hinted at another story: namely, that Ford's approach to writing was not the one that Pound was trying to get to ('his true Penelope was Flaubert'[20]). Robert Lowell writes in a Preface to the 1966 reprint of *Buckshee*: 'Pound's famous command that *poetry be at least as well-written as prose* must have been inspired by Ford, though I doubt if Ford believed this a possibility or really had much fondness for a poetry that wasn't simple, poetic, and pastoral.'[21] The method outlined in *The Good Soldier* has been applied to one mode in Ford's poetry too: 'I shall just imagine myself for a fortnight or so at one side of the fireplace of a country cottage, with a sympathetic soul opposite me. And I shall go on talking, in a low voice while the sea sounds in the distance and overhead the great black flood of wind polishes the bright stars'.[22] The 'poetry' in this prose is itself striking: 'while the sea sounds in the distance and overhead the great black flood of wind polishes the bright stars'. Though a natural assumption might be that poems have to be better written than prose, for they must achieve thematic significance in form at both local and through-composed levels, Ford's slogan retains its force in the context of then current poetic conventions exemplified, and not at their worst, by Pound's *Canzoni*.

William Rose Benét concludes his Introduction to Ford's *Collected Poems* of 1936 with a limiting judgment that evokes the ghost of Flaubert: 'What is valuable in art, as I have noted, is the particular human experience. And for that, this poet has unborrowed language, and sometimes the inevitable word' (*CP2* xi). So Ford did get the *mot juste* in his poetry, but only 'sometimes'. Bunting picks up such a hint in his 1971 Preface: 'Ford and Conrad talked too much about Flaubert but did not waste much time playing hide-and-seek with the precise word.'[23] In a lecture on his 'Precursors' Bunting reads 'The Starling' and summarizes his view of the poetry:

> He too was uncertain of his way, and published bad poems – perhaps more bad than good: yet Pound is not merely being loyal to a friend when he insists on the part Ford played in changing English poetry in the earlier years of this century. Ford at his best uses language that is not merely current but conversational. Ford at his best names *things* and lets them evoke the emotion without mentioning it. He had not the gift of monumental brevity, but he uses repetition for a kind of hypnotic effect: uses it quite consciously, without trying to disguise it.[24]

Ford himself hints that there are states in life for which the 'precise word' might be neither available not even the correct way to render the experience in 'Moods on the Moselle', a poem from *High Germany* (1911), written at about the time he was rolling on the floor to express his amusement at Pound's style:

> But it's neither death nor fleetness
> That have any utter fitness,
> Not a final joy or sorrow,
> As we press out wines. (*CP2* 115)

The idea of the *mot juste* has its own complex history, and, as already noted, it was elevated into a fetish by modernists intent on combining the principle of an exact poetic rhythm for emotions (Ford's idea of a 'personal rhythm' explains little because dependant upon an undifferentiated subjectivism) with a pseudo-scientific ideal of descriptive accuracy. But the *mot juste* compounds an equivocation related to the psychology of choice, revision, and editing.

It is ambiguous in its suggesting that there can be a right word which will effectively bring to an end the possibility of substitution. For there to be a *mot juste* implies a choice from other words less apt, and they need to remain in earshot for the justness to register. The notion that there is only one right way to put something would tend to bring writing to a halt, because in order to move forward writers have to sense possibilities for better readings. Without possibilities there cannot be imaginative activity. Without closing them down, you cannot move on. But closing them down to a flourished determinate perfection produces one kind of literary writing, not literary writing as such. Ford's staged method, as outlined early on in *The Good Soldier*, is anti-Flaubertian in its assumption of multiple ways of rendering a story, and of reiterative retelling as progression of effect. This is one reason why the poetry 'written at least as well as prose' idea detaches from Ford's example, even though sponsored by his precepts. Nor did he practise what is sometimes now called 'editing' and yet is still 'revision'. He would write his stint, then 'usually leave it unaltered' (Judd 196). As Bunting points out of his style: 'Flaubert would not have recognized it: yet nebulosities and imprecisions are much of our landscape without and within, and worth reproducing'.[25] Ford's method invites imaginative activity in reader and writer. His reputation as an inclusive and encouraging editor may also derive from a sense that there is no single right way of expressing anything.

Ford improvises on relations between *res* and *verba*,[26] as well as
on romantic feeling and modern life, at the opening of 'Champêtre'
from his late collection *Buckshee*:

> Yesterday I found a bee orchid
> But when I gave it you you never raised your eyebrows
> – 'That a bee *orchid*? … It's neither bee nor orchid!'
> Was all you said. And dropped it amongst the tea table dishes
> And went on gazing over the lake;
> As once you dropped my letters into a VI Avenue garbage can
> And went on gazing up West Ninth Street
> Towards Wanamakers. (*CP2* 303)

Ford's joke about the *mot juste* here is supported by the finely
prepared and concealed reverse rhyme of 'lake' and 'can' in
'Wanamakers'. He was adept at conjuring the sound of good writing,
but not within 'less is more' or 'dichten=condensare' theories of the
art.[27] His work sustains an idea that poetry is good not because it is
densely textured and economically accurate, but because it has an
approximative touch and improvisatory flow. At its best, his
conversational rhythms are quick and deft enough to carry forward a
great deal of circumstantial detail. Even now, poets who wish to
render the life around them could do worse than attend to the flexible
sound of his verse.

What facilitated Ford's style was a form of relationship with an
interlocutor, one which would present a mind communing privately
with an equal (one who could then help figure similarly egalitarian
relations between writer and reader): 'I should like to write a poem – I
should like to write all my poems – so that they would be like the
quiet talking of some one walking along a path behind someone he
loved very much – quiet, rather desultory talking, going on, stopping,
with long pauses, as the quiet mind works' (*CW* 156). Max Saunders,
who quotes this, adds that Ford's idea 'could scarcely be further from
the Poundian attempt to escape the prosaic altogether by re-inventing
art-speech' (Saunders I 392). Pound saw Ford as in the line of Flaubert
(an idea Ford may have wished to promote) whereas the novelist's
practice of writing whether in poetry or prose is, as I say, anti-
Flaubertian. Yet the contemporary colloquial speech that Pound took
as Ford's contribution to the development of modern poetry was not
inseparable for him from the occasioning role of the beloved

interlocutor whose indulgent presence grants permission to its intimately reiterative cadences.

By most estimates, including his own, Ford's poetry is not as well written as his prose. If the prefatory essay to the first *Collected Poems* weren't enough, in 'Dedication' he has 'E. J.' (his daughter, Esther Julia) remark:

> Then shall you take these verses out
> And say: 'He was no prosodist;
> His rhymes are false, his metres twist
> Like sinners crippled by the gout.
> But ah, his love for me was great
> And these ten fingers he has kissed!' (*CP2* 25)

Ford's poetry has attractive pitch, tone, rhythm and cadence. Yet its almost ubiquitous weakness appears to be indissoluble from his 'theory' of the interlocutor, a projected presence that the speaker announces he loves 'very much' – as in his eight-line poem '"When the World was in Building"':

> Thank Goodness, the moving is over,
> They've swept up the straw in the passage
> And life will begin. . .
> This tiny, white, tiled cottage by the bridge! . . .
> When we've had tea I will punt you
> To Paradise for the sugar and onions. . .
> We will drift home in the twilight,
> The trout will be rising. . . (*CP2* 55)

The presence of the interlocutor prompts the appearance of wishful sentiment: 'I will punt you / To Paradise for the sugar and onions ...' He mostly gets away with it here, because the move to the gesturing 'Paradise' is so quickly grounded by the shopping for provisions, but elsewhere there is less economy of emotive gesture. The occasioning relationship preeminently displayed in 'On Heaven' and the poems of *Buckshee*, though equally in 'Finchley Road' and elsewhere, is also a siren-call that threatens to sentimentalize its presentation. In 1914, in 'Mr Hueffer and the Prose Tradition in Verse', Pound wrote: 'he has given us, in "On Heaven", the best poem yet written in the twentieth-century fashion' (*P/F* 17). Yet what Violet Hunt, its dedicatee and 'onlie begetter', had said was that it evokes a 'Love without breadth, depth or thickness, without dimension. Subjectivity purely [. . . .] Not [...] the love that moves mountains, faces the 7 seas of boredom, but the mild watery variety [...] repeats the great word Agony 3 times, taking up all one line' (Judd 231). These contrasted views are by no means incompatible. What's more, William Carlos Williams's 'To Ford Madox Ford in Heaven' could not have existed had Ford himself not responded to Violet Hunt's request, as given in the subtitle to Ford's poem, that he compose a working Heaven.

In *Songs from London*, published by Elkin Matthews in 1910, poems such as 'Finchley Road' or 'The Three-Ten' display a modernity that is pointedly patchy. Yet its point is an equivocation about the modern, including critical nostalgia of a pre-Raphaelite stamp for a nobler world:

> As we come up at Baker Street
> Where tubes and trains and 'buses meet
> There's a touch of fog and a touch of sleet;
> And we go on up Hampstead way
> Towards the closing in of day . . .

Though this gives us a flavour of the then contemporary, the central part of the poem is a romantic-sentimental homage to the woman accompanying the speaker: 'You should be a queen or a duchess rather, / Reigning in place of a warlike father'. This post-Pre-Raphaelite fantasy is spun for twenty-four similar lines, concluding with the notion that you 'sometimes reach me one of your hands, / Or bid me write you a little ode, / Part quaint, part sad, part serious . . .' It's an 'Innisfree' kind of city poem, but with the twist that the best poetry is in the parts that are not privileged by the hankering cast of mind and feeling that the poem sets out to express. It ends by waking from its romantic daydream to the facts of the London scene, and a far more convincing combination of diction, rhythm, and rhyme: 'But here we are in the Finchley Road / With a drizzling rain and a skidding 'bus / And the twilight settling down on us' (*CP2* 132-3). In poems such as these Ford's best writing is firmly present-day, but his heart (to use the word so fatally re-echoing through *The Good Soldier*) is, as it were, in the wrong place. While his roll helped Pound towards writing such poems as 'The Garret', 'The Garden', and 'Villanelle: The Psychological Hour', whose modernity includes a more effectively staged double-mindedness about the urban and the pastoral, still Ford was not entirely able to follow. For example, the only verse in 'Winter Night-Song' that isn't weakened by sentimental phraseology such as 'My dearest dear, my honey-love' is the second:

> All taxi lamps and street-lights too
> Grow dim along Fifth Avenue
> And in the doorways of the shops
> Slumber the dawn-awaiting cops. (*CP2* 50)

The poem is a prime instance of Ford's problem with his interlocutor. In the verse above, with no commandeered, complicit addressee in sight, the poem sharpens and de-sentimentalizes.

There are poems that don't suffer from this trait, because the 'you' in them is differently staged: in 'That Exploit of Yours', a poem written without knowledge of Owen's 'Strange Meeting', though the Biblical call to love our enemies might be colouring the relationship between speaker and interlocutor, there is a sardonic coolness to the poem that prevents it from suffering any such weakness; and the same is true of 'The Old Houses of Flanders' where the 'you' is the impersonal pronoun alluding to author, interlocutor, and reader, though primarily by figuring the speaking subject in the second person. The dual role of the interlocutor as an intermediary point between the isolated writer and the unknown public also models Ford's sense of cultural isolation, and expresses an oblique pathos in his attempts to overcome it. Contrasted with *The Good Soldier* and its fictional narrator, Ford's poetry exposes both author figure and voice.

His best work combines a conversational free-verse line – from Whitman through Swinburne, perhaps, and therefore collaterally related to Laforgue's *Derniers vers* (as 'stolen' by Eliot) – which Ford then tags with improvised rhymes of, at their best, a wryly 'quoted' self-awareness, as in this brief passage from 'L'Oubli –, Temps de sécheresse', also in *Buckshee*:

> There is no satisfaction greater
> Than the sight of that house-side, silver-grey
> And very high
> With the single black cypress against the sky
> Above the hill
> And the palm-heads streaming away at the mistral's will. (*CP2* 308)

The epithet 'silver-grey' emerges from a reverie-like reiteration of earlier rhymes: 'winter days', and 'an infinite number of lays in Latin', and 'an infinite number of subtle greys', and 'to make up a blaze'. The best of his verse comes thus in casual patches, which are worked toward through associations of sound and rhyme, rapidly finessed, and allowed to disperse for the purpose of further movement into and out of focus. Such improvised, blurred passages can be simultaneously both highly attractive and slightly irritating. For better and worse, Ford is rarely more than half-modern in his poetry.

In his Preface to the 1913 *Collected Poems* Ford describes himself, faintly comically, as a follower of F. T. Marinetti: 'But it would be a similar hypocrisy in Mr De la Mare, Mr Yeats, or Mr Hardy to attempt to render Life in the terms of the sort of Futurist picture that life is to me and my likes' (*CP1* 27). This is the Ford whose single greatest work, under the title 'The Saddest Story', had been excerpted in the 1914 first issue of *Blast*. Yet Ford in his poetry is never more than a Futurist Toad of Toad Hall combined with a pastoralist Mole, a hybrid heard in the sound of the ranging modern cadences and the tagging English rhymes. The latter come in two types, the decorative and the functional. Bunting notes of the former: 'More often they are little lifeless piles of patched rags, sticky with commonplace adjectives, dusty with nouns out of a museum. There is metre but no rhythm, only the fatal clank of obvious rhymes.'[28] Yet a further problem even with the 'durable work' which Bunting reprinted in 1971, describing it as 'alive and, I think' with 'quite a long time to live', is that it too contains patches of the lifelessness he claims to be excluding.

Just before Ford's death, attempts were made to publish a British edition of the 1936 *Collected Poems*. Two readers' reports on the proposal have been preserved in the Unwin archive at Reading. One of these appears to be a response to the idea that there simply be a reprint, the other, commenting on a suggested selection, talks the project out of existence by raising the spectre of limited sales. Nevertheless, the first is a positive summary of what could be liked about Ford's poetry on the eve of the Second World War, when Bernard Miall observed (and a press date stamp reads 18 May 1937):

> Why a book published last year in New York by the Oxford University Press should now come to you I do not, of course, know. Presumably the more recent sales of Mr Ford's verse in the country were not such as to encourage the publishers to risk an English edition.
> If this is so, they may possibly be mistaken. There are quite a number of persons who regard Mr Ford as one of our two living novelists of the first rank; they at least might be expected to purchase. Also, the public may be getting a little weary of free verse which neither rhymes honestly nor wholly refrains from rhyme, but indulges in the sort of assonance which is fatally reminiscent of the crooner (childhood, wildwood, line, time), does not obey its own laws of scansion, is unintelligible on a first, second, and third reading,

and not worth understanding on a tenth, and is obviously derived, at not so long last, from Mr. T. S. Eliot, of whom someone is sure to remark, sooner or later, that he does not so much write poetry as practice haughtyculture.

Mr Ford is usually intelligible at a first reading; mostly his meaning leaps comfortably to the eye; his free verse respects the manners that make freedom possible. It is essentially the verse of a gentleman, an extremely English cosmopolitan, and a nephew of Christina Rossetti. And much of it is intensely personal.[29]

He concludes: 'The understanding introduction by Mr Benet, and the long, confidential preface (here an appendix) by Mr Ford, add to the interest of the edition. Whether it will sell in this country or not (and I think its chances are better than they would have been a few years ago) I think you will be well advised to publish it. There is kudos to be gained, and the desirability of keeping Mr Ford in your list.' Malcolm Barnes, however, wrote in a brief report dated 24 June 1937:

The omissions which Ford proposes from the Oxford Press (U.S.A.) COLLECTED POEMS, amount to fully two thirds of the volume. What remains for us to consider publishing will make but a slim volume of 100 pages. Reading through the whole collection (both the matter to be omitted and the remainder) I am convinced that what he is now offering us is undoubtedly the verse which would be more acceptable than the rest to English readers and possibly the stuff which will endure, if any will endure at all. Certainly they are the most readily intelligible and easily appreciable poems and contain the least part of the blank verse which Ford has turned out.

But the question is mainly whether a market could be found for it. To publish the complete Ford poems would in any case carry with it a certain amount of kudos, but to publish a selection only, carries no very appreciable kudos in comparison. Secondly I do not believe that the market for a selection would be as considerable as for the complete book. Selections seem to me to sell mostly when they are the work of poets of popularity; but, much as it may be regretted, Ford has not that popularity and his purchasers will more likely be only those who are keen enough to want everything.

Therefore I cannot predict any particular sale – a hundred or two at the most, and the only justification for publication would appear to be the possible kudos.[30]

Together these readers' reports articulate a real dilemma facing the republication of Ford's poetry, for our sense of his legendary roll in Giessen has to include the recognition that he couldn't quite take his own advice. His colloquial style of poetic speech, ideally between equals, was a means of facilitating self-expressive writing, and it did; but it also allowed for a leisurely slapdash. He is one of many writers about whom it could be said that their strengths and weaknesses are

inseparable. Those who have time for some of his poetry, as I do, may
see its unique hybrid as a valuable cultivating of Ford's own garden,
an activity he also evokes in 'L'Oubli –, Temps de sécheresse' where,
as Pound put it in *Mauberley*, the stylist 'exercises his talents / And
the soil meets his distress',[31] partially sheltered there from the *de haut
en bas* of a modernist 'haughtyculture'.

NOTES

1   *Pound/Ford: the Story of a Literary Friendship: the Correspondence between Ezra
    Pound and Ford Madox Ford and Their Writings About Each Other*, ed. Brita
    Lindberg-Seyersted, London: Faber & Faber, 1982 – henceforth *P/F*; p. 172.
2   A. David Moody, *Ezra Pound: Poet. A Portrait of the Man and His Work*,
    Oxford: Oxford University Press, 2007, p. 80 for Newbolt, and p. 114 for
    Manning and Ford.
3   Ezra Pound, *Collected Shorter Poems*, London: Faber & Faber, 1984, p. 187.
4   Pound to Harriet Monroe, 30 Sept 1914, *The Selected Letters of Ezra Pound 1907-
    1941* ed. D. D. Paige, New York: New Directions, 1971, p. 40.
5   Basil Bunting (ed.), Preface to Ford Madox Ford, *Selected Poems,* Cambridge,
    MA: Pym-Randall Press, 1971, p. vii.
6   See, for example, Joseph Wiesenfarth, 'The Ash-Bucket at Dawn: Ford's Art of
    Poetry', *Contemporary Literature* 30:2, Summer 1989, 240-62.
7   Moody, *Ezra Pound: Poet*, p. 112.
8   Donald Gallup, *A Bibliography of Ezra Pound*, London: Rupert Hart-Davis, 1963,
    p. 198.
9   Max Saunders, *Ford Madox Ford: A Dual Life*, 2 vols, Oxford: Oxford University
    Press, 1996 – henceforth 'Saunders'; I, p. 368.
10 Ford, *Collected Poems*, New York: Oxford University Press, 1936 – henceforth *CP2*;
    p. 116.
11 Ezra Pound, *Collected Early Poems* ed. Michael John King, London: Faber &
    Faber, 1977, p. 136.
12 Alan Judd, *Ford Madox Ford*, London: Collins, 1990 – henceforth 'Judd'; pp. 198,
    202.
13 Henry James, *A Life in Letters* ed. Philip Horne, Harmondsworth: Penguin Books,
    2000, p. 370.
14 Ezra Pound, *The Literary Essays*, ed. T. S. Eliot, London: Faber & Faber, 1954, p.
    5.
15 Ford, *Collected Poems*, London: Max Goschen, 1913 – henceforth *CP1*; p. 199.
16 Pound, *Literary Essays*, p. 7.
17 Pound to Elkin Matthews, 30 May 1916, *Pound / Joyce: The Letters of Ezra
    Pound to James Joyce* ed. Forrest Read, New York: New Directions, 1967, p. 285.
18 James G. Nelson, *Elkin Matthews: Publisher to Yeats, Joyce, Pound*, Madison,
    Wisconsin: University of Wisconsin Press, 1989, pp. 146-7.

19 Pound to Harriet Monroe, Jan 1915, *Selected Letters of Ezra Pound*, p. 48 and see note on p. 49.
20 Pound, *Shorter Poems*, p. 187.
21 Robert Lowell, Foreword, Ford Madox Ford, *Buckshee*, Boston, MA: Pym-Randall Press, 1966, p. xiii.
22 Ford, *The Good Soldier*, ed. Martin Stannard, Norton Critical Edition, New York and London: W. W. Norton & Company, 1995, p. 15.
23 Bunting, Preface, Ford, *Selected Poems*, p. vii.
24 Peter Makin, ed., *Basil Bunting on Poetry*, Baltimore: Johns Hopkins University Press, 1999, p. 111.
25 Bunting, Preface, Ford, *Selected Poems*, p. vii.
26 For Pound using these paired terms to praise Ford's conversation, see *The Cantos*, 4th edn., London: Faber & Faber, 1986, p. 525.
27 Ezra Pound, *ABC of Reading*, London: Faber & Faber, 1951, p. 36.
28 Bunting, Preface, Ford, *Selected Poems*, p. viii.
29 Allen & Unwin Archive, AURR 6/1/34, University of Reading Special Collections.
30 *Ibid.* AURR 6/1/35.
31 Pound, *Shorter Poems*, p. 195.

'HIS CARE FOR LIVING ENGLISH':
FORD MADOX FORD AND BASIL BUNTING

Richard Price

Basil Bunting was very briefly sub-editor, personal assistant and fac-
totum for Ford Madox Ford in Paris while the *transatlantic review*
was underway. He didn't last long in post – a matter of weeks,
perhaps in late 1923 and early 1924[1] – in any case a period
considerably less than the duration of the *transatlantic review* itself,
whose period of publication, just the calendar year of 1924, was short
enough. The briefest of surviving correspondence suggests they were
still in touch in the early 1930s.[2]

Yet nearly fifty years later Bunting remembered Ford both
fondly and respectfully. The fondness I'll return to later – perhaps it is
more significant than it seems – but first there is the selection Bunting
made in 1971 of Ford's poems for the US publisher Pym-Randall and,
in particular, his focus on Ford's literary achievement in the preface.[3]

Bunting opens that preface:

> I dare not maintain that Ford Madox Ford was a great poet or even a very good
> one; nevertheless in a few years before and after the first German war he did
> write some excellent poems which had a wider influence than anybody has
> acknowledged except Ezra Pound, and which might have more. Ford's friends
> at that time admitted Wordsworth's precept of a vocabulary taken from
> everyday speech, though they neglected it, and Yeats' further precept of
> everyday syntax, as much neglected; but Ford did not neglect them. He tried to
> write as he would speak, informally, and add to conversational diction the
> rhythms of conversation. That was rare in 1910, almost unknown.[4]

There's quite a lot in that paragraph. I think Bunting is trying to offer
a measure of Ford which will convince the reader of the
trustworthiness of Bunting's own judgement so that in turn the reader
will take Ford seriously – he 'dare not' attest to a greatness in Ford not
necessarily because Ford isn't a great poet (leaving aside the question
of what measures might be used to assess the 'greatness' of a poet – a
greatometer anyone?) but because Bunting is adopting a sound
rhetorical tactic for the re-introduction of a poet many of the book's

readers would not have thought of as a poet at all, if indeed they knew him as a novelist.

Let's not carried away with ourselves Bunting is telling us: with the sort of discriminating sensibility I have I'm certainly not going to and you shouldn't either. At the same time, though, he suggests that not only was Ford interesting in his time, but his interest has not all been consumed: he 'might have more' influence on the contemporary scene.

For this reason I'm not sure that Max Saunders, in his later, broader selection of Ford's poems, is quite right to imply that Bunting is damning Ford with 'faint praise' in this preface, if that is what is being implied.[5] Yes Bunting does go on to say that his selection is brief because there are a lot of 'lifeless piles of patched rags [in Ford's poetry], sticky with commonplace adjectives, dusty with nouns out of a museum'[6] and that does sound rather negative but in the context of Bunting's emphasis on good judgement and discrimination I still read his selection of Ford as an unequivocal but discriminating work of advocacy.

Before getting down to championing Ford on stylistic grounds Bunting first sets a wider literary context, praising Ford's verse for its synthesising and catalytic effects on others, early on in the history of modern poetry. They are 'excellent poems' of far-reaching *influence* which were not only composed of the words of common parlance but the structures of that speech, too.

There is an accusatory undertone in this passage in that only Pound is said to have willingly acknowledged Ford's innovation and, as the preface unfolds, at least one prime suspect is revealed to be not a poet at all but that other famous language hygienist, that ungrateful fosterling of Ford's, Ernest Hemingway. I think I'll have to leave it to others to see how far Hemingway is stylistically in debt to Ford, though he certainly seems to have owed Ford in other ways. Perhaps Bunting is casting his net wider, too – to Eliot, say, who may have been very interested in what Ford was writing in the years immediately before and during the First World War – but this is outside my scope here.

Bunting states that Ford's approach to vocabulary and rhythm 'was rare in 1910, almost unknown' and I suspect he is right, but such re-orientation of poetic diction doesn't isolate Ford even if it gives him special prominence as an early innovator. Paul Skinner, in his article 'Poor Dan Robin: Ford Madox Ford's Poetry' documents and discusses the various aesthetic schools of this period that Ford's poetry anticipates or with which it shares common ground.[7] Suffice it to say here that for Bunting Ford becomes a branch on the bough of the modernist family tree whose authors by and large have faith in the philosophical, sonic, poetical resources of carefully stylised contemporary speech.

That's the family to which William Carlos Williams, Chekhov and D. H. Lawrence in their different ways belong, as does Hemingway, and which, arguably, could claim an uncle in Thomas Hardy and cousins in Edward Thomas and Charlotte Mew. They deploy common speech (though not, generally speaking, working class speech) as their fundamental language carrier and have confidence in its emotional and intellectual depths and in their own sophisticated use of it.

There is also one thing in this passage that Bunting seems to be saying, by not saying it, which I find particularly interesting. His emphasis would surely lead us to think that Ford's poetry did not belong, taxonomically speaking, to the other quite different modernisms: the modernism, say, of the book or sequence as an attemptive totalising scheme (*The Cantos, A Drunk Man Looks at the Thistle, Finnegans Wake*); the modernism in which top-down views of all human civilisation and history are imposed on what are seen as the sordid disappointments of the present-day (*The Waste Land* perhaps, much of Pound); the modernism of the continued mobilisation of tales, poems and events from classical Greece and Rome, with perhaps the literature of medieval Europe thrown in for an extra didactic scourge. Bunting also doesn't refer to the collage and recycling effects that you see in, say, Eliot and Blaise Cendrars; and, especially striking for Bunting, he doesn't mention musical concepts as organising principles (or at least organising analogues). I of course simplify and de-strand these inter-braided themes – forgive a librarian's tendency towards classification.

The odd thing is that although Ford is characterised by Bunting as a moderniser of poetry for both process (rhythm and syntax) and phenomenon (vocabulary, and therefore subject), both predicated on 'the everyday', that is precisely not the sort of poet Bunting is for large swathes of his own poetry. And it is not the poet Ford often is. Rather, Bunting, perhaps more than Ford, has his Poundian frustrated-professor-with-a-view-on-everything manner (Professor Yaffle as bookend); both Bunting and Ford are very much Europhiles and classicists; and both use sequences that proceed by collage effects. Ford and Bunting are more than all that, too, but those classic modernist elements are there in both their work: yet Bunting chooses not to mention them at all. Perhaps this is another aspect of careful advocacy – relating especially to an apparently straight talking version of Modernism, which accepts how much more William Carlos Williams had been assimilated within wider culture than Eliot or Pound.

In this he is, only to a relative degree, following Ford himself. In Ford's preface to his *Collected Poems* (1914), he goes to some lengths to downplay the necessity of classical and European education (incidentally still the stock in trade of so much dreary contemporary poetry today), and the use of biblical and Irish myths in poetry. He is liberal and acknowledges poets as 'heirs of all the ages', but in preferring what he calls 'the right appreciation' of the 'facets of our own day'[8] he presents a much richer version of modernist ambition than Bunting's representation, including the challenge to the modern poet of engaging with urban spectacle, class consciousness, and crowd behaviour – all elements that Bunting does not explicitly highlight as characteristics of Ford's work, but which are in fact there.

Bunting doesn't mention Ford's championing of juxtaposition either and, most striking of all is the younger poet's neglecting to mention music as an ordering concept in Ford's work, though he is alert to broadly aural effects of which rhythm is of course one. This is surprising because Bunting is himself such a musically-attuned poet, as witnessed by a much later work of course – that exquisite sonic work *Briggflatts*, which is collected, by the way, as one of several of 'Sonatas' in his own *Collected Poems* – the culmination of a life interest in classical music.

Specifically, it is in their fondness for music that Bunting and Ford meet. They are both fascinated by music as a subject and, especially, as an analogue and example by which they organise their own work. The Ford who wrote early poems to be set to music and whose compositional skills did not desert him in later works is the Ford Bunting is especially fond of. Ford is *particularly* interested in music: as others have noted, many poems are labelled as songs, some appearing to aspire to pieces in a classical repertoire, and others, more abstractly, more tenuously, seeming to toggle from a collage (visual) structure to an almost symphonic (aural) one, or hybridise both.

Bunting does include such poems in his selection – perhaps 'On Heaven' and 'Footsloggers' as examples of the latter, but his commentary's focus is really on the spoken word. After his assertion of Ford's inspired use of speech patterns Bunting goes on to warn how this is a dangerous tactic – there's the high risk of 'letting the poem sag'. Here Bunting the yachtsman uses a sailing metaphor: to prevent that laxness 'Ford sweated up his halliards like a sailor. He took a fresh purchase and another swig again and again till the sail's last wrinkle was smoothed out'.[9]

What does he mean by this? It looks at first as if Ford is writing and re-writing to get a better expression of things – to achieve, say, the sort of tight, no-flab nonsense that the Imagist anthologies promoted – halliards hoist and then tighten a sail and the smoother the sail the more efficient it is. But it's not a re-drafting process that Bunting is talking about – this isn't honing or, that favourite craft of Bunting's, stone-masonry. Ford is not emerging as a herald of Imagism: something quite different is happening, something that rather leapfrogs Imagism in the Boy's Own chronology of literary movements and moves forward to something much more like the on-the-move observations of Objectivism. Maybe its meaning is already hinted at in that curious use of the word 'swig'.

When I first read that word I thought that Bunting meant 'swing' on a halyard ratchet, an inspired misprint that has it both ways with swinging's hearty lust-for-life tone, and swigging's repeated drinking motion (there's lust for life there, too). Bunting, distrustful of footnotes and open to the anarchy of musical effects, might well have enjoyed that misreading. In fact I should have trusted Bunting's lexis: there is no such misprint, 'swig', as a verb, is a precise nautical term for, as the *Oxford English Dictionary* has it, '[pulling] at the bight of a rope which is fast at one end to a fixed object and at the other to a movable one'.[10] The word has a literary pedigree, too: as a noun, a swig, it is used in both drinking and marine senses by Melville in *Redburn* (1849) when he describes, perhaps with an additional homo-erotic frisson, shipmates surreptitiously getting together over a brown jug of alcohol: 'Every once in a while, the men went into one corner, where the chief mate could not see them, to take a "swig at the halyards", as they called it.'[11]

So in Bunting's use of this little word there is *joie-de-vivre*, command of a precise technical vocabulary, a sense of movement, and also a tension, embodied in the metaphor, between fixed form and the 'movable' – to swig is to acknowledge a line that is held, controlled, but also to allow its free verse form, all within a structure, a vessel, that is itself, of course, moving on. Imagism's static and visual accuracies (in fact, effects) are far from what Ford is doing because there is something much more mobile, cumulative and recurring in his technique, something I would suggest, that is much more Objectivist – if that isn't to pigeon-hole Ford again, and after all one of Ford's strengths is his mercuriality. As Peter Makin says, when discussing Bunting's aesthetics: '[rhythmic play] has far greater value when the poet can articulate it into a paragraph-long progression of changes, of shifts developed for some deep analogy – or contrast – with changing meaning [....] This art, for Bunting, is the real thing: it is that for which verse, in English, essentially exists.'[12]

Bunting continues in his Preface to Ford:

> Ford and Conrad talked too much about Flaubert but did not waste much time playing hide-and-seek with the precise word. They surrounded their meaning with successive approximations instead, and so repeated in the texture of prose the pattern by which their narrative captured their theme. It is a circuitous technique, prodigal of paper. For sure, Flaubert would not have recognised it: yet nebulosities and imprecisions are much of our landscape without or within, and worth reproducing. In his best years Ford reproduced them in verse.[13]

I can't help thinking of the spiralling use Ford makes in *The Good Soldier* of sentimental and colloquial phrases his narrator deploys in strange centrifugal forms, distancing himself from his own drama. They are a kind of emotional avoidance, vain attempts to push away expressions of passion and culpability, but the reader is drawn to the trail of their heatsource and gradually infers the mess at the heart of the emotional vortex: perhaps it is not so out of place that *The Good Soldier* should have been part serialised in *Blast,* the self-proclaimed mouthpiece of the Vorticists.

Maybe this technique is a Chekhovian tactic of saying a series of only small things to get to the depths of something that cannot be said outright or without the purchase of time, perhaps it has its roots in Browning's elliptical dramatic monologues ('My Last Duchess', like Florence in *The Good Soldier*, 'had a heart'): it is certainly reliant on voice, successiveness and on levered silences so is especially suited to the stage – I think of the waves of patterning in Beckett, Pinter, Mamet – Angus Wrenn has recently written on Ford and Pinter[14] – and to the novel when it proceeds by stylised rhythmic dramatic monologue: followers of Ford may be surprised to find kin in James Kelman's novels, *The Bus Conductor Hines* say, or *How Late it Was, How Late* where remarkable speech patterning – 'nebulosities and imprecisions' – add up to complex texts of great emotional power.

At this point a case study seems appropriate. Bunting was particularly interested in Ford's 'The Starling'. He chose it to open his 1971 selection of Ford's poetry and, in his talk, 'Precursors', from the 1969-70 series of lectures he gave at Newcastle University, it is the poem that Bunting chose to exemplify Ford's work: he praises Ford and then reads the whole poem to the class.[15] As with his role in the American publication of Ford's *Selected Poems,* Bunting's public recognition of Ford's place within modernist history, his mention of Ford in these lectures, shows what an unrecognised champion of Ford both sides of the Atlantic Bunting was: in the history of Ford's reassessment, he really was an early and I believe discerning critic who never forgot Ford's literary significance and was able to re-ignite interest in his work when he had himself been only recently connected to a broader audience of readers.

Nevertheless, at first look 'The Starling' might appear an odd choice of subject for asserting Ford's modernity – it has a medieval, villagey, aspect to it and so would appear to be precisely the type of poem Ford casts doubt on in his preface to his 1913 *Collected Poems*.[16] However, Ford's own advice elsewhere in the Preface warns the reader not to take a rural *mis-en-scène* as intrinsically backwards. For example, he justifies his admiration for Hardy and Yeats whatever the location of their poems (which he characterises as rural) and asserts the primacy of 'the genuine love and the faithful rendering of the received impression' (*CP1* 28) wherever the setting.

'The Starling' is also, as I'll go on to show, a disavowal of a previous village-based life. In that way – and in others – it is actually a portmanteau poem, a manifesto poem, and so surprisingly well-suited as an illustration of Ford's aesthetic. Ford includes 'The Starling' in his *Collected Poems* and, like Bunting in the *Selected*, positions it right at the start of the book. It is also placed at the start of the collection it originally came from, *High Germany.* So Bunting may be paying homage and respect to Ford's sequencing, and perhaps remembering the impact it made as he first began to read Ford.

Introducing the poem at Newcastle he said:

> [...] Pound is not merely being loyal to a friend when he insists on the part
> Ford played in changing English poetry in the earlier years of this century.
> Ford at his best uses language that is not merely current but conversational.
> Ford at his best names *things* and lets them evoke the emotion without
> mentioning it. He had not the gift of monumental brevity, but he uses
> repetition for a kind of hypnotic effect: uses it quite consciously, without
> trying to disguise it.[17]

'It's an odd thing how one changes ...' Ford begins his poem 'The
Starling'. There's a three-dot ellipsis at the end of that sentence, one
of those pre-Pinter pauses Ford comically but sincerely codified in the
transatlantic review, where he regards it as an essential part of English
speech, something 'by which the Briton – and the American now and
then – recovers himself in order to continue a sentence' (*TRev* I [Jan.
1924] 97).[18] Angus Wrenn doesn't mention the connection between
this pause and Pinter's prosody – Wrenn is more concerned with
situational and structural similarities – but it is surely a mark of
significant affinity; it's the hard-wiring they share.[19]

As well as the signalling of an emotional or cerebral breathing
space, the pause in the poem alerts us straight away to a time
signature, warning us that the text is likely to modulate. The rhyming
couplets Ford uses for much of the poem make this transmission once
or twice rather clumsy, especially when two short lines follow each
other as they do soon enough:

> It's an odd thing how one changes ...
> Walking along the ranges
> Of this land of plains,
> In this month of rains, [...]

Plains and rains? Oof! – that is a rocky lift-off for the poem, half
nursery rhyme, half elocution lesson – it sounds as if cranes, drains
and Spain will be just around the corner. It is not a serious opening for
what is, as it turns out, a relatively serious poem.

Before the rhyme crime though, let's go back to that very first
sentence's 'It's an odd thing how one changes ...'. That's an unpoetic
thing to say, too, but it's a type of unpoetry that is much more
interesting than plains and rains. Taken literally it really isn't poetry at
all, it's surely seven words of a single sigh, one of those arresting
sighs you might make to have a listener turn to you and say, 'come on,
what's the matter?' and later you'd feel, when you had unburdened

your heart and your interlocutor was now perhaps wishing you hadn't, that you could still declare with some honesty, 'well, you did *ask* ...'.

So it looks like a low-key and even an inept beginning to a poem but I think that first line in particular is actually something of a disarming lure. Looked at more closely it gives up a bit more. It's a line about aloneness and pace. That 'one' hovers between an indefinite anybody (so bringing in all readers to sympathise – they are invited to agree, 'Isn't it though?') and a more commanding, authoritative statement – the use of an upper-class third person replacement for a first person pronoun. It is, by the way, a circumlocution, a class-based sleight of hand, that is very similar to the tactics of emotional avoidance that take place in *The Good Soldier*.

What then happens in the poem is that several kinds of non-human plurals, groups, are described, contrasting to the speaker's soli-tariness and to his sense of almost waking to find that he has been overtaken – not just by the feathered friends of the eponymous bird but by changes in his own behaviour over time; he's been overtaken by his consciousness of his own singleness. There are those plural ranges, those plains; even the weather – the rains – happening severally (and exotically). Then there are the 'the poplars [that] march along' and finally 'With a rush of wings flew down a company, / A multitude, throng upon throng, / Of starlings, / Successive orchestras of song, / Flung, like the babble of surf, / On to the roadside turf.' Not just one bird orchestra – 'successive' ones, a travelator of them!

This contrast, between the silent speaker full of thoughts, and between apparently unthinking groups, now fully and variously vocal, is *the* contrast of the poem. It's heightened by the compressed gram-mar of the stanza, pivoted on the word 'Suddenly', given its own line to dramatically pause within, and the absolute absence of the word 'I' in the sentence, so that subject and object are briefly suspended. Later in the poem the two shortest lines cut the word 'I' off at the end of the line – each line being only two syllables in any case – the subjective particularism of 'but I,' and then, later, the phrase repeated, 'but I.'

But before these we have another of those improvisational 'nebulosities' that Bunting described as part of Ford's genius – this time the comic attempt to gauge the distance of the moving starling flock 'And so, for a mile, for a mile and a half – a long way, / Flight follows flight'. It might be a nebulosity but that surely captures some-thing of the difficulty of such a measure – it isn't inarticulacy, it is a super-articulacy because it is conveying the distance in as far as it can be estimated, conveying the flocks' movement away from the speaker, and conveying the speaker's honesty as he modifies his assessment 'live': it's still faster than the status designations on Facebook and Twitter (ornithologically enough). This is something that it's easy to miss if you are not attuned to Ford's poems as dramatising speech, or thoughts dramatised as speech: they offer a different kind of linguistic density which is not necessarily visual, nor necessarily attractive as savourable vocabulary, but which, perhaps because they are not snagged by those effects, offer a different sort of sequence-of-events sophistication altogether.

The opening sentence then comes back in the third stanza:

> It's an odd thing how one changes ...
> And what strikes me now as most strange is:
> After the starlings had flown
> Over the plain and were gone,
> There was one of them stayed on alone
> In the trees; it chattered on high,
> Lifting its bill to the sky,
> Distending its throat,
> Crooning harsh note after note,
> In soliloquy,
> Sitting alone.

Chatter, dandyism, and apparently a fascination with the grating 'note after note' – there seems to be self-identification and a manifesto in this, an interest in the solitary being paradoxically all loquaciousness and volubility, an interest even in what might conventionally be regarded as ugly sounds. Ford goes on to describe the starling's ability to mimic (Ford the master of pastiche). However, after dwelling on this and – in the mechanics of the poem, executing a fair bit of it, too – Ford's speaker turns away from the starling with a near stutter of the me myself I:

> But I,
> Whilst the starling mimicked on high
> Pulsing its throat and its wings,
> I went on my way
> Thinking of things,
> Onwards and over the range
> And that's what is strange.

The reader never gets to know what the speaker is thinking about, as such – again the tender-comic banality, the blocking, of 'thinking of things': as the speaker descends into a village, which is pulsing with a multiplicity of life in anticipation of a wedding party, the reader can only infer that the speaker's rueful avoidance of both bird and then festivities – his avoidance of 'a dance / With the bride in her laces / Or the maids [...] / [...] in the stable...' – has everything to do with his inner thoughts, with what he has done in the past. He is no longer that sort of man, he bumbles, refraining from the starling's display behaviour, refraining from love and passion (while strongly signalling his enduring interest in them), until he is left finally only with himself – 'And I … I stand thinking of things.' – that double 'I' and the long pause within it: dot dot dot.

After all that refraining, it is only his own poetic refrain he has for company: 'And I ... I stand thinking of things. / Yes, it's strange how one changes.'

Bunting's preface again stresses the peculiar quality displayed here:

> There are explorations that can never end in discovery, only in willingness to rest content with an unsure glimpse through mists, an uncertain sound of becks we shall never taste: approximations. To this Ford's rhythm and diction in these poems tend steadily; to this their matter is organized with great skill. Ford leaves his hearer with no perfection to contemplate, not even a line that might become a 'familiar quotation,' but rested as though something lovely had passed, which he cannot quite recall, which yet makes it easier to put up with the day.[20]

That phrase – 'organised with great skill'. The larger structures that Ford builds – his orchestration, an orchestration that can use a mundane phrase like 'it's strange how one changes' with other cumulative effects and build them into larger and deeper works. As Max Saunders suggests it's the handling of the whole poem in which Ford excels – 'He can express complex ideas in complex forms that unfold effortlessly, as if perfectly improvised'[21] – and it's this that Bunting must have recognised early on. Many years later, when the good cop/ bad cop dynamic of Eliot and Pound's reputations, 'fighting in the Captain's tower' as Bob Dylan so agilely confined them, was in danger of monopolising wider understanding of the complex nature of modernism, Bunting returned to and remembered Ford in these tributes.

Bunting recognises that Ford is simultaneously improvisational, allowing the improvisations their place in the poem or novel, though foregrounding the improvisations as character traits – those successive approximations – and a consummate structurer of his work. For them both it is about being subtle over time, about being subtle with unpromising raw materials.

Bunting himself wants more direct yield from each of his lines – either you need a muscular tongue and a dictionary that comes in volumes to read Bunting, you need to be open to collage and jump-cuts, or else you need to suspend precisions and somehow imbibe, swig, the sound and art-cinema images (as Bunting encourages you to do in his various statements of aesthetics). Bunting recognises there are other kinds of value, sleeper value, elliptical value, that Ford's poetry can offer when it appears at first to be most prosaic. That value requires a sensitivity to what is actually being said in everyday speech but it also benefits from a broader organisation of the text to release it. Ford delivers that organisation. Ford's attention to speech vocabulary or speech rhythms is probably what Bunting is referring to when, in a letter to Bernard Poli, he describes Ford's 'care for living English' but the compressing high modernist in Bunting isn't so able to follow Ford's example in that – he is much closer to Ford when considering how a poem might be furled by the poet so that it can unfurl for the reader.

NOTES

I am especially grateful to James McGonigal and Stephen Rogers for commenting on an earlier draft of this chapter.

1   Richard Caddel, 'Bunting, Basil Cheesman (1900–1985)', *Oxford Dictionary of National Biography*, Oxford: Oxford University Press, 2004.
2   Ford to Basil Bunting, 7 Sept. 1932. Ford Archive 4605, Division of Rare and Manuscript Collections, Cornell University Library.
3   Basil Bunting, Preface, Ford, *Selected Poems*, Cambridge, Mass.: Pym-Randall Press, 1971.
4   *Ibid.*, p. vii.
5   Max Saunders, Introduction, Ford, *Selected Poems,* Manchester: Carcanet Press, 1997, p. xii.
6   Bunting, Preface, Ford, *Selected Poems*, p. viii.

7   Paul Skinner, 'Poor Dan Robin: Ford Madox Ford's Poetry', *Ford Madox Ford: A Reappraisal*, ed. Robert Hampson and Tony Davenport, Amsterdam: Rodopi, 2002, pp. 79-103.

8   Ford, *Collected Poems*, London: Max Goschen, 1913 – henceforth *CP1*; p. 20.

9   Bunting, ed., Ford, *Selected Poems*, p. vii.

10 'swig', verb, 3rd definition, in *Oxford English Dictionary,* Oxford: Oxford University Press, 1989; online version..

11 'swig', noun, 3rd definition, in *Oxford English Dictionary,* Oxford: Oxford University Press, 1989; online version. The Melville quotation is taken from the dictionary reference.

12 Peter Makin, Introduction, *Basil Bunting on Poetry*, ed. Peter Makin, Baltimore: Johns Hopkins University Press, 1999, p. xxxv.

13 Bunting, ed., Ford, *Selected Poems*, p. vii.

14 See Angus Wrenn, 'Long letters about Ford Madox Ford: Ford's afterlife in the work of Harold Pinter,' *Ford Madox Ford's Literary Contacts*, ed. Paul Skinner, Amsterdam: Rodopi, 2007, pp. 225-35.

15 Basil Bunting, 'Precursors', *Basil Bunting on Poetry*, pp. 105-17

16 See for instance: 'Love in country lanes, the song of birds, moonlight – these the poet, playing for safety, and the critic trying to find something safe to praise, will deem the sure cards of the poetic pack' (*CP1* 16).

17 Basil Bunting, 'Precursors', *Basil Bunting on Poetry*, p. 111.

18 The passage reads:

> For ourselves we limit ourselves to the use of..... to indicate the pauses by which the Briton – and the American now and then – recovers himself in order to continue a sentence. The typographical device is inadequate but how in the world..... how in the world else ? – is one to render the normal English conversation? The last one at which we attended on English soil ran as follows: (We were in our club waiting for the waiter to bring change for a cheque)
>   *First Club Member.* What sort of a feller is... er...?
> (*He points with his chin at an individual by the further fireplace.*)
>   *Second Ditto* Oh..... He's..... He's a ;;..... Er;;;;;; Er......
>   *First Ditto (Briskly)* Ah !;;;..... Ialwaysthoughtso.

19 See Wrenn, 'Long letters about Ford Madox Ford', pp. 222-35.

20 Bunting, ed., Ford, *Selected Poems*, p. viii.

21 Saunders, ed., Ford, *Selected Poems,* p. xiv.

JEAN RHYS'S *QUARTET*: A RE-INSCRIPTION OF FORD'S *THE GOOD SOLDIER*

Elizabeth O'Connor

Jean Rhys's relationship with Ford Madox Ford – both textually and in real life – was a highly fraught affair, clouded by multiple competing fictional accounts, silence, and the passage of time. Concrete, verifiable facts are few: Ford and Ella Gwendolen Rees Williams Lenglet first met in 1924 after he was shown a copy of the manuscript version of the novel she later reworked as *Voyage in the Dark* (1934).[1] Intrigued by this work, Ford published her short story 'Vienne' in the last issue of the *transatlantic review* in December 1924 and bestowed on her the professional name Jean Rhys.[2] Although her slight story appears to have produced little comment, in retrospect Rhys can be seen as one of Ford's most important 'discoveries' during his editorship, comparable to that of D. H. Lawrence in the *English Review*. Otherwise, as Ford readily admitted, his last journal did not uncover unknown writers so much as provide a home for authors such as Hemingway, H. D., Joyce, Pound, and Gertrude Stein, who were published in little magazines but often excluded from more mainstream literary journals.

After the demise of the *transatlantic review*, Ford continued his involvement with Rhys by contributing a lengthy preface to her short story collection *The Left Bank* (1927), securing her a job translating Francis Carco's novel *Perversité* (1928), and helping her obtain a contract for her first novel, *Quartet* (1928).[3] Significantly, the novel's plot bears a close resemblance to her affair with Ford. Their 'entanglement' – how Ford chose to refer to the relationship[4] – is believed to have started after Ford and his common law wife, the Australian painter Stella Bowen, invited Rhys to live with them following the imprisonment of her husband, the Dutch poet and journalist Jean Lenglet, on currency fraud charges and a passport violation.

Angered by Rhys's account of the affair in *Quartet*, Ford wrote his own fictionalized response, *When the Wicked Man* (1931), which depicts the Rhys character, Lola Porter, as an alcoholic, nymphomaniac harridan. Lenglet also aired his side of the story in three slightly different fictionalized retellings all published under the pseudonym Edouard de Nève. The first, *Barred* (1932), was translated and extensively reworked by Rhys.[5] The Dutch version, *In de Strik* (1932), follows essentially the same text as *Barred* with a few silent emendations by Lenglet, but the French version, *Sous les Verrous* (1933), reverts to Lenglet's original unedited text. Not to be outdone, Bowen put forth her own account of the affair in her memoir *Drawn from Life* (1941). Although she does not refer to Rhys by name, Bowen's rather brief account of the affair has long been granted primacy by critics largely because it is the only one purporting to be based on fact. However, as Sue Thomas points out, Bowen's account is also marked by her personal bias.[6] Ultimately, as Anne Simpson notes, the need for all four participants to revisit the affair suggests that the texts are 'necessary fictions' in which each author might painstakingly shape and reshape the actual events in order to cast themselves in the best light.[7]

Outside the confines of fiction, Rhys was notoriously silent on her relationship with Ford. Although near the end of her life she admitted to her editor Diana Athill that she started *Quartet*, 'because she was very angry with Ford and wanted to pay him back', the statements she intended for publication are quite positive and are consistent with what is known of Ford's mentorship to a host of novice writers of both sexes.[8] As she wrote to Sondra Stang, 'I learnt a good deal from him and can't think of anyone who has quite taken his place' (*Presence* 214). In interviews Rhys highlighted Ford's role in her development as a writer and stressed that he taught her the importance of clarity and concision by 'insisting' that she read French writers such as Anatole France, Maupassant, Flaubert, and Colette; he also instructed her to translate passages verging on the verbose into French and to delete anything that looks 'utterly silly'.[9]

Looking back on her relationship with Ford near the end of her life, Rhys, in her unpublished essay 'Leaving School', recounts Ford's 'programme' to train her as a writer when she lived with him and Bowen. She writes:

> So began several months of writing short stories and having them torn to pieces or praised for reasons I did not understand. 'Don't be so glib. Don't do this. Do that. Or Don't take the slightest notice of what I say or what anybody says if you are certain in yourself.'[10]

She continues, stressing that her elliptical, allusive style, use of unattributed dialogue, and a rejection of biographical exactness and referentiality are due to Ford's tutelage and relentless editing of her work. It is obvious that Ford played a central role in both the publication of Rhys's initial work and subsequent development as a writer. However, this essay will argue that one way she disregarded Ford's advice and distanced herself from his influence in *Quartet* is by responding critically to *The Good Soldier*.

Ford's influence on Rhys's personal and artistic life obviously cannot be ignored, but too often critics neglect the textual evidence to concentrate on exploring the affair's psychological and emotional effects on Rhys, speculating on the correspondence of fictional characters to real life counterparts, discussing the differences between the various accounts, or debating whose version of events is most authentic. Rather than dwell on the biographical details of Ford, Bowen, Rhys, and Lenglet's 'entanglement,' I will argue that Rhys writes back to Ford in *Quartet* by transforming and centrally responding to *The Good Soldier's* portrayal of the power dynamics of gender, class, and the male gaze. One previously overlooked key to Rhys's intertextuality is her repeated invocation of the phrase 'playing the game' and her critique of Ford's narrator John Dowell's response to it.

Several critics have commented on the similarities in plot and character between Ford's *The Good Soldier* (1915) and Rhys's *Quartet*, as both works feature a 'four-square coterie' entwined in an adulterous affair. Ford's novel centers on the philandering Edward Ashburnham – the 'good soldier' of the title – his wife Leonora, who actively manages both his estate and his love affairs, John Dowell – the novel's famously unreliable narrator – and his wife Florence, who is involved in a longstanding relationship with Edward. With obvious and intentional similarity, Rhys's novel focuses on the English art dealer/critic H. J. Heidler – the fictionalized version of Ford – his wife Lois, who is a painter and the fictionalized version of Bowen, Stephan Zelli – the Polish immigrant imprisoned on theft charges and the fictionalized representation of Lenglet – and his wife Marya – the fictionalized version of Rhys – who is taken in by the Heidlers and subsequently enters into an affair with H. J. that is aided and abetted by Lois. In *Quartet,* Rhys does away with Nancy Rufford – Leonora's ward, Edward's deepest love, and Dowell's invalid wife – and, as I discuss below, collapses her into the character of Marya.

The surface similarities between the two novels are undeniable, but they are complicated by the fact that Rhys's novel is based on the real life events of her affair with Ford. Paul Delany has tried to explain this interlacing of fact and fiction by suggesting that *The Good Soldier* is a quasi-autobiographical 'prospective' text that contains 'an emotional program that Ford was driven to act out many times in his own life, with varying partners'.[11] This suggests that one emotional source for his fiction lay deep in his psyche. Along these lines, a similar psychological mechanism may have led Rhys to fashion key elements of *Quartet* by reworking textual elements of *The Good Soldier*. Although there is no record that Rhys read Ford's novel while drafting *Quartet*, this seems a plausible hypothesis in view of the many connections between the two works that stretch far beyond similarities in plot, characters, and a shared penchant for ellipses. The extent of these connections makes it unreasonable to attribute them just to the Ford/Rhys relationship or conversations between the two writers.[12] Furthermore, both the second US and UK editions of *The Good Soldier*, which contain Ford's famous 'Dedicatory Letter' to Stella Bowen, appeared in 1927-8. It is highly possibly that she might have read the work Ford termed his 'best' novel, or even been given a copy, during this period, while she was writing *Quartet*.

In one of the earliest and most detailed investigations of the interrelationship between these novels, Judith Kegan Gardiner views *Quartet* as 'Rhys's great tribute to her literary mentor Ford Madox Ford'.[13] Gardiner primarily focuses on the similarities of plot and character between the two works and argues that Rhys transforms Ford's quintessential novel of English maleness by making the adulterous wife Marya the novel's center of consciousness (72). She fails to recognize that in addition to shedding light on the position of a woman caught between two men, Rhys subtly aligns Marya with Dowell, Ford's narrator, through her critique of the limitations of his vision. She points out that *Quartet* takes the events that Ford's narrator presumes are 'natural and inevitable' and reinterprets them as the results of 'specific social and economic situations' (71). However, Gardiner focuses unduly on Rhys's literary apprenticeship to Ford and fails to give adequate weight to the evidence of her fledgling attempts at creating her own style. She judges Rhys on how she masters such Fordian techniques as vivid and specific detail, clear prose, elliptical dialogue, wry juxtapositions, time shifts, and *progression d'effet* asserting that Rhys is 'least proficient in time shifts' (Gardiner 69). By dwelling on the ways Rhys doesn't quite measure up to Ford, whom she terms 'the self-conscious literary dictator', Gardiner never allows Rhys to come into her own as a writer. She relegates her to the position of precocious female student, who despite lending a new perspective, falls short of her male literary master. By perpetuating this patriarchal relationship, Gardiner undercuts her own arguments about *Quartet's* feminist vision.

Rhys's distinctive focus on class and economics in *Quartet* also demonstrates the way she alludes to and re-inscribes key phrases from *The Good Soldier*. For example, the narrator terms Marya's family 'quite good people', [14] which is the descriptive Dowell uses to refer to the upper class Ashburnhams who 'were descended, as you probably expect, from the Ashburnham who accompanied Charles I to the scaffold'.[15] At first glance, Rhys's use of the phrase might appear coincidental, but on closer scrutiny the stark difference in the way Rhys employs the phrase makes clear that the usage is an intentional critique of the economic and class bias of Ford's novel, specifically its focus on the upper classes. In *Quartet,* the narrator informs us that Marya's lower class relatives 'were poverty-stricken and poverty is the cause of many compromises' (*Q* 126). For Marya, these 'compromises' take the form of years spent as a chorus girl enduring 'A vague procession of towns all exactly alike, a vague procession of men also exactly alike' (*Q* 126). During 'a period of unemployment spent in London,' Marya meets Stephan Zelli, a Polish businessman she suspects is a 'bad lot', and marries him largely because she feels 'strangely peaceful when she [is] with him, as if life were not such an extraordinary muddle after all ...' (*Q* 127). In comparison, Edward and Leonora appear positively wealthy; they spend a season at the Nauheim spa every year and own an English country house. However, as Dowell's narrative eventually reveals, the Ashburnham's financial situation (like their marriage) is far from perfect. They are close to bankruptcy due to Edward's profligate spending, amorous indiscretions, and extreme generosity to his tenants. Leonora has to scrimp and save in order to repay their multiple mortgages, while attempting to maintain the illusion of affluence. Ford's novel takes pains to show that she makes important compromises due to their financial difficulties. In comparison to Marya's more desperate situation after her husband's imprisonment, which leads her to seek shelter with the conniving Heidlers, Leonora's hardships, such as foregoing new clothes, appear almost minor. Through Marya's plight, Rhys provides a window into the degradations of 'real' poverty and critiques the upper class values that Dowell takes to be sacrosanct throughout *The Good Soldier*.

While many critics have noted that Rhys infuses *Quartet* with an awareness of class and gender – especially their effects on women – by highlighting the ways bourgeois mores are perpetuated through sexual and social games, what has not been highlighted is the way that Rhys's condemnation of 'playing the game' is coupled with a critique of the power of the male gaze.[16] Nor have critics traced the roots of this refrain, which is repeated seven times throughout the novel, to Ford's *The Good Soldier*. In *Quartet* this phrase first appears when Heidler declares his love to Marya: 'She knows that I'm dying with love for you, burnt with it, tortured with it. That's why she's gone off' (*Q* 160).[17] As he delivers this confession, which is couched in terms of what his wife 'knows' rather than what he freely tells the object of his passion, Heidler gazes 'fixedly' with an 'extraordinarily hard' expression (*Q* 160). Marya tries to deny the enormity of this revelation and attributes it to drunkenness. But Heidler persists, stating that he comes into her room every night to look at her as she sleeps. Frozen by Heidler's objectifying and possessive male gaze, Marya is silent. He continues:

> Well. I kept off you, didn't I? I knew that I could have you by putting my hand out, and I kept off you. I thought it wouldn't be playing the game. But there comes a limit, you see. There comes a limit to everything. I've been watching you; I watched you tonight and now I know that somebody else will get you if I don't. You're that sort. (*Q* 161)

Rather than a passionate confession of love, the dominant theme of Heidler's speech is smug self-justification and a confident exercise of power. He tells her that he had tried to 'play the game' and maintain the standards of propriety by not giving into his carnal urges. However, now he has reached his limit and must be satisfied. Equating knowledge with the male gaze, Heidler 'knew' Marya was 'that sort' of woman who would succumb to his advances just by looking at her. His objectifying and controlling male gaze pins and blames Marya for his lust, reducing her to an object for his sexual consumption.

Marya's objectified state is coupled with an overwhelming passivity, which manifests itself in her reticence to voice her opinion or take any decisive action of her own. As Howells notes, 'She is ... an object – first of the Heidlers's charity, and then successively of

Heidler's infatuation, of Lois's jealousy and hatred, and finally of the combined contempt of the Heidlers and of her husband' (46). After she is installed as Heidler's *petit femme* in the *Hotel du Bosphore*, the narrator states: 'She never reacted now. She was a thing. Quite dead. Not a kick left in her' (194). By the end of the novel, after Heidler has broken off their affair because he has 'never shared a woman in [his] life' and an enraged Stephan has assaulted his wife on learning of her adultery, Marya has literally become an inanimate object (*Q* 209). Our last glimpse of her is lying on the floor 'crumpled up,' 'still', and possibly dead (*Q* 233).

As an object 'tossed backwards and forwards between the violent personalities' of Stephan, Heidler, and, to a lesser extent, Lois (*GS* 290), Marya closely resembles the shuttlecock that serves as such an important metaphor for *The Good Soldier*. One of the only words that Nancy Rufford, Edward and Leonora's young ward, can utter after her mental collapse following Edward's suicide, the shuttlecock serves as a pathetic representation of the way the teenager is bandied back and forth between the pair. But unlike the much more innocent Nancy, who knows that her love for Edward is wrong and actively tries to suppress it, Marya passively yields to Heidler's advances. However, like Nancy, Marya is a loser at the game and cannot survive being swatted back and forth between the opposing teams in *Quartet*'s emotion-filled game.

Marya's passivity has long perplexed critics, as everyone in the novel, even Stephan who spends most of the time in prison, is more empowered. Stating that 'there is nothing "essential" about Marya,' Howells terms her a 'blank space' that is 'constructed through other people's narrative' (46). What this assessment ignores, however, is that despite Marya's outward passivity and relative silence, Rhys provides us with accounts of Marya's un-voiced thoughts as well as extensive comments by the omniscient third person narrator who privileges her consciousness. Rather than a narrative 'blank space,' she is a multi-faceted character who experiences a range of emotions from desire to rage but is largely powerless to express them. Marya's passivity then is not a result of her 'lack of character', unresolved 'infantile longing', masochism, or one of the failures of an apprentice work.[18] Rhys consciously makes Marya into a passive object in order to highlight her inability to 'play the game' as an equal. She is subject to a whole host of forces that are beyond her control. In addition to the demands made on her by Stephan, Heidler, and Lois, Marya is controlled by her poverty, especially her economic dependence and acknowledged inability to provide for herself, by her position as a woman who violates the bonds of her marriage, by her lower class status, and by her lack of traditional family ties.

Throughout *Quartet*, 'playing the game' becomes an important refrain for the Heidlers. On a superficial level the phrase encapsulates the accepted values of society, but Rhys also uses it throughout *Quartet* to show how the Heidlers' manipulate the rules of the game to pursue their immoral desires. As the affair progresses and Marya begins to imagine herself in love with H. J., he repeatedly invokes the phrase to co-opt her into following their rules of engagement. Frustrated at having to play the part of obedient house guest to Lois's dutiful wife, while being secretly castigated by Lois and her friends, Marya balks at H. J.'s request that she must go along: '"What game?" answered Marya fiercely [....] "Yes, that is just it, it's all a game I can't play, that I don't know how to play"' (*Q* 172). The rules of the game are to protect the façade of Lois's respectability, not Marya's, while safely satisfying Heidler's urge to evoke power. Due to her impoverished state and position on the social ladder a few rungs below the middle-class Heidlers, it becomes clear that the benefits of the game do not extend to her. Moreover, Marya does not know the rules, nor does she want to learn them.

Sue Thomas has traced the roots of this recurring refrain in *Quartet* back to Ford's 1907 book *The Spirit of the People*.[19] In it Ford writes of a 'saving phrase' that, although 'in England seldom' talked or thought about is nevertheless felt 'very intimately as a set rule of conduct [...]: You will play the game'.[20] Here 'playing the game' is seen as following an unwritten series of rules that underlie all English social interaction, rules that are designed to provide pleasure, self-protection, and class stability. By comparison, the Heidlers play a game that is all about sex, class, and power and has nothing to do with the sportsman's rules of fairness. Their game is more akin to a cat hunting a mouse; the designated loser is first sadistically tormented and then killed. Furthermore, Ford's use of the phrase in *The Spirit of the People*, which Rhys likely didn't read, does not convey the sense of discreet violation of the rules of conduct in order to maintain surface appearances as she invokes the phrase in *Quartet*. It is much more probable that she borrows the game motif from *The Good Soldier*, a work that is filled with deception and places emphasis on the importance of surface appearances.

Early in *The Good Soldier* Leonora – as recounted by Dowell – laments her failed attempt at an extramarital affair after facilitating, managing, and cleaning up after her husband's adulterous indiscretions:

> And then suddenly the bitterness of the endless poverty, of the endless acting – it fell on me like a blight, it spoilt everything. Yes, I had to realize that I had been spoilt even for the good time when it came. And I burst out crying and I cried and I cried for the whole eleven miles. Just imagine me crying! And just imagine me making a fool of the poor dear chap like that. It certainly wasn't playing the game, was it now? (*GS* 13-14)

This passage with its discussion of female infidelity – attempted if not completed – and its violation of a host of unwritten English codes of conduct is closer in tone and subject matter to the usages in *Quartet*. However it is important to keep in mind that even though Leonora experiences financial hardships she keeps up the appearance of Irish Catholic respectability and recoups her husband's financial losses, unlike Marya who is unable to provide for herself, let alone recoup her husband's losses. Also unlike Marya (and almost everyone else in *The Good Soldier*) Leonora actively resists and does not engage in adulterous sexual passion. While she assists in Edward's game playing, she is unable – or unwilling – to play the game herself. Therefore, she alone actually 'plays' by the rules of the game. Unlike Rhys's description of Heidler in the seduction scene, we are given no insight into Rodney Bayham's immediate reaction to Leonora's decision nor the male coercion he has employed. However, we are much later informed that the pair eventually marries. Although it appears that we are getting Leonora's first person account, we are actually getting Dowell's ventriloquized retelling of an earlier conversation he had with Leonora. In short, we really aren't getting a critique of the sexual games of the English upper classes from an authentic female point of view.

Taking all these qualifications into consideration, I think it is far more likely that Rhys, in incorporating this refrain of 'playing the game' into *Quartet,* is actually responding to the passage that immediately follows the one quoted above, which is spoken directly by Dowell. He states:

> I don't know; I don't know; was that last remark of hers the remark of a harlot, or is it what every decent woman, county family or not county family,

thinks at the bottom of her heart? Or thinks all the time for the matter of that? Who knows? (*GS* 14)

Just as *Wide Sargasso Sea* (1966) was sparked by Rhys's desire to tell the story of the mad Creole woman in the attic in *Jane Eyre*, and *Voyage In the Dark* was fueled by her desire to relate the 'true' story of the prostitute unlike the one Anna Morgan reads about in Zola's *Nana*, *Quartet* is a response to Dowell's question. Her novel picks apart the notions of English decorum that Dowell upholds as the idealized standard of conduct in *The Good Soldier* and shows them to be nothing more than a hypocritical disguise in which the strong (the Heidlers) control the weak (Marya). *Quartet* also demonstrates that the 'harlot', Marya, has more innate decency and propriety than both of the middle-class Heidlers, whose lives are utterly concerned and consumed with appearances. Furthermore, unlike Dowell's blanket assumption that it is 'woman' – 'decent' or not – who needs to be concerned with such a mundane activity as 'playing the game', *Quartet* shows that the rules of the game are controlled by men, and it is men who have the greatest interest in maintaining a façade of propriety to hide and legitimize their more debased desires.

Furthermore, I would argue that Rhys's re-inscription of Ford's novel in *Quartet* reveals Rhys's important and often overlooked insight into her mentor's work. Just as Lois, H. J., Marya, and Stephan are all held culpable by Rhys for their actions in *Quartet*, not one of Ford's four key characters is a purely innocent victim. This is especially true for Dowell, who is commonly held to be blind to Leonora, Edward, and Florence's lies and deception. He is the self-described 'eunuch' and 'nursemaid' who claims that he is blindsided by the actions of his wife and best friend and who narrates the novel as a cautionary tale. But it is Dowell who 'plays the game' most thoroughly – so thoroughly that his narrative takes pains to conceal that he is actually 'playing the game' – and wants to make sure we don't find him out. He presents himself as a genial dupe who is lulled into a false sense of complacency by his inability to see through the pretences of his three closest associates, but Dowell is actually aware of the adulterous events he narrates far earlier than his narrative would suggest. However, his passive nature, reverence for the English gentry that he feels he has assimilated through his association with the Ashburnhams, and deep, almost erotic, affection for Edward, prevent him from taking action and exposing their 'four square coterie' for the sham it really is. Attuned to this double duplicity, Rhys constructs her narrative in order to indict all participants and, most importantly, take on the underlying hypocrisy in the way Ford treats women in his novel and the unfairness of the 'game' that Dowell is complicit in playing.

In *Quartet* Rhys does not only systematically shatter the illusions of innocence that Dowell strives to perpetuate, but also challenges Ford's belief that the 'horrors' committed in *The Good Soldier* were reflective of both the madness of a pre-War society and World War I itself. Ford seems consciously to connect the madness of a society in decline to the outbreak of World War I by having several key events in *The Good Soldier*, such as Florence's suicide and Dowell's realization of her infidelity, to Great Britain's entry into the war on August 4th. In comparison, Rhys's novel is filled with private, emotional shock, but these are more attributable to specific social, economic, and class conditions. She does not refer to the war by name or even allude to it. It is the absent presence that is always palpable but never directly named. Rhys paints a vivid picture of a society that has forever moved past both the retrospectively idyllic pre-war life of the 'four-square coterie' that Dowell records and the English country house existence he attempts to re-create in his life with Nancy. The post-war Heidler-Zelli quartet is much more corrupt, more closely fixated on status and appearances, and more ruthlessly invested in 'playing the game' than their pre-war compatriots. Indeed, the deceptions and infidelities of the Ashburnhams and Dowells seem almost quaint in comparison. In this way, Rhys re-inscribes her mentor's novel in a much darker post-war reality and penetrates beneath his analysis to emphasize the more fundamental elements of gender and class that undergird all social interactions.

NOTES

1   Destitute in Paris in 1924, Rhys showed her rough manuscript to Pearl Adam, wife of *The Times* Paris correspondent George Adam, who typed and edited it, giving the manuscript the name *Suzy Tells*. Pearl Adam showed the revised manuscript to Ford who re-titled it *Triple Sec* and published a selection in the *transatlantic review* as 'Vienne'. See Carol Angier, *Jean Rhys: Life and Work*, Boston: Little, Brown and Co, 1990 – henceforth 'Angier'; pp. 129-38.

2   The name Jean Rhys is an amalgamation of her first husband Jean Lenglet's name
     and the paternal family name of Rees. See Coral Ann Howells, *Jean Rhys*, New
     York: St. Martin's, 1991 – henceforth 'Howells'; p. 11. See also Angier 138. The
     androgynous nature of Rhys's new name is underscored in Ford's brief mention of
     her in the *transatlantic review* where, unlike his treatment of all the other male
     and female writers he discusses, does not use the honorific Mr., Mrs., or Miss.
     before her name, thus not identifying her as either a man or woman. See *TRev* II
     (June 1924), 682.
3   The translation of Carco's novel was mistakenly attributed to Ford by the
     publisher Pascal Covici (Angier 164). Ford helped Rhys secure a contract with
     Chatto & Windus for the novel that was to become *Postures*; the title was changed
     to *Quartet* with its American publication in 1929. It is important to note that Ford
     did not know the subject of this work when he offered his help.
4   Stella Bowen, *Drawn From Life*, London: Collins, 1941, p. 168.
5   Martien Kappers den Hollander, 'A Gloomy Child and Its Devoted Godmother:
     Jean Rhys, *Barred, In de Strik*, and *Sous Les Verrous*', in *Critical Perspectives on
     Jean Rhys*, ed. Pierrette M. Frickey, Washington, D.C.: Three Continents, 1990, p.
     45. See also Joseph Wiesenfarth, *Ford Madox Ford and the Regiment of Women:
     Violet Hunt, Jean Rhys, Stella Bowen, Janice Biala*, Madison: University of
     Wisconsin Press, 2005, pp. 76-8.
6   Sue Thomas shows that Bowen depicts Rhys as a racial and class other and that
     Ford's financial support of Rhys 'clearly rankled Bowen, and the resentment
     permeates her commentary'. See Sue Thomas, 'Adulterous Liaisons: Jean Rhys,
     Stella Bowen, and Feminist Reading,' *Australian Humanities Review*, 2001,
     http://www.australianhumanitiesreview.org/archive/Issue-June-2001/thomas.html.
     Letters between Ford and Bowen show that their financial support of Rhys lasted
     until at least December 1926. See Sondra Stang and Karen Cochran, editors, *The
     Correspondence of Ford Madox Ford and Stella Bowen*, Bloomington: Indiana
     University Press, 1994, p. 280.
7   Anne B. Simpson, *Territories of the Psyche: The Fiction of Jean Rhys*, New York
     and Basingstoke: Palgrave, 2005, p. 66.
8   This is apparently a paraphrased account of a letter Helen Nebeker received from
     Rhys's longtime editor Diana Athill dated September 20, 1978. Ostensibly still
     paraphrasing the letter, Nebeker adds 'though once it [*Quartet*] got going it took
     shape, and ended up not quite as she had expected'. See Helen Nebeker, *Jean
     Rhys, a Woman in Passage: A Critical Study of the Novels of Jean Rhys*,
     Montreal: Eden Press, 1981, p. 202.
9   Elizabeth Vreeland, 'The Art of Fiction No. 64: Jean Rhys,' *Paris Review*, 76
     (Fall 1979), 226 and Mary Cantwell, 'A Conversation with Jean Rhys',
     Mademoiselle, 79 (Oct. 1974), 208.
10   Quoted in Veronica Marie Gregg, *Jean Rhys's Historical Imagination: Reading
     and Writing the Creole*, Chapel Hill: North Carolina Press, 1995, p. 57.
11   Paul Delaney, 'Jean Rhys and Ford Madox Ford: What Really Happened?' *Mosaic*,
     16:4 (1998), 16. See also Sean Latham, *The Art of Scandal: Modernism, Libel
     Law, and the Roman à clef*, New York: Oxford UP, 2009, pp. 155-66.
12   In an unpublished letter (24 April 1968) to Oliver Stonor ('Morchard Bishop'),
     Rhys writes that 'Ford's book [*The Good Soldier*] puzzles me a bit. I must read it
     again slowly and be convinced that it's the saddest story' (Howells 44). While

Howells reads the excerpt as suggesting Rhys had not read Ford's novel until 1968 and, thus, couldn't possibly be writing back to it in *Quartet*, I think it is important to keep in mind that in her later years Rhys often misrepresented her reading of modernist writers and was notoriously reticent in talking about Ford. Furthermore, the portion of the letter that Howells quotes does not definitively state that Rhys read *The Good Soldier* for the first time in 1968. Rhys only notes that 'Ford's book', which Howells adds is *The Good Soldier*, 'puzzles her a bit' and that she should reread it to 'be convinced that it's the saddest story' (Howells 44).

13 Judith Kegan Gardiner, 'Rhys Recalls Ford: *Quartet* and *The Good Soldier*,' *Tulsa Studies in Women's Literature*, I (1982), 67-81 – henceforth 'Gardiner'; p. 67.
14 Jean Rhys, *Quartet,* New York: Norton, 1985 – henceforth *Q*; p. 126.
15 Ford Madox Ford, *The Good Soldier,* London, John Lane, 1915 – henceforth *GS*; p. 8.
16 See Arnold Davison, *Jean Rhys,* New York: Ungar, 1985, p. 69; Mary Lou Emery, *Jean Rhys at 'World's End:' Novels of Colonial and Sexual Exile,* Austin: U of Texas P, 1990, p. 109; Cathleen Maslen, *Ferocious Things: Jean Rhys and the Politics of Women's Melancholia,* Newcastle upon Tyne: Cambridge Scholars Publishing, 2009, pp. 42-3.
17 This phrase echoes Leonora's comment to Nancy near the end of *The Good Soldier* where she demands the girl stay with them because Edward 'is dying for love for you' (*GS* 248).
18 See Howells 46; Simpson 66; and Patricia Moran, *Virginia Woolf, Jean Rhys and the Aesthetics of Trauma,* New York: Palgrave, 2007, p. 129.
19 See Sue Thomas, *The Worlding of Jean Rhys,* Westport, Conn.: Greenwood Press, 1999, p. 83.
20 The third volume of Ford's trilogy *England and the English*, ed. Sara Haslam, Manchester: Carcanet, 2003, p. 316.

'AN OLD MAN MAD ABOUT WRITING' BUT HOPELESS WITH MONEY: FORD MADOX FORD AND THE FINANCES OF THE *ENGLISH REVIEW*

Nora Tomlinson

The *English Review* was launched at the end of November 1908, to more or less universal praise. Ford was much in demand and in celebratory mood as Violet Hunt described: 'The editor's courts were thronged socially [....] And the Review was "It" as Mr. Wells had foretold. The editor gave parties [....] I lent my maid and my spoons, or he hired the ex-butler of Sir Frederick Leighton, who had ushered in Queen Victoria to see the President of the Royal Academy'.[1] But by the spring of 1909 the mood was less celebratory, since 'it was costing its founder his life's blood in the way of money' (Hunt 51). By January 1910, when Ford had been ousted from the editorship of the review, any hint of celebration had been replaced by black depression, and Ford 'for a week of mornings [...] did not address more than three words' to Violet Hunt (Hunt 91). Some of the reasons which caused Ford to sink into such gloom were caused by an increasingly complicated personal life, but losing control of his review was a major contributor to his depression.

There are several reasons why Ford lost control of the *English Review*, which can be summarized as an inability to organize, an excessive tendency to quarrel with important contributors and supporters, and a monumental ineptness with money. The first two are well documented, but tracing the financial fortunes of the review is problematic because so much of the evidence has either vanished, or is fragmentary and unreliable. Financial records for both publisher and printer were destroyed during the bombing of London during the Second World War, though two cash books and some cheque book stubs survive among the Soskice family papers in the House of Lords Record Office. These run from 18 May to 6 July 1909 and from 7 July to 11 October of the same year. Otherwise, a fair amount of helpful incompleteness of most of the evidence means that any attempt to untangle the finances of the review is necessarily speculative.

Arnold Bennett, whose financial acumen was considerably greater than Ford's, wrote to him in October 1908, during the planning stage: 'The chief thing I wish you in connection with the English Review is plenty of capital',[2] and Conrad believed that there was 'enough capital to go on for four issues'.[3] The original capital seems to have come from Arthur Marwood and from Ford himself, though whether it was as much as Ford claimed is arguable: 'Of the £5000 that we spent on the review, Marwood paid £2200 and I paid £2800, I being generally liable for the debts of the undertaking beyond that sum'.[4] Quite where Ford could have laid his hands on such a large sum of money is puzzling, though Mizener refers to £150 borrowed from his wife.[5] Violet Hunt, who herself put money into the review, writes of the 'cohorts of relations – German Hueffers, Dutch Hueffers, Paris Hueffers' (Hunt 27) who she believed had provided financial backing. The Munster Hueffers were publishers, and may have been prepared to help. Ford himself claimed rather that the money spent on the review was his own. 'I spent a great deal of money on the Review with the definite design of giving imaginative literature a chance in England. It was my own money' (*LF* 40). The *Financial Times* for 8 March 1909 lists Ford as the general partner in the review and Marwood as the limited partner, each of them putting up £500, which sounds much more like the kind of sum which Ford could have afforded.

Ford's original plan for financing the review seems to have been some kind of profit sharing scheme. As he explained to Edward Garnett, who warned him about the dangers of this: 'I am an idealist and my ideal is to run the English Review as far as possible as a socialist undertaking' (*LF* 27-8). Some of Ford's accounts of this profit sharing scheme are so complicated and bizarre as to be virtually incomprehensible; even Conrad, who had been involved with the review throughout the entire planning stage, and who was himself intended to be a participant in the scheme, admitted that the details were not clear to him.[6] Perhaps the least obscure version is that contained in a memorandum to H. G. Wells, which is undated but almost certainly was written early in the planning stage when Ford hoped that Wells would offer both financial and editorial help with the review.

> The publisher was to bear all expenses of printing, publishing and everything except advertising and was to receive in exchange one fifth of the gross receipts. A capitalist was to be found by Mr. Hueffer to find money for advertisement and such contributors as took their payment in money. To him a share of one fifth in the proceeds was also payable. The share of Mr. Hueffer was to be one fifth. The remaining two fifths of the gross receipts was to be divided amongst the as yet unpaid contributors in the proportion of the space filled by them. (Mizener 161-2)

This scheme, of course, assumed that the gross receipts would yield sufficient excess of income over expenditure. Wells shrewdly saw the major drawback in Ford's scheme, and apart from allowing *Tono-Bungay* to be serialised in the first numbers of the review, withdrew from further involvement in its management. This led to a major falling out between the two men, though in the course of an acrimonious exchange of letters, conducted through Wells's wife, Jane, Ford was forced to admit that 'the actual profits of the first four numbers will be non-existent' (*LF* 34). In fact Ford seems to have offered contributors a choice, at least in the early days of the review. 'Will you take £2 a 1000 words, or will you take a sporting risk which might be estimated as two to one against you as a shareholder?' (*LF* 28).

A certain amount is known about the income and expenditure of the review. There were four sources of income. The first was the initial capital, the amount of which was uncertain, and which in any case seems to have run out by the spring of 1909. It was topped up from time to time by Ford's brother-in-law, David Soskice, whose bank pass book for 1909 shows numerous loans both to Ford personally and to the review itself. Most of those to the review were for £100, though there was one loan for £800 on 20 July. There was some money from the sale of shares, when Soskice tried to form a company to bale out the review. In August, William Goode and David Soskice became the first directors of The English Review Company, and £1000 was paid into the company's account. We know very little else about the company or who its other shareholders might have been, though there is a letter to David Soskice from Edward Browne, a Cambridge academic, showing not only that he purchased £300 of shares on 10 August, but that he was actively trying to persuade friends and colleagues to do the same. 'It has become vital, I think, to encourage an independent review like the ER.'[7]

There was some income from advertising, though probably not as much as there could have been. Advertising was originally the

responsibility of Stephen Reynolds, but after working for the review
for one week a month from November 1908 to January 1909, he
couldn't wait to give it up.[8] According to Ford, 'the revenue from
advertisements has been about £140 for the [first] four numbers, that
is £35 a month'. Another advertising manager, M. S. Rothwell, was
appointed, but not until September 1909, when Soskice negotiated a
new publishing contract with Chapman and Hall. At this point,
advertising revenue was about £30 a month.[9]

Finally there was the income from sales. The review sold for
two shillings and sixpence – (twelve and a half pence in modern
money) – and Ford estimated that the first two issues each sold
roughly 2000 copies, that is £250 per issue. This figure may well be an
overestimate by Ford, and even if it is accurate, it is unlikely that sales
would have continued at this level. Jessie Chambers noticed that when
she and D. H. Lawrence visited Ford in November 1909, 'there were
piles of the English Review lying on the black polished floor and on
the window seat',[10] which suggests that there were large numbers of
unsold copies. This idea is supported by the fact that when the review
went into liquidation in December 1909, no offers could be found for
15000 unsold copies of the review; Duckworth's, the review's original
publisher claimed a lien on these.[11] Income from sales therefore seems
to have been limited.

Very little is known about production costs for the review. We
have only Ford's estimate of £200 per number for 'the costs of
printing, paper, distribution, etc.' (Mizener 160). The review was
heavily advertised in other journals, including the *Athenaeum*,
Harpers, the *Nation*, the *New Age*, the *New Quarterly*, *Outlook*, the
Saturday Review, the *Spectator*, the *Times Literary Supplement*, the
Westminster Gazette, the *Glasgow Herald* and the *Daily Telegraph*.
Such advertising wasn't cheap. For example, between November 1908
and September 1909, *The Nation* carried five full page advertisements,
seven half page and three quarter page advertisements. The cost of a
full page was £10, so the cost of advertising in just this one periodical
was little short of £100. Multiply this by all the other advertisements
placed in other periodicals and the bill becomes considerable. Even in
the autumn of 1909, when the review was in many ways winding itself
down, its cash book reveals an expenditure on advertising of £72. 5/-,
which is more than double the previous month's income for
advertisements placed in the *English Review* itself.[12] Advertising was
in fact a net drain on the review's resources.

There were also salaries to be paid. It is not known how much
Douglas Goldring, the assistant editor, was paid when he was appointed in the autumn of 1908, nor how much was paid to the review's
secretary, a Miss Olive Thomas, who according to Violet Hunt, imposed some order on very considerable chaos (Hunt 22). The only
figures available are those in the two cashbooks. The first shows only
£1 paid to a 'M. Martindale'; this is presumably Ford's sister-in-law,
who may have provided some clerical assistance. The second cash
book, which covers much of the period when Soskice was running the
financial side of the review, shows Soskice himself receiving £6 a
week as business manager, Rothwell £5 as advertising manager and
Douglas Goldring £2.10/-. Ford himself seems to have been paid £6 a
week, although later he claimed that he had received no payment (*LF*
42).

Compared to production and advertising costs, salaries were
relatively a small fraction of expenditure, but when payments to
contributors are added to these, then the financial loss incurred by the
review was, as Goldring claimed, such as 'must have staggered even a
Northcliffe'.[13] Payments to contributors were by far the biggest drain
on resources. According to Violet Hunt, Ford's policy was always to
pay his contributors exactly what they asked. 'This was the editor's
system. Sometimes they didn't ask at all, or suggested modestly the
derisive sum of a couple of guineas for a forty pound article like Mr.
Cunninghame Graham' (Hunt 29). Ford himself confirmed this
system, although he was writing more than twenty years after he had
given up the review. 'I used to ask my contributors to demand any rate
of pay they liked, leaving it to their consciences to ask a fair average
price for their work [. . . .] One or two certainly asked for and got a
great deal more than they had ever imagined. On the other hand, many
of the wealthier – and not a few of the indigent – writers wrote for me
for nothing'.[14] Whether this really was the strategy adopted by Ford,
or whether he invited contributors to become shareholders in the hope
of a profit, this was clearly a system open to abuse, and the arbitrary
pricing of contributions for the review didn't lend itself to accurate
financial management.

While Ford appeared almost to take pride in his financial
naïveté, in reality he may have been rather more aware of the payment
to contributors than he allowed. Certainly, there seems to have been
some kind of limit to what he was prepared to spend. He didn't, for
example, publish anything by George Bernard Shaw, whom he

admired, because he couldn't afford him. As he wrote jokingly to
Shaw: 'I should have to increase my circulation on your account by
8,000 copies, to make it just barely pay your fee alone'.[15] Neither was
he above a bit of sharp practice in negotiations, most notably with
Arnold Bennett. When the review began, Ford and Bennett had not
met, and negotiations for a long short story were conducted through
Bennett's agent, Pinker. Ford's idea of a good price differed from that
of Bennett, who wrote indignantly to Pinker: 'I presume that Hueffer
will not argue that two guineas a thousand is so high a price that it
must be specially referred to as an inducement. I am quite willing to
accept my ordinary price, three guineas, and I do not think Hueffer
will make any difficulty as to this.' Bennett was mistaken; Ford paid
Pinker the lower price, and Bennett's response was that 'though we
have been "done", we are not favourably impressed'.[16] He indicated
his disapproval to Ford by refusing to accept an invitation to dine with
him. 'I replied in sorrow that I could not come to dinner as I considered he had done me in the eye over the price of a short story. He
wrote to ask me by how much I considered he had done me in the eye.
I replied by at least ten pounds. He sent me a cheque for ten pounds. I
attended his dinner. We have been excellent friends ever since.'[17] Not
only did they become excellent friends, but Bennett made a gift of
subsequent contributions to the review. As he explained to Pinker: 'I
am thinking of letting Hueffer print *What the Public Wants* [. . . .] I
told him I would give it him, but he said if it increased the sale he
would pay me a royalty!!! I like him! I think he can't help being
devious.'[18]

Bennett may have been right about Ford's deviousness, although
the episode reveals something of Ford's charisma as an editor. What is
not known is how many other contributors gave material to Ford without demanding payment. Edgar Jepson strongly refuted accusations
that contributors were not paid. 'I cannot think who they can have
been, for it certainly paid me and all the contributors I knew.'[19] We do
know from a variety of other sources how much some contributors
were paid. Hardy, for example, received £20 for his poem 'Sunday
Morning Tragedy' (*South Lodge* 18). Henry James was paid 40
guineas for 'The Jolly Corner', £30 for 'The Velvet Glove' and 36
guineas for 'Mora Montravers'[20] and Wyndham Lewis was paid five
guineas for each of his contributions.[21] In December 1908, Conrad
acknowledged the payment of £80 for the first four instalments of
'Some Reminiscences',[22] and the review cash book records a payment

of £25 to Conrad in late June of 1909.[23] If, as seems likely, this is
payment for another instalment of the memoirs, then Conrad received
more than £160 for the seven instalments, which is more than half of
one month's income from sales. Conrad was almost certainly a special
case, but the review published a number of other lengthy serialised
works – Wells's *Tono-Bungay*, Stephen Reynolds's *The Holy Mountain,* and Violet Hunt's *The Wife of Altamont*, and even if these
authors were paid at a lesser rate than Conrad, then the cost to the
review would have been considerable. The same cash book entry
which records the payment to Conrad also shows payments of £15 to
Ella d'Arcy, probably for her long short story 'Agatha Blount', £3
each to Ezra Pound and Eden Philpotts for poems and £2 to Edward
Thomas for a book review. This matching of payments to contributions which appeared in the June issue of the review is only inferred,
since the cash book only records recipients and not what the cash was
for.

What is outlined here is only a tiny fraction of the payments
which must have been made. However, related to what is known about
sales, it becomes clear that the review couldn't possibly have been
made to pay. The review cost two shillings and sixpence, so payment
of £20 for Hardy's poem for example, would have required sales of
160 copies simply to cover the payment, £3 for Ezra Pound's poem
would have needed sales of 24 copies , and £2 for Edward Thomas'
book review needed sales of 16 copies. Extrapolate out to the 180 to
200 pages of each issue of the review and the scale of the losses
begins to emerge. Ford himself reckoned that the first four issues
alone lost £1200, while Mizener estimated that the actual loss per
issue must have been at least £500, though he seems to have arrived at
this sum by working on Ford's own unreliable estimates and then
adding a percentage to take account of this unreliability (Mizener
160). Max Saunders estimates the losses to have been £265 per issue,
though this, too, is speculative.[24] Probably only two things can be said
with any certainty – that many sums associated with the *English
Review* are no more than estimates and that the review lost a great deal
of money.

An advertisement in the *New Age* on 25 March 1909 shows that
the review was never really regarded as a commercial proposition. 'In
supporting the English Review […] the reader will be not so much
supporting a commercial undertaking as performing a duty, since he
will be aiding in presenting to the world some of its most valuable

thought.' In later life Ford conceded that he had known 'that the Review could not be made to run on any sort of commercial lines' (*RY* 382). It would perhaps have been more accurate to say that *he* could not have run it on commercial lines. Cultural journals are not produced to make their editors rich, and the late Victorian and Edwardian period has plenty of examples of periodicals which folded for financial reasons. But it seems that Ford, by his wilful inconsistency over payments, his capacity for falling out with backers and lack of sound accounting practice, brought the *English Review* perilously close to extinction. That the review survived and even prospered financially under the ownership of Alfred Mond and the editorship of Austin Harrison shows what could be achieved under careful control of income and expenditure.[25] Nor did he learn from his experience, starting the *transatlantic review* in Paris in 1924, with the same optimism, the same limited funds and the same lack of organisation. Indeed, the situation with the *transatlantic review* was far worse than with the *English Review*, since it was published in three countries with three different rates of exchange and in competition with a far greater range of other cultural journals. He was undoubtedly 'an old man mad about writing' (*ML* 6) but he was equally, undoubtedly, hopeless with money.

NOTES

1   Violet Hunt, *The Flurried Years*, London: Hurst & Blackett, [1926] – henceforth 'Hunt'; pp. 48-9.
2   *Letters of Arnold Bennett*, vol. II, ed. James Hepburn, London: Oxford University Press, 1968, p. 227.
3   *The Collected Letters of Joseph Conrad,*, vol. IV, ed. Frederick R Karl and Laurence Davies, Cambridge: Cambridge University Press, 1990, p. 131.
4   *Letters of Ford Madox Ford*, ed. Richard M. Ludwig, Princeton, NJ: Princeton University Press, 1965 – henceforth *LF*; p. 42.
5   Arthur Mizener, *The Saddest Story: A Biography of Ford Madox Ford*, London: The Bodley Head, 1972 – henceforth 'Mizener'; p. 161.
6   *The Collected Letters of Joseph Conrad*, IV, p. 167.
7   House of Lords Record Office, Stow Hill Papers, DS 4/8, DS1, BRO.
8   *Letters of Stephen Reynolds*, ed. Harold Wright, London: Hogarth Press, 1923, p. 114.
9   HLRO, SHP, BH 2/4.

10 Chambers, Jessie, *D. H. Lawrence: A Personal Record*, London: Frank Cass, 1965, p. 169.
11 HLRO, SHP, BH 2/4.
12 HLRO, SHP, BH 2/4.
13 Douglas Goldring, *South Lodge: Reminiscences of Violet Hunt, Ford Madox Ford and the English Review Circle*, London: Constable, 1943 – henceforth *South Lodge*; p. 30.
14 Ford, *Return to Yesterday*, London: Victor Gollancz, 1931 – henceforth *RY*; p. 383.
15 *The Ford Madox Ford Reader*, ed. Sondra J. Stang, Manchester: Carcanet, 1986, p. 472.
16 *Letters of Arnold Bennett,* vol. I, ed. James Hepburn, London: Oxford University Press, 1966, pp. 119-20.
17 Bennett, letter to the editor, *Outlook* (11 Oct. 1913), 251.
18 *Letters of Arnold Bennett,* I, p. 121.
19 Edgar Jepson, *Memories of an Edwardian and a Neo-Georgian*, London: Richards, 1917, p. 149.
20 Michael Anesko, *'Friction with the Market': Henry James and the Profession of Authorship*, New York: Oxford University Press, 1986, p. 196. See also Philip Horne's chapter 'Henry James and the *English Review*' in this volume.
21 Cited in Jeffrey Meyers, *The Enemy: A Biography of Wyndham Lewis,* London: Routledge, 1980, p. 149.
22 *Collected Letters of Joseph Conrad,* vol. IV, p. 166.
23 HLRO, SHP, BH 2/4.
24 Max Saunders, *Ford Madox Ford: A Dual Life,* 2 vols, Oxford: Oxford University Press, 1996, vol. I, p. 552.
25 This is discussed in detail in Martha Vogeler, *Austin Harrison and the English Review*, Missouri: University of Missouri Press, 2008, pp. 86, 210-11, 218.

'A FEW INCHES ABOVE THE MORAL ATMOSPHERE OF THESE ISLANDS': THE PERSPECTIVES OF THE *ENGLISH REVIEW*

Simon Grimble

In any writer's mind there must be some kind of fantasy as to where he thinks he or she is writing from and the place to which he thinks his words are aimed. The place that it is from is not just the material, mundane literal place that is the writer's office or the desk in the library or wherever, but is also an imaginary place, a place possessed, perhaps, of a view on to the world – perhaps limited, but perhaps also possessed of Olympian or Parnassian power. It also clearly matters what the form of this writing is to take: is it a novel, a poem, play, or is it, in fact, an editorial – something clearly serious, important, but also necessarily transient, tomorrow's chip wrappings. One doubts that anyone ever ate chips off a copy of the *English Review* – the splendour of the binding might tend to dissuade anyone from attempting that – but still transience is part of its world: however much the post-war Ford wanted to emphasise its primary concern with important literature and to give the impression that the political content contained in 'The Month' was basically imposed on him, Ford was clearly extremely engaged with contemporary English political questions at the time of his editing of the *English Review*.[1] And so he was – he had to be – something of a 'Thunderer' himself, somebody inclined to the vehemence and certainty that is often required of the leader article: the form that, on behalf of the reader, knocks events into shape, provides a way of reading and understanding them, but which also provides a prescription, a way of moving forward, or even a fiat or a panacea. And yet this mode is necessarily problematic, to say the least, for a writer so conclusively associated with unreliable narrators – as well as with more personal accusations of unreliability.

But we can say that the *English Review* did represent the working out of a long held desire to find a vehicle for such commanding thoughts. In 1901, Ford had written to Edward Garnett, arguing for the establishment of a 'Library of Literature' that would show how 'great writers *get their effects*':

> The idea, I say keeps booming in my head—why couldn't one make some sort of nucleus, just some little attempt at forming a small heap on which people could stand and get a point of view with their heads a few inches above the moral atmosphere of these Islands. You obviously are out of sympathy with the whole drift. But wouldn't it be worth trying?[2]

Ford's ambition is to found some kind of campaign of resistance to what he thinks of as 'the moral atmosphere of these Islands'. The reference to 'these Islands' is both characteristic of Ford and telling of his attitudes: this version of Britain and Ireland is imagined as crucially cut adrift, both geographically and intellectually, from the European mainland which is also the mainstream of advanced thinking on these matters, or at least as far as Ford is concerned at this moment in time. Ford is here, as elsewhere, the descendant of Matthew Arnold and his concern that 'England is in a certain sense *far behind* the Continent':

> In conversation in the newspapers one is so struck with the fact of the utter insensibility one may say of people to the number of ideas & schemes now ventilated on the Continent – not because they have judged them or seen beyond them, but, from sheer habitual want of wide reading and thinking [....] Our practical virtues never certainly revealed more clearly their isolation.[3]

Arnold's concerns are more explicitly intellectual and political than Ford's preoccupations, as are the Continental 'schemes' that he mentions, but the central metaphors are noticeably related: those airy schemes now 'ventilated' on the Continent in Arnold's version are the opposite of the stuffy and complacent moral atmosphere that Ford refers to, a state of English cloudiness that certainly borders on a kind of pollution, and which both he and Arnold would like to disperse, or in Ford's case, to get above, at least by 'a few inches'. This is, of course, a self-ironising gesture about elevated views – 'a few inches' is clearly not very far, but still the desire is there, the desire to be both outside a polluted and corrupting atmosphere but also to see it for what it is – with the essential help of others. But, as often with Ford, through the letter he is edging towards defeatism and pessimism, even if the effect of that is to make others sympathise with him, and therefore join him. For the central focus of Ford's account is the desire to form that 'nucleus' which is also a 'heap', and by that he means some kind of collaborative and collective endeavour, an avant-garde which also has some of the spirit of political reaction (embodied in his anxieties about the 'drift') but which is also composed of fellow feeling and mutual support, and which also needs to find a form in which to embody itself: a publication, a periodical. At the same time, Ford is confessing his own feelings of potential cultural disintegration of which he himself, and those artists like him, are at least partially an embodiment: the heap that he wants to form to gain his point of view does sound like a form of waste itself, just like the 'heap of broken images' in *The Waste Land*. One question is whether this will be the kind of heap on which one can stand, at least for some period of time, or one, like Winnie's heap in Samuel Beckett's *Happy Days*, into which the protagonist will slowly sink. Another related question is the character of the heap in itself: what kind of material is it made of? This is the question considered in H. G. Wells's *Tono-Bungay*, published in the first numbers of the *English Review*: the heaps that Wells considers are heaps of 'quap', the radioactive material that George Ponderevo plans to steal from an island off the coast of Africa in order to boost his uncle's flagging business. For Wells, these heaps are toxic yet extremely valuable; it is Wells's comment on money and high-octane capitalism, with its capacity to burn up traditions and identity, but also on what he thinks it symbolises as an essential element of the universe:

> It is in matter exactly what the decay of our old culture is in society, a loss of traditions and distinctions and assured reactions. When I think of these inexplicable dissolvent centres that have come into being in our globe—these quap heaps are surely by far the largest that have yet been found in the world, the rest as yet mere specks in grains and crystals — I am haunted by a grotesque fancy of the ultimate eating away and dry-rotting and dispersal of all our world. (*ER* I [March 1909] 742)

Ford is similarly haunted by anxieties about the dispersal of the valuable aspects of culture, yet it is on the top of the best of these traditions that he wants to make his stand. These hopes and fears would be represented by the publication of the *English Review*, with its assembling of both traditions and newness, both the foreign and the local, with its sense of collaborative enterprise co-existing with Ford's feelings of suspicion and fears of betrayal, with its optimism feeding off its pessimism (and vice versa), along with its heroic and yet very self-ironising dramatisation of the editor, forever setting off on quixotic assertions of lost causes, with the help of a crew that is like a ship's crew, a 'nucleus crew' being the essential members of a ship's crew, but which is also like a band of conspirators, or a revolutionary cell. As Andrzej Gasiorek has argued, there is a strong element of anarchism in Ford's thinking, even whilst things splitting apart are exactly what he fears.[4] And yet Ford is also a more straightforward moralist or cultural critic in an Arnoldian sense: he is concerned that 'the moral atmosphere of these Islands' is unintellectual, liberal in an unthinking sense (emphasising the validity of the individual response in opposition to more 'objective' standards: Ford's version of Arnold's 'doing as one likes'), ensnared in sexual hypocrisy which prevents clear speaking on such issues, dated in its forms of expression, unable to render its own time in the language of its own time, but also subject to a philistine press, the threatening representative of the contemporary demos.

In all of these things Ford, and the *English Review*, are both outsiders and insiders, insurgents and embattled defenders. Opposed to that lack of confidence which means that he can only hope to get 'a few inches' above the moral atmosphere is the hope that one could be on the inside of power, and to be seen and acknowledged as one 'in the know', connected to the great and the good. On 2 November 1908, *The Times* carried an advertisement for the forthcoming *English Review*, which claimed, amongst other things, that 'editorial comment [was] to be provided by the communications of statesmen and diplomatists'.[5] It remains obscure how exactly this editorial comment was to be provided: would the 'statesmen and diplomatists' write it themselves? Or would they somehow provide it through their 'communications' to the editor and his writers? But clearly Ford did want to impress on potential readers this sense that his periodical was connected to such people, and therefore to high politics, in important ways. At the same time, there is something slightly garbled about this statement: the last date of usage for the noun 'diplomatist' employed by the *OED* is 1860, although the word was still being used in the early twentieth century. But Ford's use of it implies that there was something dated, wilfully slightly archaic, in his conception of the high politics to which he wishes to be connected. This in turn raises the question of how reliable the 'editorial comment' is to be: is this editor really 'in the know'? Or is he some kind of fraud? Ford clearly did want some of that gentleman's club spirit that emerges in Arnold's account of his conversation in the Athenaeum Club with Disraeli about his coining of what the former Prime Minister calls his 'current phrases' ('such as Philistinism, sweetness and light, and all that'[6]), and in his friendship with C. F. G. Masterman, a minister in the Liberal government at the time of the publication of Ford's *English Review*, Ford did indeed possess *some* of those connections. But what kind of authority did he have for such pronouncements as the following, issued during the Dreadnought crisis of 1909, when British public opinion, alarmed by the growing German navy, demanded that Britain should build eight of the new Dreadnought battleships:

> But we have it on good authority that at least one Continental Power would welcome an informal intimation from the Foreign Office that Great Britain, as being the Power most open to damage at sea, would consider an increase of the fleet of any other nation as an unfriendly action directed against herself, and we have no doubt whatever that once this action were taken, several other Powers would join ourselves. (*ER* II [June 1909] 585)

Here Ford is connected to the corridors of power both at home *and* abroad (even if the insights he is privy to can only be whispered to him): he is truly Arnoldian in that sense, with international culture operating closely in tandem with international relations, and in this scheme the *English Review* situates itself in the mid-Channel in a positive sense, looking over to the Continent but also back to England. It may also be important to remember where Ford had been living in the early years of the twentieth century: at Winchelsea in East Sussex, where he was both close to the respective homes of Henry James and Joseph Conrad, but also looking over the Channel towards the Continent, to where, at the outbreak of the First World War, for James, 'just on the other side of that finest of horizon-lines history was raging at a pitch new under the sun'.[7] Even before the war, for both Ford and James there was a sense that history was – if only partially – elsewhere, over that horizon, because England suffered from 'insularity', to use James's word, but both Ford and James position themselves as look-outs, watch-men, who are sensitive to what is not just 'within the rim', but to what is beyond it too. There were further pragmatic reasons for their choice of location: within reasonable commuting distance to London, the place where reputations were made and lost and which supported a whole network of cultural relationships (dining clubs, literary agents, and so forth), and yet far enough away to claim a reasonable distance from both London's fashionable preoccupations, and, also, far enough away to make property, and therefore the life of the English gentleman of letters, affordable. Finally, there they were also close enough to access the ferries that would take each across the Channel and towards the 'freedom' of Ostend, Paris, Italy and so on. But still it is unclear whether those kinds of connections were sufficient to support Ford's claimed-for position as international man of affairs, and to see the *English Review* as the organ for the propagation of those insights.

Instead, the much more common emphasis in Ford's editorial writing for the *English Review* was on the disconnection of the English man of letters from such kinds of political power or influence, because the cultural and political landscape, in the absence of a self-consciously public culture, tended to fragment into individualism (and gentlemanliness), unlike the world elsewhere that is France and the Continent. As Ford wrote in the *English Review*:

> The English man of letters of any distinction lives apart, dotted over the face of the country, each one isolated, as it were, upon a little hill. He has no Academy like that of the Immortal Forty; he belongs to no movement and in consequence the Art of Letters in England has practically no social weight and practically no contact with the life of the people. It is with the attempt to form some such meeting-place that THE ENGLISH REVIEW has set out upon its career—that the attempt is foredoomed to failure we know very well, for to attempt to form a combination of strong individualists is obviously the attempt of a madman. (*ER* I [March 1909] 797)

So, instead all of the men of letters being united on Olympus or Parnassus or even in the halls of the Académie Française, 'each one [is] isolated, upon a little hill' (one of the South Downs each, say). Ford is noting the tendency of distinguished English men of letters of the period to live 'dotted over the face of the country' rather than in London. The English 'republic of letters' therefore has to operate over these greater distances, rather than through inhabiting a position on the left bank of the Seine, which, in Ford's imagination at least, represents that meeting-place, as well as a kind of standing power in relation to both the state and political and cultural life in general: 'contre le pouvoir' in various senses but also a power in its own right. The 'English' position of distinction 'upon a little hill' does have its advantages: it means that the English man of letters has the certain distance already mentioned above – the position of partial withdrawal that he has taken up means that he may be more able to practice the 'disinterestedness' that Arnold had wanted to characterise the function of criticism, a freedom from the pressures of political party or religion or commerce, in order 'to learn and propagate the best that is known and thought in the world'.[8] Certainly, Ford, Conrad and James wanted to get away from those things. But it also tends to lead, in Ford's mind, to a flourishing of individuals who can then not be united in a common practice and a common space, 'for to attempt to form a combination of strong individualists is obviously the attempt of a madman'. In this case, Ford's attempt to use the *English Review* as that surrogate meeting-place means that he, the editor, is that 'madman', attempting to unify these various isolated, strong-willed, possibly eccentric, possibly insane figures (like the madman, who is necessarily one of the 'strong individualists' himself). But because of the social structure, these thoughts can only be ever untimely meditations, ones which portray the editor as an alienated outsider, who desperately tries to move the men of letters from their little hills onto his temporary 'heap', but agonises about the Art of Letters and its lack of 'social weight'. This, he worries, is particularly the case with James and Conrad, because their extreme eminence (more of an Alp than a little hill), means that they threaten to disappear out of sight:

> Mr. Conrad and Mr. James stand so far above any other imaginative writers of to-day that their significance and their importance are apt to be a little lost. They stand, moreover, so far apart one from another that they have, as far as any literary movement is concerned, an entire want of unity or cohesion. (*ER* III [Nov. 1909] 660)

As discussed above, Arnold's idea of disinterestedness implies having some kind of distance from the world and its preoccupations – in order to better understand them. But James and Conrad have such distance that they seem disconnected from the world – unable either to unite with it or with each other to form the coherent avant-garde, if we take the progressive view, or even collectively to defend the little hill on which they can take their last stand.

But one can also see, in Ford's account, why one would want to be at such a distance. The pages of 'The Month' repeatedly show an antagonistic relationship between this editor and the political culture of the present, even if Ford did still aspire to be a person of importance in that culture. 'The Critical Attitude' of January 1910 begins with the question, ahead of the January 1910 election that would act as a kind of referendum on Lloyd George's 'People's Budget' of 1909 and the constitutional standoff that it had produced: 'Could anything to be more depressing than the present state of public

affairs?' (*ER* IV [Jan. 1910] 329). He goes on to profess his disaffect-
ion with both of the predominant political parties, citing primarily
their materialism and lack of principle, which in turn is inciting the
nation as a whole into a 'class war': 'On the one side there is little or
no talk of liberty or of any of the higher things, on the other there is no
talk at all of the old traditions or of the finer things. And from both
side come perpetual cries of "Grab"' (329). In this process of cultural
decline the parties are singularly aided by the work of the 'periodical
Press', in particular 'the lower Conservative Press', which 'is all-
devouring, is all present':

> It seems to taint the food we eat; it seems to render miasmatic the air we
> breathe. It is more vulgar than the vulgarest of demagogues; it is more
> mendacious than the most irresponsible of speakers at a street corner. Yet the
> lower press has taken in hand, has controlled, for the first time, the entire
> fortunes of the Conservative party. (330)

This vision of the corrupting and inescapable power of the new
popular press – clogging hearts, eyes and lungs, and dragging down
the level of public debate to such dismal levels – is obviously part of
wider anxieties about the changing position of the press, especially
since the outbreaks of 'jingoism' that marked the Boer War.[9]
However, Ford also shows some derision for 'the Liberal Press' in its
tendency to ignore or to underplay those aspects of contemporary life
which it finds unsightly but to which it does not have a straight
answer: in particular, its underreporting of 'deportations' of political
agitators in India: ('DEPORTATIONS! The comfortable Liberal
imagines two or three happy agitators seated beneath the palm-trees,
eating rare fruits in a climate cool and more salubrious than that of
their own provinces') (*ER* IV [Jan. 1910] 332). He also deplores its
unwillingness to consider fairly and honestly the question of votes for
women, which Ford strongly supported. He directs particular attention
to those subjected to force-feeding whilst on hunger-strike: 'In the
barbarous and never sufficiently to be reprehended Middle Ages this
punishment was known as the *peine forte et dure*. Liberal newspapers
have not, so far as we have been able to discover, claimed yet for Mr.
Gladstone the honour of this splendid revival' (333).

The question here, and for Ford in general in the *English
Review*, is what is the force of his irony and sarcasm? The review had
been set up as a neo-Arnoldian project to embody disinterestedness
and the critical attitude and to provide for the publication of various

kinds of august imaginative literature. However, it had also been founded in a spirit of pessimism: Ford may have been against the inheritance of Romanticism in various ways, but the founding of the review was also in one sense a romantic gesture; one doomed to failure. The two 'communications' that Ford says he has received in advance of the publication of the first number are scarcely encouraging blessings: the one given by George Bernard Shaw is 'taken at once as a benediction and as a prophecy of disaster' (*ER* I [Dec. 1908] 157). Ford extemporises on a metaphor of the *English Review* as a boat, being rowed out to sea for the first time, but there seems to be an implied fear that it will soon be holed below the waterline. As this is the case, then it would seem difficult for Ford to generate the kind of confidence which would repel his tendency to display a kind of strangely undirected irony. Many of Ford's contributions to 'The Month' – and especially those which are directed largely to political considerations and are not primarily literary in focus – are very discontinuous in nature: the tone is notably uneven, even if his lashings out seem to be pretty fairly spread around. This unevenness is present right from the beginning: in the first version of 'The Month' he imagines the topics will include 'the production of a well-flavoured book, the commencement of a historic series, the production of a play not too shallow, the chronicling of a symphony, the opening of a gallery containing fine etchings' (158). A 'well-flavoured book'? 'Fine etchings'? This sounds like the critic as belles-lettristic gourmand (and there is certainly something of that in Ford) – but it also raises the possibility that Ford doesn't believe in any of it, that there is something incredible, even despicable about the fruits of his own labour.

We can develop this point further by considering the range of Ford's targets in the *English Review*. In no particular order they include but are not limited to: a critique of England as 'the country of Accepted Ideas' (160), a complacent, unintellectual, uncritical land where one might imagine nothing ever really changes, and one which is basically hostile to, or at least unmoved by, the higher, more exacting standards embodied in the work of the true artist. It is also implied that England should pay attention to these things for its sake as much as for the artist's, for 'Flaubert said that had the French really read his "Education Sentimentale" France would have avoided the horrors of the *Débâcle*. Mr. James might say as much for his own country and for the country he has so much benefitted by making it his

own' (160). It's clear that Ford doesn't just want an equivalent to the
Académie Française; only a really detailed understanding of Flaubert's *L'Education Sentimentale* will do the job of preventing national
crises. So, the implication is that if the kinds of standards and
awareness that Flaubert and James embody were to be recognised and
even incorporated into the practice of the life of the nation (in some
way, however unclear that might be), then various potential national
disasters could be warded off. On the other hand, the pages of 'The
Month' describe England as a country that is, in fact, going through
sudden, radical changes, a country that is seething with tensions of
various kinds. However, Ford seems to assume that these tensions are
not exactly the product of various competing ideas, about class,
progress, the role of the state and income distribution: they seem
instead to be the product of various instincts which could not be
characterised as having reached the level of 'idea'. For example, to
return to the example of 'the lower Conservative Press', Ford
imagines it as 'all-devouring', as if were some kind of monster, but
also as an entity that pollutes anything and everything, tainting the
food we eat, making the air we breathe 'miasmatic'. In these senses it
seems to relate to fears about degeneration that had proliferated in the
general biologising of social theory since the publication of Darwin's
The Origin of Species in 1859. The press, by generally pandering to
humanity's 'lower instincts', becomes a monster which pollutes as
well as devours, stopping anything from being seen clearly, but also
furthering the desire of the editor to find a way to get 'a few inches
above the atmosphere of these Islands'. But in this desire Ford is
located in a tradition of thinking about 'the condition of England' that
even predates the dissemination of Darwin, but which is bound up in
other, more literal forms of pollution. In 'The Fogs of London' in his
My Past and Thoughts, the Russian political organiser and theorist,
Alexander Herzen, had written about what it was like to live in
London, as an exile, in the middle of the nineteenth century:

> There is no town in the world which is more adapted for training one away
> from people and training one into solitude than London. The manner of life,
> the distances, the climate, the very multitude of the population in which
> personality vanishes, all this together with the absence of Continental
> diversions conduces to the same effect. One who knows how to live alone has
> nothing to fear from the tedium of London. The life here, like the air here, is
> bad for the weak, for the frail, for one who seeks a prop outside himself, for
> one who seeks welcome, sympathy, attention; the moral lungs must be as

strong as the physical lungs, whose task it is to separate oxygen from the
smoky fog. The masses are saved by battling for their daily bread, the
commercial classes by their absorption in heaping up wealth, and all by the
bustle of business; but nervous and romantic temperaments – fond of living
among people, fond of intellectual sloth and of idly luxuriating in emotion –
are bored to death and fall into despair.[10]

Ford would doubtless class himself, with his own family history
of immigration as well as interest in and sympathy for 'Continental
diversions', as one of those 'nervous and romantic temperaments',
who had suffered his own fall into despair during his breakdown in
1904. There is also no doubt that he wanted to transcend or cut
through those 'fogs' – which are, clearly, as much intellectual and
social as they are visual – before they finished off this particular
member of the weak and the frail. Or perhaps not quite so weak and
frail, as Ford had, along with Herzen, to some extent trained himself
into withstanding this. As Herzen goes on to say, out of this
experience of solitude in London, 'I learnt a great deal'. But for Ford,
out of all this cloudiness and lack of clarity, which also seems to
symbolise, to some extent, stupidity, and the possibility of being
stupefied oneself, as well as an unfatal solipsism as you wander
through the fogs unable to see or recognise anyone else, through this
shines both the desire for 'welcome, sympathy, attention' and the
necessity for violent gestures, even if they are buried amongst the
editorial pages of 'The Month':

We may never have a Parthenon: perhaps one day we may nerve ourselves,
say, to the extent of being proud of the National Gallery or of cleaning out
from that Augean stable, the Tate, its huge proportion of dreary and inane
canvases. (*ER* I [March 1909] 798)

Those 'dreary and inane canvases': both ugly in a depressing
way that is not even really worth describing (and which is inclined to
make you 'aweary' and wish that you were dead, according to
Tennyson's 'Mariana') and stupid, 'inane', which in a way is worse
than stupid, because it is trying to be something more than it is. No
wonder Ford thinks we should nerve ourselves to complete this
Herculean task, but he doesn't seem hopeful, even if he really wants to
do it. But his fear is in a sense justified, that the fogs of pollution and
inanity, are in some way contagious, in that the editor himself, despite
his desperate desire to get 'a few inches above the atmosphere of these
Islands', may himself be guilty of what he accuses others of, a certain

'cloudiness of spirit'. In his review of Masterman's *The Condition of England*, he laments his friend's own inability to produce a sense of clarity about what exactly the condition of England is: 'And so Mr. Masterman wavers from despondency to hope, wavers from hope to caution and ends by saying he cannot tell where we stand' (*ER* III [Aug. 1909] 182-4).

It is this uncertainty about where he himself stands that produces the characteristic uncertainty, or perhaps undecidability, of Ford's tone.[11] The irony that pervades much of his fiction and, often, his autobiographical writing, can turn into sarcasm when Ford comes to take up the position of leader-writer or editorialist in the *English Review*, where he therefore comes to take on the mantle of the man of letters, despite the fact that he had commemorated 'The Passing of the Great Figure' in an early number of his own periodical. By this he had meant that the high Victorian days of Gladstone, Tennyson, Ruskin, Arnold and others had ended, to be replaced by a present day where no similar figures had such a commanding relationship to their audience, due to a variety of social and intellectual changes, which meant that the high liberalism which Ford associated with high Victorianism was now challenged by a partially democratised, enlarged but damaged public sphere: we can see an early version here of F. R. Leavis's 'Mass Civilisation versus Minority Culture'. But, still, to be the editor of a journal with such august hopes as the *English Review* meant that Ford was still in some sense continuing this role of 'the great figure' himself, even if it felt somewhat diminished. The sarcasm emerges as Ford struggles to deal with the uncertainties built into the situation, and it seems to take on two primary forms. Firstly, there is a very uneven kind, where the reader could be unsure as to what exactly the force of his irony is. For example, as Ford continues his examination of the question of the force-feeding of suffragettes on hunger-strike in jail, he discusses the position of the Home Secretary, Herbert Gladstone, the son of W. E. Gladstone – four-times Liberal Prime Minister and 'great figure' himself – who was in a position of overall responsibility for the treatment of those women. Ford remarks on the irony of the situation, given that W. E. Gladstone had frequently protested against the harsh treatment of political minorities in other European countries in the 1870s and 1880s. 'It has been reserved for Mr. Gladstone – oh, sacred name, whose echoes bear in their skirts gracious and fluttering whispers of the word "Liberty!" – it has been reserved for Mr. Gladstone to cause the maltreatment of women in our own gaols' (*ER* IV [Jan. 1910] 333). It is hard to know exactly what to make of those echoes and their skirts, except that perhaps Ford is not happy about any of these things: he is not happy about the force-feeding of the women, he is not happy about pious philanthropic liberalism of the (first) Gladstonian kind, but which itself seems to be associated with misguidedly altruistic upper-class females, but he is also not happy with Herbert Gladstone for breaking the Gladstonian covenant. It is even harder to see what is entirely meant by this when one reads the piece in its original context: it is buried in the course of an extremely long paragraph, which is dense and allusive, like a modernist novel, but which does not say 'this is a modernist novel: therefore it is going to be dense and allusive, and you, the reader, had better be prepared for that'. The uncertainty of the tone seems to be related to the fact that Ford is not quite sure of his hold on his audience: on the one hand, one can suspect that some readers of the *English Review* on occasion skipped over much of the contents of 'The Month' – or read a few paragraphs, and then abandoned it. On the other, and further complicating the situation, other parts of the readership would have been representatives of various political camps, who could have found Ford's views to be a potentially disturbing mix of sympathies and opinions. Which, in a sense, was the problem: Ford's fear of not being listened to, and of not having real power, makes him more likely to react in the first place.

But there is another kind of tone in the *English Review*: one where we know exactly what is going on. The word 'sarcasm' comes from the Greek, σαρκάζειν, 'to tear flesh', and so it aims to do violence to that which it criticises, but it also suggests the possibility that it is the critic's own flesh that can be torn. We find this in the publication of 'On the Objection to the Critical Attitude' in February 1910, when Ford already knew that the *English Review*, at least under his editorship, had already failed. He was then prepared to say what he – *really* – thought, about the reasons for its failure:

> In these islands critics have been extraordinarily rare. When they have arisen they have been listened to with dislike and dread, or with a show of respect. Then they have been patted out of the way. If a slug should enter a bee-hive these industrious insects will, if they can accomplish it, slay him with their stings, but failing this, and in any case, they set to work and cover him with wax. They pack the wax down, they smooth it over: they extinguish, in fact, that poor slug until he reposes beneath a fair monument, a respectable protuberance from which escape neither groans nor foul odours. Now our

islands are the bee-hives, and what is the critic in England, when direfully he appears, but just a slug? He lives if he has a chance, suspected, dreaded, applauded. Then he disappears. He is covered with the wax of oblivion. So it has been with, let us say, Hobbes, Matthew Arnold, and Mr. Ruskin, who, being dead, are nearly as much forgotten as, let us say, the inventor of the safety bicycle. (*ER* IV [Feb. 1910] 532)

And so Ford attempts to bite back, through the wax: but what does he taste? Not so much the blood of the complacent, unintellectual, emollient great British public (the reader should note that we are back to 'these islands' again), but, one would guess, just more wax: if he did get through, however, then one would have to remember that the bees can provide not just wax but also stings. He also does not want to hurt his readers, who are, of course, the heroic few who have stuck it out to the end, but he does want to satisfy them, just as he wants to satisfy himself. And to be able to give out the superiority of judgment and criticism is very satisfying. It is not a satisfaction that lasts, or that changes anything, but, at the moment that it is pronounced, it is very satisfying. And, of course, what he says is in one way true, as well as being funny in a bitter way: the condition of being a critic, of culture and society, does tend to mean that you might well be forgotten and sent to oblivion, just because to be a critic is to criticise something in particular, which you then stand in relation to, and if the entity that you criticise disappears or loses centrality, then your point (and your criticism) tends to get lost: just as many readers would now struggle to understand the point of *Culture and Anarchy* (1869) without some understanding of the historical context, whilst they would be very much able to 'enjoy' or 'apprec-iate' *Great Expectations* (1861) or *Middlemarch* (1872). This situation is particularly signified by the form in which these critical reflections are generally embodied: in periodical or in other kinds of occasional publication, which, until the recent advent of digital and online resources, meant that your words could very much suffer the same fate as the inventor of the safety bicycle; here today and gone tomorrow. One could try to recover this situation, as Ruskin's editors, E. T. Cook and Alexander Wedderburn, did in their contemporaneous *Library Edition* of Ruskin's complete works (1903-12; all 39 volumes). But then they worried that what they were producing was not so much a monument as a mausoleum, and it is true to say that Ruskin would come to be seen as increasingly dated after the publication of that edition: just another part of the Victorian past that would need to be sloughed off by the moderns. So, there is not even a view from the monument or mausoleum: that particular 'heap' is only raised when the critic is dead, and so he will never get to stand on it, in order to get those crucial 'few inches above the moral atmosphere of these Islands'. But others might, if they spare the time.

But, in all this, we should also see Ford as a representative figure and not purely as an exceptional one. His uncertainty, his contradictory positions, portray both his anxiety and our anxiety at facing a world which we do not wholly understand, and whose depravity, in whatever form it emerges, tempts us into the superiority of condemnation. And so we should also to some extent resist seeing his work, as it were, teleologically: somehow always aimed at the finished achievement of *The Good Soldier* or *Parade's End*, or instead as something that can be stripped down to providing some of the originating principles behind 'modernist literary doctrine'. If instead, we think of Ford in a more actively historical sense, we can see him as a particularly sensitive and intelligent witness to the 'atmosphere' of his times even as he wants the *English Review* to cut through or disperse the 'miasma', or to rise those crucial few inches above it.

NOTES

1 'To imagine that a magazine devoted to imaginative literature and technical criticism alone would find more than a hundred readers in the United Kingdom was a delusion that I in no way had. It must therefore of necessity be a hybrid, giving at least half its space to current affairs. Those I did not consider myself fit to deal with. I knew either nothing about them or I knew so much I could not form any opinions': *Return to Yesterday*, London: Victor Gollancz, 1931, p. 310.
2 *Letters of Ford Madox Ford*, ed. Richard M. Ludwig, Princeton, NJ: Princeton University Press, 1965, p. 15.
3 Matthew Arnold, letter to Jane Martha Arnold, 28 March, 1848, *The Letters of Matthew Arnold*, vol. I, ed. Cecil Y. Lang, London: University Press of Virginia, 1996, p. 98.
4 Andrzej Gasiorek, 'Ford Among the Aliens', *Ford Madox Ford and Englishness*, ed. Dennis Brown and Jenny Plastow, Amsterdam: Rodopi Press, 2006, pp. 63-82.
5 Advertisement for *English Review* in *The Times* (2 November 1908), 9.
6 Matthew Arnold, letter to Francis Bunsen Trevenen Whately Arnold, 21 February, 1881, in *Letters of Matthew Arnold*, vol. V, p. 135.
7 Henry James, 'Within the Rim', *Within the Rim and Other Essays*, London: Collins, 1918), pp. 16-17.

8   Arnold, 'The Function of Criticism at the Present Time' [1865], *Essays in Criticism; First Series*, London: Macmillan, 1898, p. 37.

9   Cf. G. M. Trevelyan, 'The White Peril', *Nineteenth Century and After*, 50:298 (December 1901), 1043-55.

10   Alexander Herzen, *My Past and Thoughts* [1868], trans. Constance Garnett, abridged Dwight Macdonald, London: University of California Press, 1973, p. 445.

11   For more on these questions see the chapter on Ford in Simon Grimble's *Landscape, Writing and 'the Condition of England', 1878-1917 – Ruskin to Modernism*, Lampeter: Edwin Mellen Press, 2004.

LIBERALISM AND MODERNISM
IN THE EDWARDIAN ERA:
NEW LIBERALS AT FORD'S *ENGLISH REVIEW*

John Attridge

The *English Review* is well known for combining imaginative writing
with political and social commentary, but discussions of its political
content have tended to be summary, bundled up with an overview of
the review as a whole or preoccupied with the politics of its editor.[1]
This essay fills in some of the detail in our picture of the review's
politics by identifying a previously unnoticed bloc within its list of
contributors, several of whom were associated with a form of Liberal
collectivism known to Edwardian observers as New Liberalism.[2] In
what follows I will trace the presence of this group of writers in Ford's
magazine, suggest how and why they may have ended up there, and
finally propose an oblique and unexpected correlation between their
political outlook and Ford's own.

The *English Review*'s political content, along with its social and
cultural commentary, was corralled in a section called 'The Month',
located at the back of each issue after the monthly dose of poetry,
serial fiction, short stories and drama. Notwithstanding the credo of
'No party bias' (*ER* I [Dec. 1908] 159) proclaimed in Ford's first
editorial, contributors to 'The Month' tended to come from the left of
the political spectrum, whether Liberal or socialist, although Ford's
own pseudonymous Tory 'Declaration of Faith' was a notable
exception (*ER* IV [Feb. 1910] 543-51). Most critics agree that 'The
Month' was Liberal in outlook: Ralph Hermann Ruedy notes that 'the
English Review supported most of the standard Liberal causes of the
day', including especially the defence of constitutional democracy
overseas; Frank MacShane says that from mid-1909 it was no more
than a vehicle of 'propaganda for the Liberal party'; and Ann Bar
Snitow remarks that Ford's own editorials were imbued with the
confidence of 'Gladstonian liberalism'.[3] Eric Homberger dissents
slightly from this consensus, placing the review's political tone

somewhere between William Morris's medievalism and the Fabianism of H. G. Wells.[4]

If the *English Review*'s broadly Liberal sympathies are not in doubt, however, none of these commentators has pointed out the close affiliation of several of Ford's contributors with *New* Liberalism, a collectivist strain of Liberal thought that had its heyday in Britain around the turn of the twentieth century.[5] This collectivist turn within Liberalism reflected a more pervasive trend in late-Victorian political discourse towards concern for the 'social question' and urgent reflection on the state's role in ameliorating social ills.[6] The New Liberal response largely consisted in rethinking the relationship between the individual and society, departing from the ethos of unchecked individualism that had characterized Victorian Liberalism. New Liberal theorists like L. T. Hobhouse turned to an organic model of society to accomplish this rethinking. As Hobhouse wrote in 1911:

> No one element of the social life stands separate from the rest, any more than any one element of the animal body stands separate from the rest. In this sense the life of society is rightly held to be organic, and all considered public policy must be conceived in its bearing on the life of society as a whole.[7]

The rights of the individual were no longer to be assessed in isolation from the social organism:

> in the matter of rights and duties which is cardinal for Liberal theory, the relation of the individual to the community is everything [....] An individual right, then, cannot conflict with the common good, nor could any right exist apart from the common good.[8]

This notion of rights being contingent on the common good, coupled with the New Liberal principle of self-development or self-realisation, led logically to what J. A. Hobson described in the *English Review* as 'that saner, more positive and progressive conception of liberty which identifies that word not with absence of restraint but with presence of opportunity' (*ER* III [Nov. 1909] 686). From a practical perspective, this positive conception of liberty was a justification for activist government and the politics of social welfare. As the journalist and Liberal MP J. M. Robertson put it in 1912: '"Laissez-faire" [...] is not done with as a principle of rational limitation of State interference, but it is quite done with as a pretext for leaving uncured deadly social evils which admit of curative treatment by State action'.[9] Needless to say, critics of the new movement did not always bother to distinguish between New Liberalism and outright socialism.

To my knowledge, only Paul Peppis has discussed the *English Review* in the context of New Liberalism. For Peppis, however, this term reduces to the policies of the 1908 Asquith Liberal government, 'men who [...] favored a strong state and a strong empire'.[10] 'The *English Review*'s politics', he says:

> mirror the attitudes of the (New) Liberal government during this period of perceived internal unrest and external competition: domestically the *Review*'s policies are more progressive and socialistic; internationally its policies are closer to those of the Tories, more conservative, patriotic, and imperialist.[11]

But the extent to which New Liberal ideology can be equated with the legislation of the Edwardian Liberal *Party* is not so easily ascertained: 'the gulf between the ideas and policies of official Liberalism and the new liberals was often immense', cautions Michael Freeden.[12] Hobhouse, for one, was profoundly sceptical of Liberal Imperialist politicians like H. H. Asquith and R. B. Haldane, whose rhetoric of state efficiency clashed with his own conception of Liberal principles.[13] It is also surprising to see an attitude of patriotic imperialism ascribed to the New Liberal ethos. J. A. Hobson, another primary architect of New Liberal doctrine, vociferously deplored British imperialism: his *Imperialism: A Study* (1902) was a seminal and widely read critique. (Indeed, Hobson aired his views on inevitable decolonization in the *English Review* itself, in a September 1909 article entitled 'South Africa as an Imperial Asset'.) Moreover, Peppis infers the review's 'policies' largely from Ford's editorials, without discussing the several articles written by New Liberal contributors (although he does mention Hobson's contributions in passing).[14] Whether or not the *English Review* can be shown to 'mirror the attitudes' of a putatively '(New) Liberal' government, the appearance in its pages of significant New Liberal theorists surely merits attention in this context.

The New Liberals were not a strictly defined club, but two New Liberal contributors to the *English Review* are easy to identify: Hobson and Hobhouse, the pair of journalists and maverick social scientists described by Freeden as 'the two most profound of the liberal thinkers of the period'.[15] Hobhouse contributed only one article to Ford's review, in December 1909 on the constitutional crisis, but Hobson published six articles there between July 1909 and January

1910, making him the review's most prolific political writer behind Ford himself.

In addition to these two eminent theorists, three lesser known New Liberal associates also wrote for the *English Review*. There were, first, the foreign policy specialists H. W. Nevinson and H. N. Brailsford. Nevinson and Brailsford were prominent Liberal journalists who wrote regularly for the weekly *Speaker* and later the *Nation*, where Hobson and Hobhouse were also regular contributors. More importantly, however, all four men were also regular participants at H. W. Massingham's weekly *Nation* lunches, a gathering that provided, along with the Rainbow Circle discussion group and the South Place Ethical Society, 'the semi-institutionalized foci' of New Liberal activities.[16] (Nevinson later recalled of these lunches that Hobson rivaled G. K. Chesterton as resident wit, but this quality is not apparent in Hobson's *English Review* writings.[17]) Nevinson contributed two articles to the *English Review*, on Balkan politics and women's suffrage, and Brailsford contributed three, on the Young Turks, European militarism, and the Foreign Office's lack of accountability.[18] None of their contributions was directly concerned with the finer points of New Liberal theory, but Nevinson's suffragist piece does demonstrate his familiarity with the New Liberal vocabulary. Extending the franchise to women, Nevinson argued, was not only a question of justice, but also a recognition 'that their happiness, like our own, lies, if anywhere, in the realisation of self [....] The assertion of self, the fulfillment of function, is the final object of life' (*ER* III [Nov. 1909] 695). The idea that self-realisation occurs through participation in society, along with the principle of self-realisation itself, were commonplaces of New Liberal writing. Hobson, for example, in his *English Review* essay 'After the Destruction of the Veto', defined the state 'as an instrument [...] to secure full opportunities of self-development and social service for all citizens', a conception that was, he added, 'foreign to the Liberalism of the last generation' (*ER* IV [Dec. 1909] 111).

Another contributor, the Liberal MP G. P. Gooch, was also a participant in the Rainbow Circle group ('the ideological core of advanced social, and especially liberal social, thought'), bringing the total number of contributors to the *English Review* associated with the New Liberal movement to five.[19] Even without this supporting cast, moreover, the series of six essays by Hobson, the least topical of which were collected in his book *The Crisis of Liberalism* (1909), constitutes a significant presence at the review.[20]

However, we cannot conclude from Hobson's frequent appearances and the contributions of his New Liberal comrades that Ford was sympathetic to the New Liberal ethos, because Hobson began writing for the review *after* Ford's brother-in-law David Soskice had assumed partial responsibility for its political content. The financial history of the *English Review* is notoriously snarled, but it is sufficient to note here that when Ford's capital ran out in April 1909, the Russian émigré Soskice formed a committee to manage the review's finances pending its sale to a suitable buyer, in return for partial control over the political section.[21] Arthur Mizener states that the agreement was formalized on 16 May, and Nora Tomlinson has recently discovered from Soskice's bank pass book that his loans to Ford commenced in that month, although it took until August for Soskice to form The English Review Company, with himself and William Goode as directors (Mizener 188). According to Tomlinson, the cashbooks of the review indicate that Soskice was acting as business manager from July 1909.[22] Ruedy observes that 'The Month' did increase in size around this time, doubtless reflecting Soskice's influence, although he also finds that 'the general nature of the views expressed was consistent throughout Ford's editorship'.[23]

Ford did not relish the prospect of Soskice and his committee harnessing 'The Month' to their own agenda. In 1909 he wrote to his wife Elsie of 'struggling to keep Soskice from turning the Review into a Whig. Socialist organ', and in June that year he predicted grimly that 'If S. wins the R. will become a Socialist organ pure & simple'.[24] As late as 8 June Ford continued to resist Soskice's control of 'The Month', telling him that he had agreed to 'commission a number of friends of your own of a purely partisan nature' only as a gesture of 'friendship and affection'.[25] The only contributors answering to this description around June are Brailsford, a colleague of Soskice's at the short-lived Liberal daily *Tribune*, whose first articles appeared in the May and July issues, and Hobson, whose first essay appeared in July.[26] In this 8 June letter to Soskice Ford also again voices his objection to 'turning the review into a purely Socialist organ', which he claims would lose the review both readers and advertising. A letter from Soskice to Ford dated 13 August, moreover, states that he does indeed have an essay from Hobson in hand, presumably 'South Africa as an Imperial Asset', which appeared in September.[27]

To Soskice's involvement, then, can be attributed Brailsford and Hobson's appearances in 'The Month', as well as, presumably, that of Hobhouse, who also wrote for the *Tribune*. To some extent, that is, Soskice did change the political composition of the review, Brailsford, Hobson and Hobhouse contributing ten essays between them from May 1909 to January 1910. At the same time, however, Nevinson had written on the Balkans in the first number of the review, at a time when Ford still had complete editorial control over 'The Month'. It does seem likely that Nevinson came to the *English Review* through Soskice, with whom he was connected through Brailsford and his circle. However, the fact that Ford published Nevinson's foreign affairs commentary while still in full command of the review suggests that he did not recognize Nevinson as one of Soskice's 'friends of a purely partisan nature', even though Nevinson's ideological commitments were very similar to those of Brailsford and Hobson. This is confirmed by Ford's January 1910 editorial, in which he alludes to both Nevinson and Brailsford as two of the *Daily News*'s 'most attractive writers'.[28] But however Ford may have felt about these two foreign affairs writers, Hobson's articles must on the whole have struck him as partisan hectoring.

If any writer commissioned by Soskice was going to turn the review into a 'purely socialist organ', as Ford put it, it was surely the rogue economist and anti-imperialist J. A. Hobson. More than Brailsford and Nevinson, Hobson used his *English Review* articles to formulate explicitly New Liberal principles. His essay in July 1909 on 'The Significance of the Budget', for example, voiced a central New Liberal belief about the social generation of wealth, construing the Chancellor of the Exchequer David Lloyd George's taxes on land and industry as 'the first half-conscious recognition that taxation rightly means the assumption by the State of a socially earned income' (*ER* II [July 1909] 800). His article on 'The Extension of Liberalism', moreover, clearly defined the break between liberalisms old and new, arguing that true 'equality of opportunity' required the redistribution of land ownership and the nationalisation of electricity, education, transport, and the legal profession (*ER* III [Nov. 1909] 673). As I have already noted, Hobson called in this essay for a 'more positive and progressive conception of liberty which identifies that word not with absence of restraint but with presence of opportunity'. Hobson's highly literal, rather lurid January 1910 article on 'Social Parasitism', meanwhile, vilified capitalists and land-owners, the illicit appropriators of socially earned income: 'The persons who live upon "economic rent" or upon the interest of property obtained otherwise than by their personal exertions belong to this parasitic species' (*ER* IV [Jan. 1910] 349).

Hobson's October 1909 article, 'The Task of Realism', is particularly interesting because it directly refers to the journal in which it appears, giving us some idea of how Hobson saw the *English Review* and its aims. What Hobson calls 'realism' is a contemporary descendent of Enlightenment Reason, defined as 'the persistent strenuous desire to reach, present and represent facts, not excluding fictions, illusions, superstitions, but disentangling this sort of facts from the others' (*ER* III [Oct. 1909] 552). The spirit of 'realism' is also distinguished by its tendency towards synthesis rather than fragmentation: it occurs simultaneously in 'religion, politics, art, science, literature', and tends 'to reverse the dissociative current, which everywhere made for separation, and to lay the main intellectual and spiritual stress on harmony and unity' (551). It is this quality of holism, achieved by spanning a variety of fields, that makes the *English Review* an appropriate platform for realist views. Hobson concludes that:

> those who accept the view that experiments in collective self-consciousness, as a means of accelerating and directing the 'urge of the world' towards human enlightenment and well-being, are likely to yield great results, will recognise that a rendering of realism in many fields of thought and art is the most profitable use for such a Review. (554)

What seems particularly to have attracted Hobson to the *English Review*, then, was its combination of imaginative writing with social and political commentary, which represented an effort to tie together the many manifestations of 'realism' into a single *Zeitgeist*. In this way, Hobson's perception of the review confirms Mark Morrisson's reading of its will to integration: its 'attempt to shore up what Ford saw as the fragmentation of a culture by turning to a semimytho-logized vision of cultural cohesion'.[29]

Ford, whose pseudonymous 'Declaration of Faith' in February included the avowal that he was a 'sentimental old-fashioned Tory' entirely satisfied with the existing House of Lords, would not have endorsed Hobson's radical reform agenda (*ER* IV [Feb. 1910] 544). Even so, his 'Declaration of Faith' does seem to refer obliquely to Hobson's essay on 'Social Parasitism', which had appeared the previous month. Ford claims that 'I should like to see legislation introduced which would press hard upon, which would exterminate, all the purely parasitic classes' and that 'I think I should even be inclined to confiscate all profits made by investments after a reasonable interest had been paid' (545-6). This echoes the language and thinking of Hobson's essay, which had seconded Lloyd George in arguing that unearned increment should be disposed of by the state. Like Tietjens in *Some Do Not . . .*, whose 'High Toryism' is practically equivalent to 'the extreme Radicalism of the extreme Left of the Left', Ford's 'Declaration of Faith' cuts across traditional political boundaries, seeming to adopt part of Hobson's position while rejecting his program as a whole.[30] The wording of the article suggests that, at the very least, Ford had unconsciously absorbed the terms of Hobson's polemic, framing Ford and Hobson fleetingly as improbable ideological bedfellows.

In spite of this incidental correspondence, it seems clear that Ford published Hobson's collectivist theses only under protest. Nonetheless, I want to close by suggesting a point of intersection between the ideology of New Liberalism and Ford's own political sensibility. In his editorial for December 1909, 'The Passing of the Great Figure', Ford reflected on the gap separating the Victorians from the moderns. 'In the Victorian Era', he writes, 'an official altruism reigned as the unquestioned standard whether of the religious or of the agnostic – a sentimental altruism embracing all humanity, all races, all types' (*ER* IV [Dec. 1909] 104). Ford evoked a similar theme in his April 1909 editorial, 'Blue Water and the Thin Red Line', which criticized the pro-Empire demagoguery of Joseph Chamberlain. Chamberlain, Ford says, 'gave us the Boer War which swept away, as if with one breath, nearly all traces of Victorian culture', deposing 'the Great Figure, and the Great Figure's hold upon popular imagination', and replacing them with xenophobic populism: 'Damn the foreigner!' is Chamberlain's alleged catchcry (*ER* II [Apr. 1909] 141). Two years later, in his memoir *Ancient Lights*, Ford stated that as a result of the Boer War 'principles had died out of politics', and this remark may be taken as a gloss on his criticism of Chamberlain as a demagogue.[31] In each of these statements, the Victorian era – and particularly the Victorian public sphere – is characterized by a certain quality of idealism, the consensus of 'sentimental altruism', the agency of 'principles' in politics, the absence of vulgar demagoguery.

The public idealism that Ford misses from post-Victorian England was especially associated with the Liberal tradition. Ford says as much in his May 1909 editorial, 'Little States and Great Nations', which links the shift marked by the Boer War to the Austro-Hungarian annexation of Bosnia-Herzegovina, formalised in April 1909. 'What the Boer War so efficiently began', he writes, 'the Balkan settlement has consummately ended' (*ER* II [May 1909] 358). Ford's point is that the failure of the Great Powers to uphold the Treaty of Berlin against Austria-Hungary's expansion, allowing smaller nations to be bartered as geopolitical pawns, was a betrayal of England's nineteenth-century role as beacon of liberty:

> For, from the time of Napoleon until, let us say, 1870, England was *la grande nation*. It was the nation of Reform Bills, of Constitutional freedom, of Humanitarian ideals; it was the land that sent Byron to Greece, it was the land that gave hospitality to Mazzini, to Cavour, to Garibaldi – and even to Louis Napoleon; it was the champion of oppressed nationalities. (358)

Ford's references to Reform Bills, and to Mazzini, Cavour and Garibaldi, the heroes of Italian unification, suggest that what he has in mind is the Gladstonian Liberal tradition, which was associated with the righteous fostering of democracy at home and abroad. He may have been thinking of such high watermarks of Liberal sentiment as Gladstone's 1862 speech on Italian affairs, in which he deplored Austria's imperial presence in Italy, and Garibaldi's triumphant reception in London two years later. This link to the tradition of Liberal idealism is made still more explicit in his editorial for July 1909, 'Splendid Isolations', in which Ford wrote:

> For Liberalism to be effective there must be behind it a certain glow of humanitarian faith, a certain visionary quality, an absolute incapacity to temporise. So that when we remember the late Mr. Gladstone's splendid and rhetorical handling of the Balkan question we feel bitterly ashamed of Sir Edward Grey's. (*ER* II [July 1909] 763)

By failing to defend the cause of constitutional democracy in Persia and Turkey, and of national sovereignty in Bosnia and Herzegovina, the foreign secretary Edward Grey had departed from what Ford called the 'blind, but fine, following of a sentimental tradition' (764). These expressions of nostalgia for sentimentalism, idealism and altruism in political discourse seem to link the Victorian atmosphere of great figures specifically to a Liberal tradition, one characterized by the *agency* of ideals in a mass democracy and personified, as Ford suggests, by the great Liberal premier William Gladstone. Gladstone's passionate rhetorical defence of clearly defined ideals, such as Reform at home and national sovereignty in Italy and Bulgaria, had confirmed idealistic oratory – what Ford calls 'splendid rhetoric' – as a core component of Liberalism, whereas contemporary politics was conducted in a comparatively prosaic and uninspiring idiom (or so Ford thought).[32]

Ford was likewise disappointed by the tone of the debate over Lloyd George's redistributive 'People's Budget', which was blocked in the House of Lords in 1909. In his editorial for January 1910, the month of the ensuing general election, he described this conflict as 'a class war simply and solely for money', in which each party had betrayed its traditional ideals. 'On the [Liberal] side', Ford complained:

> there is little or no talk of liberty or of any of the higher things, on the other side there is no talk at all of the old traditions or of the finer things. [...] About neither party is there a breath of principle or a sign that either has any real comprehension of its traditional significance. (*ER* IV [Jan. 1910] 329-30)

In short, Ford concludes gloomily, 'With a Press sinking daily to an even lower level, with two dominant parties sinking always to lower levels of appeal, there seems to remain no scintilla of hope for anything not purely materialistic in the concerns of the State' (338-9). As in his other laments for the sentimentalism and principle of the Victorian public sphere, Ford sees contemporary politics as suffering from a dearth of ideals, an expulsion of the 'higher things' from political discourse.

Robert Green has suggested that 'the prevailing direction of Ford's work of this period was towards the past, towards an aristocratic but doomed conservatism', and Andrzej Gasiorek argues cogently that the *Parade's End* tetralogy examines and ultimately rejects the possibility of a Tory Radicalism with its roots in the eighteenth century.[33] However, in 1909 Ford's nostalgia also seems to have had a more immediate object in the Victorian era, the age of altruism and sentiment, and the prime political manifestation of this age seems to have been not conservatism but the Gladstonian Liberal tradition. It was the Gladstonian vocabulary of high political idealism, which Gladstone had deployed against the Ottoman oppression of Bulgaria in the 1870s, that Ford found lacking in Sir Edward Grey's more reserved handling of the Balkan question.

Interestingly, this same January 1910 editorial also contains an appreciative allusion to Brailsford and Nevinson. Having opened the piece by asking 'Could anything be more depressing than the present state of public affairs?', Ford goes on to deplore the government policy of force-feeding suffragette hunger strikers, and notes that one of London's Liberal daily newspapers 'has recently lost its three most attractive writers, disgusted by its policy with regard to the actions and aspirations of women who desire the Suffrage' (333). I don't know who the third journalist was, but two of these attractive writers were almost certainly Brailsford and Nevinson, both of whom resigned from the *Daily News* in October 1909 over its failure to condemn the force-feeding of prisoners.[34] Nevinson was once described by St. Loe Strachey as a modern day knight errant, and Ford doubtless appreciated this principled act of resigning in protest as an example of political idealism, in the grand Liberal tradition.[35]

What I want finally to suggest is that Ford's overt concern with the agency of ideals and sentiment in politics does align him, in an unexpected way, with New Liberalism. In spite of their penchant for abstruse theorizing, Hobson, Hobhouse and their comrades did not abandon the idealism and humanism of the Liberal tradition; these were, rather, explicit elements in their ideology. Brailsford, in a 1947 memoir of Hobson, put it succinctly: 'the ideals that move us are also facts among the visible and measurable realities'.[36] Hobhouse, similarly, wrote in 1907 that 'the people are prepared to move if intelligible and inspiring ideals are set before them'.[37] Or, as he put it in his 1911 manifesto *Liberalism*, 'Great changes are not caused by ideas alone; but they are not effected without ideas. The passions of men must be aroused if the frost of custom is to be broken or the chains of authority burst'.[38] *Liberalism* also acknowledged the import-ance of Gladstone's rhetorical legacy:

> Gladstone was a moral rather than an intellectual force. He raised the whole level of public life. By habitually calling upon what was best in men, he deepened the sense of public responsibility and paved the way, half unconsciously, for the fuller exercise of the social conscience.[39]

For New Liberalism, moral forces were necessary in politics because a healthy state requires the participation of its constituent members. Unlike, say, Fabian socialism, New Liberalism insisted on the conscious participation of each individual in the pursuit of the common good, and the idealism of a Gladstone was salutary as a means of raising the tone of public life and awakening the social conscience of the people. (The degree to which the state might act coercively where such awakening did not occur is one of the more troubling aspects of New Liberal ideology.[40]) Quite apart from its high-minded concern with justice, New Liberalism also advanced a pragmatic argument for idealism in politics, maintaining that without ideals the *polis* is inert. This is not far from Ford's lament for the 'higher things', and the 'certain glow of humanitarian faith' without which Liberalism is ineffective. Although Ford might have been sceptical of the jargon of New Liberalism and its militant collectivism, this new incarnation of Liberalism nonetheless echoed his own concern about the decline of ideals in the public sphere.

We still read the *English Review* – and rightly so – because of the astonishing calibre of its literary roster, and especially for the future titans of an embryonic modernism who wrote there. If Ford had not been able to attract and select contributions from the rising generation of Pound, Lawrence, Lewis and Forster; if he had not been in a position to combine their names with those of late-Victorian luminaries like Hardy and James, protomodernist craftsmen like Conrad and, of course, himself, Edwardian doyens like Bennett, Galsworthy, Hudson and Wells, notable up-and-comers like Walter de la Mare and Edward Thomas, and the Russian trinity of Chekhov, Dostoevsky and Tolstoy in original translations; if he had not amassed this crop of literary talent, the *English Review* would not be the rich and fascinating source that it is. Recent scholarship, however, has reminded us of the social and political context in which this aesthetic achievement was embedded, and with which it was literally bound together in the fifteen numbers of Ford's *English Review*. While the review's political content – sometimes musty, sometimes topical – may not in itself command an enduring interest, close attention to the tropes and currents that traverse this content can help to situate the review more concretely in the complex public culture of its day, as well as yielding new perspectives on Ford's own political outlook. J. A. Hobson's essay on 'The Task of Realism' suggests that the *English Review* appealed to the period's nostalgic longing for holism, as opposed to the modern phenomena of specialization and the fragmentation of the public sphere. This may be why Hobson was attracted to periodicals like the *New Age* and the *English Review* which combined social commentary with aesthetic concerns. The New Liberal connection, moreover, suggests an interesting perspective on

Ford's own political writings. Ford's nostalgia for the politics of sentiment and ideals can easily be written off as whimsical or amateurish, but the corresponding New Liberal doctrine of ideals in public culture precludes such a dismissive attitude, qualifying the apparent eccentricity of Ford's beliefs by situating them in a context of comparable views. Perhaps the most urgent observation that can be gleaned from a close reading of the review's political content, however, is the extent to which a periodical is a polyphonic, if not a cacophonic artifact. The best approach to such a farrago is perhaps not as a coherent political intervention susceptible of classification, but rather as an archeological record of interrelated tropes and discourses, a microcosm of the complex public culture in which it takes part.

NOTES

1   Ralph Hermann Ruedy, for example, gives an excellent but necessarily synoptic overview of the review's political and social commentary. Ruedy, 'Ford Madox Ford and the *English Review*', PhD thesis, Duke University, 1976. Paul Peppis's interesting discussion is an example of a political reading of the review that focuses on Ford's editorials and the review's literary content rather than analysing its political essays. Peppis, *Literature, Politics, and the English Avant-Garde: Nation and Empire, 1901-1918*, Cambridge: Cambridge University Press, 2000.

2   An important figure in the movement, J. A. Hobson, later offered this reflection on the origin of its name: 'The term "New Liberalism" was adopted by [Herbert] Samuel and others as rightly descriptive of its aims. That "New" Liberalism differed from the old in that it envisaged more clearly the need for important economic reforms, aiming to give a positive significance to the "equality" which figured in the democratic triad of liberty, equality, fraternity.' *Confessions of an Economic Heretic*, London: George Allen & Unwin, 1938, p. 51.

3   Ann Barr Snitow, *Ford Madox Ford and the Voice of Uncertainty*, Baton Rouge: Louisiana State University Press, 1984, p. 236.

4   Ruedy, 'Ford Madox Ford and the *English Review*', p. 104; Frank MacShane, '*The English Review*', *South Atlantic Quarterly*, 60 (1961), 317. Eric Homberger, 'Ford's *English Review*: Englishness and Its Discontents', *Agenda* 27:4–28:1 (1989-1990), 61-6 (p. 64).

5   Michael Freeden offers 1886 as a tentative start date. *The New Liberalism: An Ideology of Social Reform*, Oxford: Clarendon, 1978, p. 2.

6   Freeden writes that 'The concern of liberals with problems of social reform was of course part of a general movement of progressive thought that had existed as an undercurrent in the first half of the nineteenth century and gradually swelled to become a dominant factor in social thought towards the end of the Victorian era'. *The New Liberalism*, p. 5.

7   L. T. Hobhouse, *Liberalism and Other Writings*, Cambridge: Cambridge University Press, 1994, p. 35. As Hobhouse acknowledges elsewhere in this monograph, his organicism closely resembles that of the Idealist philosopher T. H. Green, although Freeden questions the extent to Green was a direct influence on New Liberal ideology (*The New Liberalism*, pp. 16-17).

8   Hobhouse, *Liberalism*, p. 61.

9   Quoted in Freeden, *The New Liberalism*, p. 34.

10 Peppis, *Literature, Politics, and the English Avant-Garde*, p. 26.

11 *Ibid.*, p.29.

12 Freeden, *The New Liberalism*, p. 195.

13 On Hobhouse's antipathy for the Liberal Imperialists, see Stefan Collini, *Liberalism and Sociology: L. T. Hobhouse and Political Argument in England 1880-1914*, Cambridge: Cambridge University Press, 1979, pp. 83-4.

14 Peppis, *Literature, Politics, and the English Avant-Garde*, p. 26.

15 Freeden, *The New Liberalism*, p. 9.

16 *Ibid.*, p. 4. Hobson recalls the attendance of Nevinson and Brailsford in Hobson, *Confessions*, p. 82.

17 H. W. Nevinson, *Fire of Life*, London: James Nisbet, 1935, p. 214.

18 Nevinson published 'Notes on the Balkans, with a Table' in December 1908 and 'Women's Vote and Men' in November 1909; Brailsford published 'The Counter-Revolution in Turkey' in May 1909, '"The Hush in Europe"' in July 1909 and 'The Control of Foreign Affairs: A Proposal' in December 1909.

19 Freeden, *The New Liberalism*, p. 257. Hobson recalls Gooch's presence at the meetings in Hobson, *Confessions*, p. 95.

20 'The Task of Realism' (Oct. 1909) became 'The Task of Reconstruction' and 'The Extension of Liberalism' (Nov. 1909) became 'The Equality of Opportunity' in the book.

21 On the Soskice arrangement and the various other projects to finance the review see Arthur Mizener, *The Saddest Story: A Biography of Ford Madox Ford*, London: The Bodley Head, 1972 – henceforth 'Mizener'; pp. 186-8; and Max Saunders, *Ford Madox Ford: A Dual Life*, 2 vols, Oxford: Oxford University Press, 1996, vol. I, pp. 252, 293-4.

22 See Nora Tomlinson's chapter, '"An Old Man Mad About Writing" but Hopeless with Money: Ford Madox Ford and the Finances of the *English Review*' in this volume.

23 Ruedy, 'Ford Madox Ford and the *English Review*', p. 95.

24 Ford to Elsie Hueffer, no date [1909]; and Ford to Elsie Hueffer, June 1909: Ford Madox Ford Collection, Division of Rare and Manuscript Collections, Carl A. Kroch Library, Cornell University Library. Quoted with the kind permission of Cornell University, and Michael Schmidt. The undated letter was written while Ford was harassed with 'finding capital' for the review, which suggests a time-frame after or shortly before the money ran out in April 1909.

25 Ford to David Soskice, 8 June 1909, Division of Rare and Manuscript Collections, Carl A. Kroch Library. Quoted with the kind permission of Cornell University, and Michael Schmidt.

26 On *The Tribune*, where Hobhouse and Brailsford were among the chief writers, see Barry Hollingsworth, 'Benckendorff's 'Bête Noire': *The Tribune* and Russian Internal Affairs 1906-1908', in *Poetry, Prose and Public Opinion: Essays*

Presented in Memory of Dr. N. E. Andreyev, ed. William Harrison and Avril Pyman, Avebury: Aldershot, 1987.

27 David Soskice to Ford, 13 August 1909, Ford Archive, Cornell University Library.

28 Ford, 'The Critical Attitude: Women's Suffrage – the Circulating Libraries – the Drama – Fine Arts, Etc.', *ER* IV (Jan. 1910), 333. This allusion is discussed below.

29 Mark S. Morrisson, *The Public Face of Modernism: Little Magazines, Audiences, and Reception, 1905-1920*, Madison: University of Wisconsin Press, 2001, p. 48.

30 Ford, *Parade's End*, New York: Penguin Books, 2001, p. 79.

31 *Ancient Lights*, London: Chapman & Hall, 1911.

32 Patrick Joyce argues that the tone of nineteenth-century Liberalism was an essential element of its political identity. Gladstone's oratory, he writes, 'involved feeling the faith, but also feeling reason as itself a form of faith: [...] the tenets of Gladstonian Liberalism involved the rationality of free and informed public discussion, and this was expressed in the serious and didactic nature of Liberal rhetoric'. Patrick Joyce, *Democratic Subjects: The Self and the Social in Nineteenth-Century England*, Cambridge: Cambridge University Press, 1994, p. 100.

33 Robert Green, *Ford Madox Ford: Prose and Politics*, Cambridge: Cambridge University Press, 1981, p. 27; Andrzej Gasiorek, 'The Politics of Cultural Nostalgia: History and Tradition in Ford's *Parade's End*', *Literature and History,* 11: 2 (2002).

34 H. N. Brailsford, 'Nevinson, Henry Woodd (1856–1941)', rev. Sinéad Agnew, *Oxford Dictionary of National Biography*, Oxford University Press, 2004; online edn, Oct 2009 [http://www.oxforddnb.com/view/article/35206, accessed 2 Dec 2009]. Nevinson and Brailsford were well-known supporters of women's suffrage, and were also both married to suffragists. Jane Brailsford contributed a story to the *English Review* in September 1909 under her maiden name of Malloch.

35 Nevinson, *Fire of Life*, p. 241.

36 H. N. Brailsford, 'The Life-Work of J. A. Hobson', in *L. T. Hobhouse Memorial Trust Lectures*, London: 1947, p. 11.

37 L. T. Hobhouse, 'The Career of Fabianism' (1907), quoted in Collini, *Liberalism and Sociology*, p. 93.

38 Hobhouse, *Liberalism*, p. 24.

39 *Ibid.*, p.51.

40 For a discussion of some potentially illiberal implications of L. T. Hobhouse's social vision, see Collini, *Liberalism and Sociology*, pp. 124-6, 139.

THE *TRANSATLANTIC REVIEW* (1924)

Stephen Rogers

The early days of the *Transatlantic Review*, before it became apparent that by no conceivable chance could it be made to pay, were great fun.[1]

Suzanne W. Churchill and Adam McKible have argued: 'The story of modernism in magazines is a tale of complex entanglements between high art and intellectual thought, mass culture, and the commercial marketplace.'[2] In this chapter I attempt to disentangle some of these threads in relation to the history of the *transatlantic review*. Unfortunately, much of the material that would aid a comprehensive study of the *transatlantic* was lost in a fire in 1929 at the offices of Duckworth, the English publisher. Subsequently, further damage was done to whatever records survived by enemy action in 1942 and by another fire in 1953.[3]

Ford Madox Ford's second attempt to edit a magazine resulted, of course, in the *transatlantic review*; a venture that is usually supposed to have not quite matched his success with the *English Review*. The origins of the magazine are not entirely clear, but it seems that Ford responded to a suggestion of his brother, Oliver Madox Hueffer, who was then living in Paris.[4] In 1923 Ford had praised Harold Monro's *Chapbook* (he was then living in Monro's house in the South of France), so he may already have been thinking of editing a magazine again. By the early twenties the idea of the modernist magazine had received a boost by the arrival in Europe of the 'Lost Generation' writers, eager to experience life and to experiment with literature. Titles such as *Gargoyle* (1921-2), edited by Arthur Moss, *Secession* (1922-4), edited by Gorham Munson and Matthew Josephson, and *Broom* (1921-4), edited by Harold Loeb, had begun to appear; and in many ways these publications looked back to the pioneer work done by Ford in producing the *English Review*. Ezra Pound seems to have encouraged the new project from the outset. However, it is unlikely that anything would have resulted if it had not been for the financial encouragement provided by John Quinn, the American lawyer and patron of the arts. Ford had some money to

invest, having recently sold his former Sussex home, Cooper's
Cottage. These beginnings, though providing the encouragement
necessity to turn an idea into a reality, also contained some of the
reasons for the project's downfall, to which I will return in more
detail. Apart from the issue for August 1924, which was edited by
Ernest Hemingway, Ford was responsible for each issue. The magazine ran for twelve monthly numbers – Volume I, 1-6 (Jan.-June,
1924) and Volume II, 1-6 (July-Dec. 1924). The editorial offices were
based at 29 Quai d'Anjou, on the Ile Saint-Louis in Paris. Copies were
of Quarto size, and originally bound with blue and white covers,
which was later replaced by blue and buff covers in an attempt to
avoid the fact that the early numbers had quickly dirtied, making them
difficult to sell as they appeared to be old issues. Each number was a
fairly bulky 120 pages, including adverts. The price in Paris of a
single issue was 7, 5 francs; although annual subscriptions of 75
francs were encouraged. The Paris based Transatlantic Review Company worked in association with the London publishing house of
Duckworth and Co. and with Thomas Seltzer in New York.

Money was always a problem, and ultimately was the cause of
the magazine's failure. Cyril Connolly, who had some practical knowledge of the problems faced by editors, observed that:

> Magazines require two animators: an editor and a backer (or angel) [....] The
> life of a little magazine depends on three things: the resources of its angel, the
> talents of its editor and the relationship between them. Where there are angels
> there are wrangles, where there are editors there are creditors [...] it is as
> simple as that. With a good angel and wise editor, contributions flow in and
> ultimately the public is formed for them: they shape the times which they
> reflect. Most little magazines fail because they cannot wait, the backer loses
> too much money or the editor makes too many mistakes.[5]

Ford was both a backer and editor, having about £400 from the sale of
the Sussex cottage. Pound persuaded John Quinn to provide $2000,
which was supplemented by Ford's £400 plus an extra £35, which
appears to have been Stella Bowen's contribution. She also seems to
have decided that the project was worth investing in and drew upon
some capital she had in Australia. As Alan Judd records, she 'could
not help seeing how lovely it would be for him if he could have his
review'.[6] Quinn's involvement was crucial; however, as Timothy
Materer has indicated, the relationship between Quinn and Pound had
been in decline, with Quinn both unwell and annoyed that Pound had

not taken his advice in relation to the prosecution of the *Little Review* for obscenity, which he felt took the campaign for artistic liberty naïvely too far by openly trying to flout the obscenity law. Even though things had been patched up, Quinn had become 'less interested in avant-garde art', though on his visits to Paris in 1921 and 1923, he had visited the studios of painters he supported, including Braque and Picasso.[7] Nonetheless Quinn was persuaded to support the *transatlantic* and even installed his companion, Jeanne Foster, an actress and poet, as New York editor. Quinn's illness and death were significant factors in the magazine's eventual failure, but so too was Quinn's suspicion of Americans in Paris. Quinn's last communication with Pound was through the medium of Foster, to whom he wrote on 23 August 1924: 'I don't think he [Pound] ought to stay in Paris. He is too kind-hearted. Vagrant Americans impose on his kindness'.[8] Quinn might well have said as much of Ford. It was probably views like this that led Ford to comment to Hemingway that whilst no American could be a gentleman, Quinn was.[9]

    The editorial office, measuring a meagre 15 feet by 6 feet, at 29 Quai d'Anjou, was in fact located up some stairs at the back of the shop that William Bird used to run his Three Mountains Press. Pound provided a secretary called Marjorie Reid, and two sub-editors – the then unknown Basil Bunting and a White Russian, who soon disappeared with some proofs. There were initially some rather confused negotiations between the financial backers and Ford, who had markedly different sets of objectives. The sticking point was over the inclusion of work by James Joyce. As has already been mentioned, the *Little Review* had been suppressed and had to defend itself in court in the United States over the inclusion of sequences which were to become part of *Ulysses*, which in itself of course was banned from the country until 1936. Ford is credited by Joyce with making a stand about the inclusion of Joyce's work: 'Mr. Hueffer has been made editor of a new Paris Review. The editorship was offered by a financial group on condition that nothing of mine was published in it. Mr. Hueffer then declined it. Finally the group gave in.'[10] Bernard Poli suggests that these backers were contemplating a very different kind of magazine incorporating 'horse racing and a touch of salacious literature'[11] and had entertained the idea of Frank Harris as editor. Harris was in severe financial trouble, having in 1922 left the editorship of the New York-based *Pearson's Magazine*, which had pioneered the association of literary content and the promotion of consumer culture, and he was finding it difficult to publish his autobiographical *My Life and Loves* because of its sexually explicit content – indeed copies of this publication were seized by the French police in 1923. If the backers were worried about the inclusion of Joyce's work, they might equally have been concerned that Harris' name as editor might have brought them into conflict with the authorities. Though there remains the suspicion that as long as the magazine was not actually suppressed then the suggestion of some furtive sexual content might be good publicity. However, these mystery backers soon withdrew their interest from the project. Apart from 120 francs which had been paid to Ford in advance to cover salaries, no money had been forthcoming; and no formal agreement reached.[12]

The agreement with the original backers had been to call the magazine the 'Paris Review'. However, the change of name to the *transatlantic review* led to the obtaining of valuable advertising by the *Compagnie Transatlantique* shipping line.[13] It is worth noting that the transatlantic crossing was an extremely prestigious and profitable business in the 1920s. In 1924, the company's most famous ship, the *S. S. France*, was converted to be an all first-class ship. The *S. S. Paris* – the line's flagship until the launch of the *S. S. Normandie* in 1935 – had been launched in 1921, and was, a showcase for French culture to rich Americans eager to sample European sophistication. Undoubtedly, the *transatlantic review* tried to capture the economic advantages of this moment, with its appeal to the cultural aspirations of this new kind of traveller.

The first issue of the magazine opened in a manner that might be said to prefigure its precarious financial situation. The first segment under the title 'The Transatlantic Review Advertisements: Paris Section' was vacant except for the simple phrase, 'To let'. This was balanced by the declaration that 'the transatlantic review contains and will contain no unpaid advertisements except for exchanges with other reviews or publishers'.[14] It also immediately becomes apparent that with its great reliance on work in the English language, and with its first legitimate advert entitled 'Tours in France' provided by the American Express Travel Department, that the review was not aimed at a French audience. Indeed, it seems likely that a cultivated and affluent American audience was being targeted. A point suggested by the character of M. de la Penthièvre in Ford's later novel, *Vive Le Roy* (1936), tends to back this up: 'You will be going to the American Express Company, of course [....] All Americans go to the American

Express Company the first morning they are in Paris'.[15] Later travel adverts were perhaps more closely associated with the French perspective, feeding off the association with French North African colonies, but with an eye on rich American customers, Cie Générale Transatlantique advertising 'Sunny North Africa /Morocco/ Algeria/ Tunisia/ A delightful trip to the Garden of Allah!'[16] Other adverts included those for 'The Corner Bookshop', W. H. Smith & Son, 248 Rue de Rivoli, Paris, which was described as selling American and English magazines and newspapers, as well as providing English Tea Rooms.[17] This would seem to have been an early and enterprising attempt to diversify the role of the bookshop and seems to imply a conscious response to the contemporary success achieved by Lyons. There was, then, a general association made between a content of avant-garde literature and art, and an international and cosmopolitan readership (though with a strongly American bias), suggestive of a leisured life-style of latter-day grand tourists.

Ford reacted forcefully in defence of the role of the *transatlantic review*, suggesting that 'we – the writer and his collaborators – are here to put before the world a picture of the world's real mental activities which are centred in the world's imaginative arts' (*TRev* I [Apr. 1924] 196). It is a definition that locates Ford's position as editor as being in opposition to 'solemnised and portentous journalism' with its emphasis on 'semi-official utterances' on the topics of the day, ranging from political economy to international football. Instead Ford offered his near manifesto:

> Now we are a review – we survey, report and offer documents in support of such views as we presume to hold. We have a definite policy and carry it out with industry and determination. These factors constitute a Review, having actuality and a bearing on the life of the day. A miscellany is a notebook, a magazine a periodical intent on giving pleasure – a periodical of escape from the world. That we are not: we bring the world – the most important side of the world – directly to your doors. (196)

Ford noted that in the first number of the *Cornhill* – along with the serialization of Trollope's *Framley Parsonage* - was an advert for Ford's Eureka Shirts. This circumstance led him to speculate 'if Thackeray in his padded editorial throne realized what a milestone in the history of civilization his advertising pages set up?' and concluded that, 'it is pretty safe to say that the influence of advertising on Literature is practically to stifle all comment on such good work as has not got a considerable advertising capital to back it' (*TRev* I [May 1924) 360). The precarious funding of the *transatlantic* meant that it could not do without advertising, and Ford's comments seem to be a protest against the economic conditions that hamper art and which would have a direct effect on his periodical.

For Ford the magazine was to provide support for the emergent wave of writers then congregating in Paris, which he referred to as: 'the modern more-or-less-Movement for which we more or less stand' (*TRev* I [Apr. 1924] 209). This sentence reveals the extent perhaps that Ford was wary of producing a coterie magazine. Indeed, he could be blamed for printing praise of those outside this grouping of 'moderns' if his purpose had solely been to produce a magazine with which to promote the avant-garde. However, Ford's notion of editor was, as it had been with the *English Review*, based on getting into print that which he regarded as the best of its time whether or not that work was experimental. The magazine is usually celebrated for publishing Ezra Pound, Gertrude Stein, Ernest Hemingway and James Joyce. Actually there were tensions; and the magazine 'dramatized the generational struggle between the older group Ford had been part of and the newer one he attempted to join. It is the story in miniature of the aggressive American victory on the literary and cultural battlefield of post-war Europe.'[18] Ford's stated intention had been of 'widening the field in which the younger writers of the day can find publication, the second that of introducing into international politics a note more genial than that which almost universally prevails' (Poli 37). Essentially for Ford this involved communication between peoples through the medium of literature.

Much has been made of the three literatures – British, American and French; but in reality Paris only provided a base, a neutral territory where British and American could meet on more or less equal terms. Ford describes this situation in the manifesto: 'There is no British Literature, there is no American Literature: there is English Literature which embraces alike Mark Twain and Thomas Hardy with the figure of Henry James to bracket them' (Poli 37). Such a formulation, of course, excludes French literature. Indeed, French language texts were in the minority in the *transatlantic*. The range of material that was published in the magazine was wide, embracing the avant-garde work of Stein, Joyce, George Antheil, Ezra Pound, Ernest Hemingway, H. D., Mary Butts, Djuna Barnes, the Baroness Elsa von Freytag-Loringhoven, Dorothy Richardson, John Dos Passos, William

Carlos Williams and Joseph Conrad. In French, work by Paul Valéry, Jean Cassou, René Crevel, also appeared. But Ford was not solely committed to providing an exclusive platform for the avant-garde, and work by Catherine Wells (Mrs. H. G. Wells), Havelock Ellis, A. E. Coppard and Ethel Colburn Mayne also found a place. Ford classifies these contributors in a different way, compiling lists in which authors are listed as being either 'well-known' or as 'belonging to the most modern schools of to-day' (*TRev* II [Oct. 1924] xiii]. Each issue advised that 'The editor receives contributors and friends at the Paris office on Thursday afternoons from 4 to 6.'[19] Ford's role seems to have been conceived as a paternal, even grandfatherly figure, who would, in the manner of the *English Review*, preside over the emergence of new talent, in effect young American talent. Ford's stance was to represent the magazine's politics: 'The politics will be those of its editor who has no party leanings save toward those of a Tory kind so fantastically old fashioned as to see no salvation save in the feudal system as practiced in the fourteenth century – or in such Communism as may prevail a thousand years hence' (Poli 38).

Eugene Jolas and Elliot Paul (the editors of *transition*) later praised the *transatlantic review* as one of the magazines that had done most to promote the work of the new American writers that emerged in the 1920s:

> Thanks to the *Little Review, Broom, Secession, The Transatlantic Review, This Quarter*, and in earlier days to the *Dial*, the work of such writers as Gertrude Stein, Sherwood Anderson, Ezra Pound, Ernest Hemingway, William Carlos Williams, E. E. Cummings, Ben Hecht, Malcolm Cowley, Hart Crane, Kay Boyle, Emmanuel Carnevali, Yvor Winters, Elsa von Freytag-Loringhoven, Robert McAlmon, Djuna Barnes, Matthew Josephson and others was made known to a more or less limited company.[20]

These were the American writers credited with the will to experiment. However, if the *transatlantic review* can be credited with a role in promoting these emerging American writers, it is desirable that we know something of the magazine's circulation. Indeed, it is symptomatic of one of the problems faced by the *transatlantic* that this praise came from the coterie of Left Bank Americans who constantly threatened to overturn Ford's venture.[21] Ford's conception of the magazine was based on the model that had served him well, critically, if not financially, with the *English Review*. His idea was for a critical review that would combine the work of the most promising newcomers with more established figures, as we have seen. In essence this was not only a sound idea in terms of the magazine's internal structure, but the formula of combining the known with the unknown should have ensured that a broadly-based readership was created that would secure the magazine's success. Perhaps, if stable funds had been available at the outset, it might have been possible for the magazine to offer a consistent editorial approach. As it was, Ford's position was always threatened, and when he was away in the United States, Hemingway and his American friends turned the magazine into one that reflected their narrower concerns.

It should not be imagined that this westward gaze was established wholly outside of Ford's conception for the *transatlantic*. Indeed, as Ford wrote in the retrospective Preface to *Transatlantic Stories* (1926), and in a language that hints at the following development of his notion of geographically and historically shaped maps of essential cultural production that he links with 'Middle Westishness':

> the evolution of races, cities or even civilisations brought about by the crowding out of Far, Wild or Pioneer Wests. This happens politically, as is exemplified by the British occupation of India or the French eastern colonies; it happens financially as when the great banks, British or North American, having nothing else to do with their plethora of money, exploit for their own purposes the Middle, the Near or the Far East; it happens when we Anglo-Saxons, finding the struggle for life too much for us at home, settle or cheapness, convenience and rational life, in France – to the East of our native lands. We are here as an exemplification of the fact. We are all Middle Westerners.[22]

It might with justness be argued that this comment represents Ford at his most pragmatic, adjusting his position to account for changes in cultural production that he himself could not influence. In this preface Ford referred to the role of the *transatlantic* as an experiment, an attempt, in as scientifically respectable a manner as possible, to trawl in an unbiased way for the most up-to-date manifestations of literature. In part this was seen to be an element of post-war reconstruction, so the interest was in those new shoots emerging from the world ravaged by war. It is interesting to note that Ford distances himself a little from this objective by declaring that the notion was one stimulated by anonymous 'promoters'. What he did find was 'a very considerable and extended movement' with 'the gift of telling the real thing in life from the pinchbeck'. It was a reaction to what he saw, or saw retrospectively, as 'before the war too much hypocritical idealism, too much moral gasconading, too much posturing in letters. And too much of it has survived'.[23] Was this sentence added as an after-thought? He records the opinions of a young American, who Ford suggests, shares the American uncertainty about how much Ford was in earnest if he truly wanted his magazine to sell:

> 'You should write about how it feels to be an English editor with all American contributors. That is what America wants. That will make your book sell in America. America is interested in …'
> 'But,' I said, 'our contributors were French and English as well as American and I have the European publishers to consider.'
> He said – with an enormous gravity, weighing every word:
> 'France is … *fichu*. England is *fichu*…. Your English and French contributors were … *fichus*…. Your English publisher is … *fichu*. … What America wants is to hear your experiences as an English editor with all American contributors….'
> Well, I have given America what, according to this gentleman, she wants…. I wonder whether she will know whether I have been really in earnest or no.[24]

The desire of these young Americans was to reject the past, and accept a commercial present, at least at home in America. Ford was perceptive to appreciate and acknowledge, whether in earnest or not, that this was an indication of the global mind-set. It was a united 'hatred of knowledge: a definite shuddering at the idea of the pre-war knowledges that led, all inevitably, to the late war'. A world in which Ford's 'historic contemplations and comparisons' seemed to be made redundant by the 'desire to forget the standards of pomps and parades that used to sway us'.[25] Ford claimed that he could accept such a situation, though he made it clear that he could not partake of such a world-view having been brought up in different cultural conditions, 'lumbered up by all the bric-a-brac of monumental ideals that we used to have'.[26]

The case of the *English Review*, under the editorship of Austin Harrison in the early 1920s, was perhaps illustrative of the contemporary dilemma facing editors. Aleister Crowley records that he attempted to put pressure on Harrison to promote the magazine in America. The plan apparently got as far as eliciting the support of influential American editors, who 'being editors of periodicals whose combined circulation must be in the millions' were to introduce the *English Review* to an American audience. Crowley claims that 'H. L. Mencken himself came to see us, and he formulated a plan of action which would have certainly succeeded and put Harrison's circulation up to

thirty thousand at the lowest estimate within a few months'.[27] The plan
would have meant that two editions of the magazine would have been
produced, the 'bulk of the contents was to be identical, but a proportion to cover matters of local interest in the respective countries'.[28] The
project came to nothing, with Harrison putting too high a price on an
agreement with Otto Kahn, who was to finance the project by
amalgamating the *English Review* with his ailing *Forum*. The result
was that the magazine continued its circulation's steady decline,
having, as Crowley maintained, 'lost interest for the educated classes
whose taste it was designed to please'.[29] Apart from Crowley's
obvious need to denigrate a publication that had for a brief period
seemed likely to offer him the opportunity to make some money at a
time of financial need, there remains sufficient evidence to suggest
that his criticism was fair. Moreover, the criticism touches upon the
difficulty of maintaining interest in a periodical publication against an
unpredictable intellectual and economic background. Crowley thought
the way forward was to pander to the taste and interest of students of
the occult, a group that he felt Harrison underestimated as an audience
for such a magazine. In relation to the *transatlantic*, we may wonder
to what extent Ford understood his audience. Indeed this touches upon
the difficult question of whom a magazine is designed to please. It has
been taken that modernist little magazines were seen as productions
meant only to satisfy a small group of writers and/or artists, and a
number of their friends and associates. On the other hand, commercially run magazines were run on the basis of appealing to the widest
audience possible.

     The *transatlantic* had a circulation of about 5000 copies per
issue, which meant that it performed rather better than other modernist
magazines of the period such as the *Little Review* (circa 2000
subscribers) and *transition*, of which 'No more than 4,000 copies of
any issue were ever printed and paid subscriptions never exceeded
1,000.'[30] The *transatlantic review*'s relatively wide circulation, though
tiny compared with that of mass-market magazines such as *Vanity
Fair* (96,500), was aided by the fact that it was run on more commercial lines than many other little magazines; for instance it was able to
pay contributors, though this was no doubt in part due to the financial
assistance provided by John Quinn. However, it should be remembered that, like most other similar magazines, many copies remained
unsold, or were given away. It would have been understood that
contributors and other interested parties could promote the magazine

and so to a degree these unsold copies were considered as loss-leaders. Whether or not, or how much, the magazine was able to exploit such marketing strategies as making copies deliberately scarce and collectable is open to conjecture. The presence of Joyce and Stein, at least, would certainly have enhanced the magazine's collectability.

The mid-twenties were not easy times to launch a magazine; there were numerous alternatives competing for what must have been a very small and specialized market. As a literary review, the *transatlantic* was a space in which experimental work could be found along with broader cultural discussion; as Mark Morrisson and Jack Selzer have pointed out: 'the value of understanding the connection between avant-gardism and the larger culture that produced it was not lost on Ford'.[31] Such an understanding goes back to the pre-war period of the *English Review*. The *transatlantic review* was not one of those 'little magazines' that could afford to publish without thought to the necessities of commerce. Indeed the model provided by hybrid periodicals, with a mixture of review and original contributions, like the *Mercure de France*, the *Revue des deux mondes* and the *Nouvelle revue française* had proved that such a format could be successful.[32]

NOTES

1 Stella Bowen, *Drawn from Life*, London: Collins, 1941, p. 116
2 Suzanne W. Churchill and Adam McKible, 'Modernism in Magazines', *The Oxford Handbook of Modernisms*, ed. Peter Brooker, Andrzej Gasiorek, Deborah Parsons & Andrew Thacker, Oxford: Oxford University Press, forthcoming 2010.
3 See Senate House Library, University of London, website @ http://www.aim25.ac.uk/cats/14/1758.htm (consulted 19/10/09). Papers of Gerald Duckworth & Co.
4 According to Joseph Wiesenfarth, 'Ever possessed by projects that needed doing, Oliver conceived the idea for *the transatlantic review* ...'. 'The Genius and the Donkey: The Brothers Hueffer at Home and Abroad', *Ford Madox Ford's Literary Contacts*, ed. Paul Skinner, Amsterdam: Rodopi, 2007, p. 129.
5 Cyril Connolly, 'Fifty Years of Little Magazines', *Art and Literature,* I (March, 1964), 108-9.
6 Alan Judd, *Ford Madox Ford*, London: Collins, 1990, p. 345.
7 Timothy Materer (ed.), *The Selected Letters of Ezra Pound to John Quinn, 1915-1924*, Durham, NC and London: Duke University Press, 1991, p. 10.
8 *Ibid.*, p. 175.
9 Ernest Hemingway, *A Moveable Feast*, New York: Scribner's, 1964, p. 87.

10 *Letters of James Joyce*, ed. Stuart Gilbert, London: Faber and Faber, 1957, p. 204.
11 Bernard J. Poli, *Ford Madox Ford and the 'Transatlantic Review'*, Syracuse, NY: Syracuse University Press, 1967 – henceforth 'Poli'; p. 21.
12 *Ibid.*
13 See Max Saunders, *Ford Madox Ford: A Dual Life*, 2 vols, Oxford: Oxford University Press, 1996, II, p. 137.
14 *TRev* I (Jan. 1924), unpaged.
15 Ford, *Vive Le Roy*, Philadelphia: J. B. Lippincott, 1936, p. 8.
16 *TRev* I (Apr. 1924), III.
17 *Ibid.*, I.
18 Warren Henderson, 'The Transatlantic Review', Alvin Sullivan (ed.), *British Literary Magazines: The Modern Age, 1914-1984*, Westport, CT: Greenwood Press, 1986, p. 463.
19 For example, see *TRev* II (Nov. 1924), unpaged.
20 Eugene Jolas and Elliot Paul, 'A Review', *transition*, no. 12 (March, 1928), 140.
21 The idea of the coterie was self-consciously part of the dynamic of modernism. This was reflected in the title of the British magazine, *Coterie* (1919-21), and later by *New Coterie* (1925-7).
22 Ford, *Transatlantic Stories, selected from The Transatlantic Review*, London: Duckworth, 1926, pp. ix-x.
23 *Ibid.*, p. xxix. Robert Graves developed a similar theme about continued disingenuousness in the post-war period in his play, *But It Still Goes On* (1931).
24 *Ibid.*, pp. xxvii-xxviii.
25 *Ibid.*, p. xxx.
26 *Ibid.*, p. xxxi.
27 Aleister Crowley, *The Confessions of Aleister Crowley: An Autohagiography*, edited by John Symonds and Kenneth Grant, London: Routledge & Kegan Paul, 1979, p. 894.
28 *Ibid.*
29 *Ibid.*, p. 893.
30 Dougald McMillan, *'Transition': The History of a Literary Era, 1927-1938*, New York: George Braziller, 1975, p. 23.
31 Mark S. Morrisson and Jack Selzer, eds, '*Tambour*: A Snapshot of Modernism at the Crossroads', Harold J. Salemson, ed., *Tambour*, Volumes 1-8, Madison, Wisconsin: The University of Wisconsin Press, 2002, p. 19.
32 See Morrisson and Selzer, *ibid.*, pp. 12-13.

EDITING THE *TRANSATLANTIC REVIEW*: LITERARY MAGAZINES AND THE PUBLIC SPHERE

Andrzej Gasiorek

For Continuity

Ford Madox Ford had a talent for getting himself into awkward spots of one kind or another. His middle name could have been 'Muddle' rather than 'Madox'. He also had a talent for making literary capital out of his difficulties by transmuting them through writing, often providing several versions of the same events. Ford's editorship of the *transatlantic review*, the literary magazine that ran for twelve issues in 1924, is a case in point. Ford fell into the job by happenstance. He bumped into his brother on the streets of Paris and was promptly asked by him to edit a review for which backing had already been secured. After numerous difficulties with personnel, finances, and organisation had been resolved, the first issue appeared in January 1924. The *transatlantic* began its topsy-turvy career in an atmosphere of 'purposeful confusion', as Douglas Goldring put it.[1] It was to carry on that way. Ford's reminiscences reveal that the review continued to exist amidst confusion throughout its short life before it gradually 'staggered on its way towards death'.[2]

The *transatlantic review* didn't last long, but it occupies an important place in the history of the post-war 'little magazines' and literary reviews that promoted contacts between Europe and America, most notably the *Little Review*, *Broom*, *Secession*, the *Criterion*, *This Quarter*, and *transition*. Ford's aims in editing the *transatlantic* were several: to bring together in one journal contemporary writing from various aesthetic traditions and national backgrounds; to encourage communication between writers and artists from different societies in order to unite them 'in some sort of common activity'; to contribute to the cultural reconstruction of post-war Europe; to publish the most interesting writing of the day; and to establish continuities between pre- and post-war literature and art, in keeping with his claim that his

real country was not England but 'that invisible one that is known as
the kingdom of letters' (*IWN* 186, 248).

Prior to the publication of the first number of the *transatlantic
review*, Ford issued a prospectus. It indicates that there was a clear
continuity between his aims in this second foray into editing and his
earlier aspirations for the *English Review*. Ford's passion for conscious literary artistry and for civic awareness remained undimmed.
His new literary magazine had only two goals; one was 'purely
literary', while the other was 'disinterestedly social'. He described
these goals as follows: 'The first is that of widening the field in which
the younger writers of the day can find publication, the second that of
introducing into international politics a note more genial than that
which almost universally prevails. The first conduces to the second in
that the best ambassadors, the only nonsecret diplomatists between
nations are the books and the arts of nations'.[3]

Paris had been chosen as the review's headquarters, Ford
claimed, since it was the only possible 'centre' for a journal aiming 'to
spread comprehension between the three nations', partly because so
many aspiring writers gravitated towards it, and partly because 'it is
only in France that you will find an equal glory accorded to all writers
from Racine back to Villon' (Poli 39-40). The city was also the site
par excellence of cultural exchange. Ford, in short, saw Paris as the
only possible location from which he could launch a review that
would bring about artistic renewal not by breaking with a European
literary heritage but by building on it.

In practice, however, the *transatlantic review* didn't pursue
these laudable aims as decisively as Ford's circular suggested it would
do. Various reasons can be adduced to account for this: the exigencies
of publishing a monthly journal, which may struggle to find good
copy and has to deal with unreliable contributors; Ford's desire to
publish writing that he personally valued, irrespective of the 'school'
or 'tendency' it represented; the tension between Ford and his co-
editor Ernest Hemingway over the direction the *transatlantic* should
take, specifically whether it should aggressively promote American
literature rather than various kinds of writing, and whether it should
aim for a wide readership by publishing a broad range of work or cater
to a small coterie by concentrating on exclusively 'modern' texts;
finally, Ford's belief in the importance of the literature of the past,
which led him to publish work that a younger generation often
considered to be irrelevant to their concerns. In his fine study of the

review, Bernard J. Poli observes that this lack of clarity about editorial aims was visible from the outset. He suggests that most readers of the *transatlantic* would have been 'puzzled about the literary objectives of the review: in what sense would it be "transatlantic"? What was the basis for a Franco-Anglo-American literary brotherhood?' (Poli 51).

These questions go to the heart of the *transatlantic review*'s difficulties. In truth, there was no clear-cut basis for confraternal relations between the three countries shortly after the First World War, especially when we consider that such iconoclastic, anti-traditional movements as Dada and Surrealism were emerging at this time. Ford was passionate about French literature, but he was primarily interested in a tradition of conscious artistry whose roots lay in the nineteenth century. He was not drawn to the 'radical' experiments of Dada and Surrealism that were beginning to receive so much attention in the early 1920s and which appeared only sporadically in the *transatlantic review*. Ford was receptive to literary innovation and eager to advance the cause of modernist and avant-garde writing, but he was also looking for ways to reinvigorate the literature of the present by connecting it with the writing of the past. To many of those associated with the *transatlantic* (and certainly to those involved with Dada and Surrealism) this was an unsustainable position. Paris Dada and the Surrealism that emerged from it were in different ways hostile to the literature of the past and saw their work as a break with it, while significant emerging American writers were either developing a modern nativist literature that rejected European predecessors or writing fictions that explored the nature and boundaries of language. None of these groups could in practice escape all influence, but that was scarcely the point, which was that they sought to liberate themselves from precursors in the name of new ways of evoking human experience. Ford, in contrast, remained wedded to the belief that – however 'modernist' they were – contemporary writers could still learn from earlier writers and literary traditions.

In retrospect, this difference in attitudes is visible in the views of Hemingway and Ford. It might fairly be said that the two men didn't so much collaborate on the *transatlantic review* as fight over it. Egged on by Pound, who was irked by what he perceived as Ford's editorial timidity, Hemingway sought both to radicalise the *transatlantic* by publishing overtly experimental work (most notably Gertrude Stein's *The Making of Americans* and Elsa von Freytag-Loringhoven's poetry) and to promote American writers above all others.

Ford, on the other hand, believed that the review should support 'any work of any type that is good of its type'. He insisted that while the *transatlantic* was sympathetic to 'newer sincerities', it had not been set up to proselytise on behalf of particular movements. The review was 'not a critical organ, our main purpose being to present the reader with works of art. With works of art of sincerity and freshness of method. To that we subordinate anything else' (*TRev* II [Nov. 1924] 549-50).

For Pound and Hemingway, this approach felt like a compromise that weakened the magazine. Hemingway wrote to Pound that Ford 'ought to be encouraged, but Jesus Christ. It is like some guy in search of a good money maker digging up Jim Jeffries at the present time as a possible heavy weight contender [. . .] anything Ford will take and publish can be took and published in Century Harpers etc, except Tzara and such shit in French. That's the hell of it.'[4] This diatribe points to another issue that bedevilled the *transatlantic* during its one-year existence. What, exactly, was its attitude to experimental writing? How interested, really, was it in French writers and Europeans (such as Tzara) who wrote in French? Did it aim to facilitate a productive interaction between European and American literature or did it wish to act as a showcase for writers whose work the two editors happened to like?

There was relatively little French writing in the *transatlantic*, and it is generally agreed that the review had more impact in England and America than in France, where it was virtually ignored. There was no sustained engagement with Paris Dada and French Surrealism in its pages, though it did publish such writers as Jean Cocteau, Georges Pillement, Philippe Soupault, and Tzara. But Hemingway was contemptuous of such 'shit in French', as we have seen. In May 1924 he announced that Dada was dead. In July he made fun of Cocteau's and Tzara's knowledge of English, parodied Dada 'nonsense', and, with heavy irony, asserted the superiority of its American variant: 'how very much better dadas the American dadas, who do not know they are dadas, unless, of course, Mr Seldes has told them, are than the French and Roumanians who know it so well' (*TRev* II [July 1924] 103). When Hemingway published Elsa von Freytag-Loringhoven's Dada-inspired poetry, he did so to score off Ford, who dismissed her writing and tried to exclude it from the review. Ford, in turn, admired individual works by some French writers, such as Soupault's *A La Dérive*, for example, but never showed any interest in Surrealism's and Dada's search for the unconscious through experiments in automatic writing, their passion for the aleatory, and their scepticism about the category of the aesthetic.[5]

Why was there so little interest in Dada and Surrealism at the *transatlantic review*? Poli simply observes that Ford had 'no particular sympathy for the noisy members of that group' (Poli 74), which is correct but is something of an understatement.[6] Ford was a great supporter of experimental literature. He wrote that his sympathies were 'altogether with revolutionary work and with no other' and that he 'would rather read work of Miss Stein or Mr. Joyce or look at the work of Picasso himself than consider the work of a gentleman who wrote like Thackeray or drew like Apelles' (*IWN* 162). But neither Dada nor Surrealism met with his criteria for what constituted significant literary work. Why was this? I would suggest that entirely different conceptions of how European culture should be regenerated after the First World War were at stake here. The French literature Ford admired and sought to defend was being cast to one side by Dada and Surrealism. These iconoclastic movements were threatening to destroy the arts in which Ford so passionately believed. Three issues are salient in this context: Ford's stress on the importance of maintaining continuity with the past; his commitment to the aesthetic as a category; and his conviction that imaginative writing was a key component of a properly functioning public sphere. To understand why Dada and Surrealism might have been seen by Ford as hostile to the values he upheld – and thus why they did not feature prominently in the *transatlantic review* – we need to turn to his earlier editorship of the *English Review* and then to consider a different magazine: the *Little Review*.

The *English Review* and the Civil Sphere
When he was making preparations for the publication of the *transatlantic review*, Ford wrote to his former assistant Douglas Goldring. 'Alas', he observed of this second attempt to run a literary magazine, the '*Transatlantic Review* will be the old *English Review* all over again'.[7] Ford's letters to other former collaborators and possible future contributors in late 1923 sound the same note: the new review was to continue the project launched in pre-war years.[8] That project had been conceived in literary and cultural terms. Ford sought to publish work that would not have been acceptable to other journals of the day, to promote the claims of younger writers, and to defend the

canons of conscious artistry – derived primarily from European, and mainly French, models – that were central to his aesthetics. The review also had a wider purpose. It aimed to ascertain the extent to which literature was engaging with and representing modern life in all its seemingly bewildering aspects. The writers Ford valued (and whom he had published in the *English Review*) were aesthetically meticulous; their seriousness of artistic purpose disclosed a considered understanding of the craft of writing that for Ford served as a model for how social problems should be approached. He was explicit about this connection in *The Critical Attitude* (1911). Noting that some commentators had objected that the *English Review*'s pages 'rang the changes too continuously upon a certain set of names', Ford admitted the charge.[9] But he argued that chief among the *English Review*'s several purposes had been 'the furthering of a certain school of literature and of a certain tone of thought'. The latter, he explained, should be conceived as 'a critical attitude' (*CA* 4).

For Ford, however, the creation of a specifically 'English' literary journal upon these lines was 'a contradiction in terms' (*CA* 4) because the English were in his view hostile to critical thinking and to conscious artistry alike. Since 'nothing will make the Englishman adopt a critical attitude' (*CA* 5), the *English Review* should have been regarded as one of those 'insane enterprises' (*CA* 4) that had no hope of succeeding in its aims. This exaggerated rhetoric served a polemical purpose. But it also articulated a serious claim: modern life had become so varied and so complex that unillusioned thought was more than ever required to make sense of it. Ford argued that because this kind of thinking seemed cold and dispassionate (even inhumane), it was widely distrusted; readers feared its corrosive qualities and ignored its hortative dimensions. Instead of grasping that reflection on the problems of modernity enabled them to be understood and confronted, such readers saw the critical attitude as the destroyer of established values and habitual forms of life. Ford's view, in contrast, was that in a rapidly changing society accepted mores and customs were in any case being overthrown. An intellectually quiescent stance *vis-à-vis* social transformation was thus self-defeating.

There was also a further difficulty: the rise of specialist and professional cadres who arrogated political, scientific, and technocratic expertise to themselves.[10] For Ford, this parcelling up of areas of expertise had troubling cultural consequences for the *polis*, which, he argued, was becoming more atomised and fragmented. Furthermore, when the task of comprehending modern existence was allotted to professionals of various kinds, communal understanding of social life was further eroded. This was because while specialised professionals might be experts in their respective fields they were unable to provide an overarching analysis of society as a whole:

> The moment that questions at all abstract leave the broad ways of black and white, the great bulk of humanity abandons for good the consideration of such questions at all. And nothing is more difficult than, at the present moment, to diagnose the exact condition. All questions have become so exceedingly complicated, there is so little opening for moral fervour that the tendency of the great public is more and more to leave all public matters in the hands of a comparatively few specialists. Practical politics have become so much a matter of sheer figures that the average man, dreading mathematics almost as much as he dreads an open mind, is reduced, nevertheless, to a state of mind so open that he has abandoned thinking – that he has abandoned even feeling about any public matter at all. (*CA* 114-15)

Ford had earlier claimed that the English were noteworthy for their desire to muddle through in affairs of state, preferably keeping reflection to a minimum. This *ad hoc* and bovine approach to political issues was bad enough – though perhaps just about practicable in relatively settled societies – but it was disastrous in an unstable world characterised by far-reaching processes of social rationalisation. For Ford, the abandonment of the public sphere to specialists – who are given charge of politics and public administration – prevented the majority of people from participating in their own governance. The fatal result of this shift in power was that the wider community, which was increasingly unable to comprehend the world around it, still less get to grips with policy matters, gradually lost any sense of active citizenship and became the victim of those who would manipulate it. The 'critical attitude' enjoined upon its readers by the *English Review* was a corrective to intellectual and civic capitulation.

We might think that Ford's well-known advocacy of conscious artistry would lead him to neglect the social usefulness of imaginative literature. This would be a mistake. Despite his sympathy for a tradition of thought that valued aesthetic autonomy over art's utilitarian applications, Ford never took the view that emphasis on their autonomy severed the arts from the society in which they were produced or prevented them from commenting on its dilemmas. He insisted that only the most consciously conceived arts had the capacity to interpret and to revalue contemporary life, precisely because they were attentive to its complexity and thus aware of the difficulties involved in representing it.

There was a clear civic dimension to the *English Review*'s editorial programme. Ford was in the 1900s preoccupied with the consequences of social change for participatory citizenship. The *English Review* sought to assert the social value of the arts by arguing that they played an indispensable role in the maintenance of a properly functioning public sphere. It presented itself as a journal that had come into being to counteract the maleficent influence of specialisation, uncritical thinking, and writing that failed to engage with contemporary reality, which, Ford maintained, had become 'so fragile, so temporary, so evanescent, that the whole stream of life appears to be a procession of very little things, as if, indeed, all our modern life were a dance of midges' (*CA* 186). Ford's belief that modernity was the site of perpetual change informed his belief that the arts were a vital component of the body politic: 'The artist to-day is the only man who is concerned with the values of life; he is the only man who, in a world grown very complicated through the limitless freedom of expression for all creeds and all moralities, can place before us how those creeds work out when applied to human contacts, and to what goal of human happiness those moralities will lead us' (*CA* 27-8).

Specialisation was a danger because it impeded communication across different kinds of human endeavour and, by its very logic, eroded the capacity of citizens to participate in public life. For Ford, the creation of professionalised groups whose expertise was necessary to the functioning of modern societies but whose knowledge and skills were beyond the comprehension of those who hadn't been similarly trained meant that these societies were becoming ever more atomised. If specialisation had the tendency to isolate tightly organised professional cadres from each other then this state of affairs left the wider public floundering in a sea of ignorance. In this situation, the artist's public function was to resist the dispersal of communal bonds. His task was 'to awaken thought in the unthinking', and this meant 'that the artist should consider himself as writing for the uninstructed man *bonae voluntatis* – for the absolutely uninstructed man who is of his own type' (*CA* 64). Imaginative writers were to communicate the experience of their fellow citizens and to extend the 'human knowledge and human sympathy' (*CA* 67) that an increasingly compartmentalised society needed. The value of the arts lay in their capacity to go beyond randomly gathered data, to discern the significance of apparently unrelated phenomena, and to weld the constituent features of modern existence into a meaningful whole. 'It is only the imaginative writer', Ford wrote, 'who can supply [a picture of the life we live], because no collection of facts, and no tabulation of figures, can give us any sense of proportion' (*CA* 33). Literary magazines like the *English Review*, then, existed to give this kind of imaginative writing a chance to address as wide a readership as possible.

Dada and the *Little Review*
Ford published a characteristically digressive essay in the *Little Review* in 1920: 'W. H. Hudson: Some Reminiscences'. It's hard to imagine that the *Little Review* would have printed this essay five years later. By this time it had become a boldly polemical 'little magazine' absolutely committed to advancing the cause of the most innovative writing and painting. European and New York Dada were central to this programme. The *Little Review* prided itself on being at the forefront of post-war avant-gardism and delighted in the opprobrium heaped on it by more stuffy periodicals, taking this as proof that its cultural mission was necessary. In the years between 1919 and 1925 the *Little Review* regularly published work by Sherwood Anderson, Louis Aragon, Djuna Barnes, Mary Butts, E. E. Cummings, Elsa von Freytag-Loringhoven, Marsden Hartley, Ernest Hemingway, James Joyce, Mina Loy, Robert McAlmon, Ezra Pound, Dorothy Richardson, Philippe Soupault, Gertrude Stein, Tristan Tzara, and William Carlos Williams; it also printed illustrations by, among others, Hans Arp, Max Ernst, Naum Gabo, Juan Gris, George Grosz, Wassily Kandinsky, Fernand Léger, El Lissitzky, Joan Miro, Francis Picabia, Man Ray, Kurt Schwitters, and Vladimir Tatlin. The *Little Review* saw itself as a 'little magazine' that had a specific function in America, one that was '*performed by at least a dozen reviews in France and by eight or ten in England*', that is, the establishment of 'some intellectual communication between England, France and America by presenting the best of the creative work produced in those countries today'.[11] This was how Ford conceived the *transatlantic*, except that he did not share the *Little Review*'s high valuation of English literary magazines. He argued, in fact, that he had started the *transatlantic* because there was no serious review in England dedicated to literature and the arts:

It is the greatest blot on the face of Anglo-Saxondom that it has never been able to support a review devoted entirely to the Arts [. . . .] It seemed, therefore, my duty, if there was any chance of the existence of such a periodical, to do all I could to bring it into being. (*IWN* 296)

A comparison of the *Little Review* with the *transatlantic review* shows how the latter closely followed the format of what was clearly a precursor magazine. But in many respects the *Little Review* may be said to have outdone the *transatlantic* before it even got started. It not only published more and lasted longer than the *transatlantic* but also introduced the English-speaking world to most of the writers and artists that Ford and Hemingway would publish. The *transatlantic*'s capture of the first parts of Joyce's *Work in Progress* (later the centre-piece of *transition*'s 'revolution of the word') and of Stein's *The Making of Americans* were significant literary coups, but the majority of the writers it showcased were reasonably well known to those who kept abreast of developments in the modern arts. A reading of the back numbers of the *Little Review* between the years 1919-24 also reveals that its editorial policy was self-consciously 'radical' in a way that Ford's was not. This 'radicalism' was visible in its championing of Dada and its defence of the very writer considered by Ford to be more or less a charlatan: Baroness Elsa von Freytag-Loringhoven.

The *Little Review* had been publishing Freytag-Loringhoven's work since 1918. But after the Spring 1921 issue the presence of Dada was more noticeable in its pages. In that issue there appeared a Dada manifesto (in French), and this was followed by a 'Picabia Number' in Spring 1922, which included writing by Cocteau, Ribemont-Dess-aignes, Tzara, and Picabia himself. At the back of this issue, under the heading 'DADA', the editors appended a comment from Harriet Monroe claiming that the *Little Review* 'is headed straight for Dada; but we could forgive even that if it would drop Elsa von Freytag-Loringhoven on the way'. Monroe's observation was met head-on by 'jh' (Jane Heap) who described Freytag-Loringhoven as 'the first American dada' whom the *Little Review* was delighted to publish because of the challenge to literature that she represented. The *Little Review* intended to 'drop the baroness – right into the middle of the history of American poetry'. Was Monroe hostile to Dada, she inquir-ed, because it 'laughs, jeers, grimaces, gibbers, denounces, explodes, introduces ridicule into a too churchly game?' Dada, Heap asserted, had 'flung its crazy bridges to a new consciousness'.[12]

A key feature of Dada was the challenge it offered to existing conceptions of literature and art through its hostility to 'high' cultural seriousness and to aesthetic sycophancy. By dropping the baroness into the heart of American writing, the *Little Review* was trying to blow it apart. Hemingway's use of Freytag-Loringhoven's work in the *transatlantic* served the more limited purpose of goading Ford into being more 'radical' and mocking his apparent conservatism. Ford was later able to refer to this conflict lightheardedly when he wrote of his fellow editor: 'he assisted me by trying to insert as a serial the complete works of Baroness Elsa von Freytag Loringhofen. I generally turned round in time to take them out of the contents table' (*IWN* 309). Given that Hemingway had a low opinion of Dada, and of Tzara in particular, it is clear that his inclusion of the Baroness in the *transatlantic* was an aggressive, provocative act. A text like Tzara's 'Monsieur Antipyrine's Manifesto' was in fact opposed to key values that Ford and Hemingway shared. Declaring that 'DADA remains within the framework of European weaknesses, it's still shit, but from now on we want to shit in different colours so as to adorn the zoo of art with all the flags of all the consulates', Tzara insisted that 'art isn't serious, I assure you'.[13] In a 1924 lecture delivered once at Weimar and then again in Jena, he argued that art didn't 'have the celestial, general value that people are pleased to accord it', that he had no interest in 'a pictorial, moral, poetic, social or poetic renovation', and that the 'beginnings of Dada were not the beginnings of an art, but those of a disgust'.[14]

Freytag-Loringhoven's work functioned in the *Little Review* as a Dada-inspired battering-ram with which bourgeois decorum, aesthetic sentimentalism, and cultural propriety could be beaten down. Dada rejected accepted artistic canons in favour of experiments in automatic writing; psychic derangement; spontaneous 'happenings'; nonsensical prose, poetry, and manifestoes; theatrical provocations of the public; and satirical absurdist humour. Leah Dickerman has suggested that Dada enacted a 'radical subjectivity' that offered 'an assault on the public, communicative functions of language'.[15] It was this doubled aspect of Dada, which was evident in Freytag-Loringhoven's texts, that so troubled her vociferous critics who argued that her work destabilised subjectivity by embracing solipsism and 'madness', while it decomposed language to such an extent that literature's capacity to communicate was called into question.

Freytag-Loringhoven's work (especially her poetic text 'The Cast-Iron Lover') caused the most intense debates in the *Little Review*. Two angry letters were published in the October 1919 issue, one simply demanding: 'Are you hypnotized, or what, that you open the *Little Review* with such a retching assault upon Art'. Freytag-Loringhoven's writing was seen as an attack on the category of 'art' itself, and not as a contribution to or extension of it. Heap defended this writing by suggesting that it represented an 'Art of Madness'.[16] In the next issue Maxwell Bodenheim followed suit, arguing that an art 'that steams, boils, sweats and retches' was needed to break away from the 'sanctimonious' and over-refined views of art that were still culturally dominant.[17] Heap, in turn, maintained that although Freytag-Loringhoven's explorations of the psyche were indeed 'unhampered by sanity', they were motivated by conscious choice: 'Madness is her chosen state of consciousness'.[18] Freytag-Loringhoven added that 'jh' (Heap) understood her 'perfectly', arguing that she sought to control the emotion of insanity and to 'take it by the neck and make Art out of it'.[19] In her recent assessment of Freytag-Loringhoven's career, Amelia Jones suggests that she was indeed radical in her assault on the category of 'art', since she 'performed a kind of unhinged subjectivity that most of the other artists of her day only examined or illustrated in their work'.[20]

Surrealism developed out of Dada in complex ways, but it was motivated by the same disgust spoken of by Tzara. Like Dada, it rejected not only 'ordinary' reality but also the bourgeois social order predicated upon it. Its attempts to break free from accepted patterns of thought were orientated towards destroying the social compact no less than the 'mind forg'd manacles' that constrained the individual psyche. Embracing paradox, Surrealism enacted its revolt against the literature and the arts of the past on the terrain of the aesthetic even as it sought to destroy that terrain in order to proclaim its contempt for a socially and psychologically oppressive culture.[21] Its insistence on freedom from existing (perhaps one should say 'dominant') artistic models went hand in hand with a search for visionary modes of apprehension that could release the individual from conventional ways of seeing and thinking. The Surrealist act of literary creation was an existential commitment, the sign of a new authenticity, a plunge into the unknown that departed from previously established and accepted aesthetic canons. By following a rule-breaking strategy and insisting on the importance of chance, spontaneity, and ephemerality,

Surrealism undermined the concept of artistic discipline and its concomitant: the well crafted artifact. And if Paris Dada was more overtly anti-art than its Surrealist successor, then this is simply a matter of emphasis. Both movements sought new modes of expression that decisively broke with the aesthetic as a category. Hans Richter, for example, described Dada as 'a tireless quest for an anti-art' and as 'an artistic revolt against art', while Breton wrote: 'Tuer l'art est ce qui me paraît aussi le plus urgent.'[22]

Tradition, Cosmopolitanism, and the *transatlantic review*
Ford's and Hemingway's respective aesthetic views may not always have been consonant, but the two men had more in common with each other than either of them did with Surrealism and Dada. Neither of them was sympathetic to the iconoclastic assaults on literary tradition and on the concept of the aesthetic that were prominent in these movements. Hemingway primarily wanted to publish new American writers in the *transatlantic*; in pursuit of this aim he tried to wrest control of the review from Ford. Some critics have considered that he was successful in this regard, to the review's detriment.[23] Be this as it may, we need to acknowledge that Ford himself valued much of the American literature that Hemingway was promoting so sedulously. But throughout 1924 Ford continued to show relatively little interest in the equally new French writing. The reason for this disregard can be traced to his convictions about aesthetics, tradition, and the function of the arts in civic life.

Ford's 'Stocktaking' essays in the *transatlantic* make it clear that he was concerned to defend culture from English philistinism. He 'imagined the review', Max Saunders argues, 'as a lone voice speaking against the Anglo-Saxon mistrust of the arts' (Saunders II 156). There is a direct continuity here between this aspiration and the 'critical attitude' fostered in the pages of the *English Review*, which had been established to give imaginative literature a chance in England. Sub-titled 'Towards a Re-valuation of English Literature', Ford's 'Stocktaking' essays dismissed academic professionalism; expressed his admiration for French clarity of writing and thinking; mocked Anglo-Saxon philistinism, the struggle against which was ostensibly one of the main reasons for publishing the *transatlantic*; insisted that literary technique was more important than subject matter and that good writing was neither moralistic nor didactic; and maintained that imaginative literature had the capacity to civilize human beings by helping them to understand other people. A vital feature of Ford's position in his *transatlantic* editorials was his anti-elitist conviction that literature should be intimately bound into everyday existence. Disapprovingly citing Shelley's claim that he was writing for the 'highly refined imaginations of the more select classes', Ford argued that as a result of this kind of view the arts 'have been so forced out of all contact with or inspiration from the "masses" of Anglo-Saxondom that, inasmuch as any human manifestation that is taken in hand by any coterie or Class of the More Select must speedily die, so literature in Anglo-Saxondom has after growing more and more provincial [. . .] died' (*TRev* I [Feb. 1924] 61).

Ford's conception of the arts was a constructive one. It rejected elitist views of the aesthetic, fostered communication both within and across national boundaries, and defended cultural cosmopolitanism. Unlike some avant-gardists, Ford didn't want to break with the arts and culture of the past (which, for some avant-garde writers and artists, were considered to be fatally compromised) but sought rather to renovate post-war society by establishing continuities with the past. This had nothing to do with some sort of slavish abasement before literary tradition; it entailed a personal critical engagement with tradition, in all its multiple aspects.[24] So inasmuch as Ford remained committed to innovation, he was certainly not hostile to earlier artistic achievements. Dada's and Surrealism's revolt against literature (and, more generally, against the aesthetic as a category) was anathema to Ford, who sought to sift the literary tradition for what could still be learned from it, hoping in this way to maintain links between past and present. He was thus impatient with those who seemed indiscriminately to have turned their backs on earlier writing, irrespective of whether they aligned themselves with Dada, Surrealism, or American nativism.[25]

Writing in an uncharacteristically vituperative vein, Ford described Waldo Frank and Robert McAlmon, for example, as the 'two worst writers' he had encountered in Paris. They were 'violent ignorers of the past', an attitude he thought was justified for the kind of work they were trying to produce, but which nonetheless revealed a self-defeating disregard of the lessons that could be learned from others, since the problems of writing 'are so very complex that one is very foolish if one ignores all the pointers that all the dead have found into the labyrinth that the thing is' (*CE* 269-70). This insistence on the value of continuity and craftsmanship was later reiterated in *The*

March of Literature (1938): 'Technique is simply what lies below the art of pleasing. You must study a great many books that have pleased men to see how they have pleased. When you have learned that you will be fully equipped'.[26] Alan Young has argued that many writers whose modernist antecedents lay in pre-war England were in the 1920s concerned 'to stress the necessity, in the process of continual renewal that art demands, for awareness of whatever can be profitably absorbed from other cultural traditions'.[27] This was certainly true of Ford. Alan Judd puts it well when he observes of Ford: 'Always conscious of tradition and of being part of it himself, he wanted others to see its benefits and progress' (Judd 346).

Ford conceived of 'tradition' in aesthetic terms, but he insisted that the aesthetic had an important social function. Dada's and Surrealism's scepticism about the aesthetic were opposed to Ford's high estimate of its liberatory power. Tzara's claim that 'there is great destructive, negative work to be done' in order that the 'complete folly of a world left in the hands of bandits who have demolished and destroyed the centuries' be finally exposed was countered by Ford's claim that the *transatlantic review* existed to present 'as many of the art activities of the world as we can get in; we are here for that and no other reason' (*TRev* I [Apr. 1924] 200). Where Breton argued that Surrealism's experiments with automatic writing 'had nothing to do with any aesthetic criterion' and contrasted this anti-aesthetic project with Joyce's '*imitation* of life', which then trapped Joyce 'within the framework of art',[28] Ford saw Joyce's work as the discovery of 'a new continent with new traditions', argued that its complexity made it 'a bridge between Anglo-Saxondom and the Continent of Europe' (*CE* 217, 219-20, 238), and insisted that he valued it above all for its purely literary qualities.

Critics who have written on the *transatlantic* have emphasised that Ford saw it as a bridge between the past and the present (and, of course, as a bridge between the two reviews Ford edited). Hemingway was no more interested in this maintenance of links to the past than were Surrealism and Dada. Bernard Poli remarks that once Hemingway had pushed the *transatlantic review* in the direction of avant-gardism, it was riven by a conflict between two rival conceptions of the form a literary magazine should take. Hemingway wanted it to be a polemical 'little magazine' that was 'part of a movement which tried to destroy old values and accepted ways of writing to create a new literature' (Poli 75). Ford, in contrast, had no desire to militate on behalf of any specific avant-garde tendency, believed that literary reviews should publish all kinds of writing, resisted the devaluation of the aesthetic that he discerned in such movements as Dada and Surrealism, and believed that continuity between the past and the present should be maintained. He had made this last point clear in his original prospectus, explaining that the *transatlantic* would follow in the footsteps of the *English Review* by publishing the work of 'old and eminent writers', backing 'with energy' recently established poets and novelists, and printing 'the first words of many, many young giants as yet unprinted' (Poli 40). When he looked back on the review's achievements in his closing editorial, Ford insisted that the *transatlantic* had been conceived as a non-aligned review of the arts that aimed 'to promote greater cordiality in international relationships so that the arts might work in a better atmosphere' and also 'to provide a place for publication for such sincere commencing authors as the world might hold' (*TRev* II [Dec. 1924] 684).

As in the case of the *English Review* there was a clear civic impetus behind this conception of a literary magazine's public function. In political terms, Ford's editorial project should be seen as a reconstructive rather than a revolutionary one. Writing about the *transatlantic* in *It Was the Nightingale*, Ford explained that his 'fine idea' had been that 'communication should be established between that Sun, Paris, and the furthest satellites, and between them and Paris'. The result of such interchange would be that the politician 'would be moved to give the Arts a higher place in his body politic' (*IWN* 260). Ford's goal, in short, was to promote the view that the arts were inherently civilizing because they fostered the exchange of experiences and ideas, and thereby contributed to the forging and maintenance of a vibrant public sphere. Elena Lamberti argues that Ford's ideal of a literary republic should be seen as a 'virtual community'; Ford, she argues, sought to create 'a "network" of transnational correspondences which move[d] around the values of the Arts and Literature, values that he [saw] as universal and unbiased'.[29] Ford, we might say, was committed to modernism but did not on that account seek a rupture with history. The arts of the past were part of a continuous tradition whose resources – when selectively and critically parsed – were still needed by post-war society. As an editor, Ford urged his readers to follow him in believing that the arts were among the most important constitutive features of a viable public sphere.

NOTES

1   Douglas Goldring, *Trained for Genius: The Life and Writings of Ford Madox Ford* [originally published in England as *The Last Pre-Raphaelite*], New York: E. P. Dutton and Co., 1949, p. 230.

2   Ford, *It Was the Nightingale*, London: William Heinemann, 1934 – henceforth *IWN*; p. 342.

3   Bernard J. Poli, *Ford Madox Ford and the 'Transatlantic Review'*, Syracuse, NY: Syracuse University Press, 1967 – henceforth 'Poli'; pp. 38-9.

4   Ernest Hemingway, *Selected Letters, 1917-1961*, ed. Carlos Baker, London: Granada, 1981, p. 116.

5   It is revealing that when Ford praised this book he aligned it with Conrad's work. See 'Literary Causeries from the *Chicago Tribune Sunday Magazine*, 1924': in Ford, *Critical Essays*, ed. Max Saunders and Richard Stang, Manchester: Carcanet Press, 2002 – henceforth *CE*; pp. 232-40 & 235.

6   Ford's lack of interest in Surrealism cannot be doubted. Surrealism receives no mention in either Poli's study of the *transatlantic* or in the second volume of Max Saunders's definitive biography of Ford.

7   Max Saunders, *Ford Madox Ford: A Dual Life*, 2 vols, Oxford: Oxford University Press, 1996 – henceforth 'Saunders'; vol. II, p. 141.

8   See *Letters of Ford Madox Ford*, ed. Richard M. Ludwig, Princeton, NJ: Princeton University Press, 1965, pp. 152-60.

9   Ford, *The Critical Attitude*, London: Duckworth, 1911 – henceforth *CA*; p. 3.

10 For more on this aspect of Ford's thinking, see John Attridge, '"We Will Listen to None but Specialists": Ford, the Rise of Specialization, and the *English Review*', in *Ford Madox Ford: Literary Networks and Cultural Transformations*, IFMFS 7, ed. Andrzej Gasiorek and Daniel Moore, Amsterdam and New York: Rodopi, 2008, pp. 29-41.

11 *Little Review* VI:11 (Apr. 1920), p. 62.

12 *Little Review* 'Picabia Number' (Spring 1922), p. 46.

13 Tristan Tzara, *Seven Dada Manifestos and Lampisteries* trans. Barbara Wright London: Calder, 1992, pp. 1-2.

14 *Ibid.*, 'Lecture on Dada', pp. 110 & 112.

15 Quoted in Dafydd Jones, 'Introduction: *der Holzweg der Holzwege*' in Dafydd Jones, ed., *Dada Culture: Critical Texts on the Avant-Garde*, Amsterdam: Rodopi, 2006, p. 18.

16 See 'Concerning Elsa von Freytag-Loringhoven', *Little Review,* VI, No. 6 (October 1919), 56.

17 Maxwell Bodenheim, 'THE READER CRITIC', *Little Review,* VI, No. 7 (November 1919), 64.

18 Evelyn Scott, 'The Art of Madness', *Little Review,* VI, No. 8 (December 1919), 48 and 49.

19 Evelyn Scott, 'jh', and Elsa von Freytag-Loringhoven, 'The Art of Madness' *Little Review,* VI, No. 9 (January 1920): 25-9.

20 Amelia Jones, *Irrational Modernism: A Neurasthenic History of New York Dada*, Cambridge, Massachusetts: MIT Press, 2004, p. 5.

21 See André Breton, Paul Eluard, Philippe Soupault, *The Automatic Message, The Magnetic Fields, The Immaculate Conception* trans. David Gascoyne, Antony Melville and Jon Graham, London: Atlas, 1997, p. 12.

22 Hans Richter, *Dada: Art and Anti-Art* trans. David Britt, London: Thames and Hudson, 1978, p. 7; Breton is quoted by Richard Sheppard, 'Introduction' in Richard Sheppard, ed., *New Studies in Dada: Essays and Documents*, Driffield: Hutton Press, 1981, p. 8.

23 Alan Judd, *Ford Madox Ford*, London: Collins, 1990 – henceforth 'Judd'; pp. 356-7.

24 For more detailed discussions of this issue, see Max Saunders, 'Tradition and the March of Literature: T. S. Eliot and Ford Madox Ford' *T. S. Eliot and the Concept of Tradition*, ed. Giovanni Cianci & Jason Harding, Cambridge: Cambridge University Press, 2007, pp. 185-200.

25 See Jason Harding's valuable remarks about Eliot's similar resistance to Dada's 'aesthetic nihilism' in *T. S. Eliot and the Concept of Tradition*, p. 96.

26 Ford, *The March of Literature*, London: George Allen & Unwin, 1939, p. 420.

27 Alan Young, *Dada and After: Extremist Modernism and English Literature*, Manchester: Manchester University Press, 1981, p. 82.

28 André Breton, *Manifestoes of Surrealism* trans. Richard Seaver and Helen R. Lane, Ann Arbor: University of Michigan Press, 1972, p. 298.

29 Elena Lamberti, 'Real Cities and Virtual Communities: Ford and the International Republic of Letters' in *Ford Madox Ford and the City*, ed. Sarah Haslam, Amsterdam: Rodopi, 2005, p. 142. See also Lamberti's chapter, '"Wandering Yankees": The *transatlantic review* or How the Americans Came to Europe' in this volume.

'WANDERING YANKEES':
THE *TRANSATLANTIC REVIEW* OR
HOW THE AMERICANS CAME TO EUROPE

Elena Lamberti

On 3 February 1924 President Woodrow Wilson died in Washington; only a few years earlier, he had been among the promoters of a League of Nations aiming to establish and maintain a peaceful community world-wide. Wilson's idea of peace was based on an idealistic vision of a transnational brotherhood of nations; he did not believe in the long-term effects of a peace imposed by winners upon the vanquished because this would simply sediment rage and resentment, in time fuelling new conflicts. He trusted international diplomacy as the only agency capable of creating a new brotherhood of nations. His project was articulated in the famous 'Fourteen Points', some of them addressing contingent situations, others establishing principles of international politics which, in his intention, were meant to redesign the world after the tragedy of the Great War. Due to historical and political reasons, Wilson's project remained unfulfilled: the League of Nations, established in 1919, replaced by the United Nations Organisation in 1945 and finally disbanded in 1946, did not accomplish its original mandate and was a forlorn hope. Similarly, the *transatlantic review*, the new literary review that Ford Madox Ford published throughout the year of Wilson's death was doomed to remain an interesting but a forlorn hope; also this original project couldn't but surrender to the new historical and cultural contingencies of the new post-war age.

World War One left Ford sick and tired of the London literary and social worlds, so much so, that he secluded himself for a few years and devoted himself to the society of 'cabbages, goats and the flowers of the marrow plant'.[1] In 1923, he moved from England to Paris, committed instead to the re-evaluation of English and International Letters. The prospectus he wrote to promote his forthcoming review clearly reveals that, at that time, Ford was idealistically convinced that literature and the arts remained the only civilising agencies capable of bringing and consolidating peace across nations:

The *Transatlantic Review*, the first number of which will appear on January 7th, 1924, will have two only purposes, the major one, the purely literary, conducing to the minor, the disinterestedly social.

The first is that of widening the field in which the younger writers of the day can find publication, the second that of introducing into international politics a note more genial than that which almost universally prevails. The first conduces to the second in that the best ambassadors, the only nonsecret diplomatist between nations are the books and the arts of nations. There is no British Literature, there is no American Literature: there is English literature which embraces alike Mark Twain and Thomas Hardy with the figure of Mr. Henry James to bracket them.

The aim of the *Review* is to help in bringing about a state of things in which it will be considered that there are no English, no French − for the matter of that, no Russian, Italian, Asiatic or Teutonic − Literatures: there will be only Literature [. . . .] When that day arrives we shall have a league of nations no diplomatists shall destroy, for into its comity no representatives of commercial interests or delimitators of frontiers can break.[2]

That day never arrived, and Ford's hope, like Wilson's, remained unfulfilled. Ford was soon to discover not only that American literature *did* exist, but also that it was about to conquer Europe. Ironically, his own *transatlantic review* had a role in such a conquest, as it became a solid outpost for the new Yankee army. The American shock-wave certainly hit Ford's review. But the *transatlantic* did not collapse because of Hemingway & Co., as Ford himself later suggested, but because 'nothing was simple' in Paris, as Hemingway more convincingly acknowledged.[3] What at the time was read as an evident editorial failure (and it was: there were only 12 months of troubled publication), can now be reconsidered not only in the light of this historical and cultural complexity, but also in terms of the review's lasting cultural heritage. Such a reassessment might even bear out Frank MacShane's definition of Ford's 1924 review as not just another 'little magazine' in post-war Paris; but 'essentially the bringer of America to Europe'.[4]

As Malcolm Bradbury pointed out, 1924 was 'another remarkable Modernist year', especially if you were in Paris:

Breton's review *La Révolution surréaliste* was founded, and Surrealism, which also published its manifesto that year, proclaiming a new revolution of consciousness, replaced Dada as the spirit of the new. It was a season of transition: Conrad, Anatole France, and Franz Kafka all died that year. But Cocteau had published *Poésie, 1916-1923*, Mann *The Magic Mountain*, Kafka *The Hunger Artist*; and Hemingway himself was now a published writer with in our time, which won him small sales but much local attention. He was also developing a more combative style and strategy. Ford Madox Ford had now started a magazine, the transatlantic review (Paris was a lower-case city). 'It seemed to me that it would be a good thing if someone would start a centre for the more modern and youthful of the art movements, with which, by 1923, the city, like an immense seething cauldron, bubbled and overflowed,' Ford noted, though he was hardly alone in the idea; and he took on Hemingway as his assistant editor.[5]

Bradbury is right: Ford was hardly alone and Paris was a lively cauldron boiling with new ideas and movements; however, it was only Ford who – following Ezra Pound's suggestion – took on Hemingway as his assistant editor. This is an important factor in understanding not only how Americans came to Europe, but also how the 'making of Americans' evolved in post-war Paris. Critics have acknowledged that, between 1919 and 1941, Sylvia Beach's bookshop, Shakespeare & Co., constituted the headquarters of the American 'lost generation', promoting and supporting the works and the ideas of the young expatriates; what is still underestimated is the role played by Ford's transatlantic in demonstrating and even accelerating their coming to town. Generally speaking, Ford's Parisian review is often mentioned in the background of various 1920s memoirs which have created the lasting myth of the lost generation. An exception is Bernard J. Poli's volume dedicated to the history of the transatlantic review published in 1967; however, though this valuable account of the magazine helped reassess Ford's fortunes as a neglected writer, it did not encourage further analysis of the role played by Ford's review in promoting the American literature of the time. While retrieving Ford's role as a writer and an intellectual, Poli missed the challenge posed by MacShane only two years earlier. In fact, MacShane's hyperbolic definition of the transatlantic as 'essentially the bringer of America to Europe' constitutes an interesting point of departure from which to assess the truer and lasting legacy of Ford's review. Notwithstanding Ford's original intentions (to establish an 'International Republic of Letters'), the transatlantic review was not a new English Review, bringing various traditions together and scouting for new literary talents; similarly, it was not an outstanding literary review mirroring what was blooming in Paris at the time – a task that was better accomplished by other reviews. The transatlantic review was the one which bore witness to the dawning Americanisation of the twentieth century. In 1924, America elected a new President, Calvin Coolidge, who became famous for one lasting motto: 'the business of America is business'. And Ford was to Wilson what Hemingway was to Coolidge.

Hemingway performed the role of Ford's assistant editor fully embracing the spirit of the 'wandering Yankee' whose praise is sung by Lt Pinkerton in Puccini's famous opera, *Madama Butterfly*. First staged two decades earlier, Puccini's opera unveiled uncanny scenarios presenting some tragic side-effects of unbalanced trans-national relationships.[6] While the Victorian age was blurring, the young, happy and self-assured Pinkerton introduces his audience to the dawn of the new American age:

> The whole world over,
> on business and pleasure,
> the Yankee travels all danger scorning.
> His anchor boldly he casts at random [...]
> until a sudden squall
> upsets his ship, then up go sails and rigging.
> And life is not worth living
> if he can't win the best
> and fairest of each country [...]
> and the heart of each maid.
> 'America for ever!'

Pinkerton's happy ballad is counterbalanced by the equally farsighted comments of the more sympathetic Sharpless, the American Consul in Nagasaki, who underlines that Pinkerton's (and therefore the Yankee's) attitude is:

> A very easy gospel
> which makes life very pleasant,
> but is fatal in the end.[7]

Certainly, it was fatal for poor Butterfly, not for Pinkerton; similarly, twenty-years later, in 1924, it was fatal for poor Ford, not for Hemingway.

The new twentieth-century spirit that was somehow prefigured in Puccini's opera (the Italian composer even dared to include in his opera score a fragment of the US national anthem to emphatically accompany Pinkerton's vision) had started to materialise soon after (and through) World War One. America was now internationally acclaimed as the pre-eminent nation and old Europe was acknow-ledging the relevance of the cultural productions coming from the new

world. In a very short span of time, America became a model and a
myth to be referred to and, later, to be deconstructed; it became the
key to understanding actuality. The glamorous twentieth-century myth
of America originated first and foremost in post-war Europe through
the works of young expatriate writers; such a myth was immediately
associated to the idea of freedom at a time when new totalitarian
regimes were consolidating in both Western and Eastern Europe.[8]
Thus, as Bradbury noted: 'The whole spirit of transatlantic encounter
had changed, reflecting not just the collapse that had taken place in
European civilisation around the war, but the fast-changing balance of
cultural and moral power'.[9] The *transatlantic review* reflected this
historical and cultural situation, which pervaded the world of the arts
and the world of business and politics alike. Through Hemingway
(and Pound), Ford's review offered a stage to a noisy army of
wandering Yankees coming to Europe, travelling 'all danger
scorning', ready to 'win the best and fairest of each country'. Just like
Consul Sharpless, all Ford could do was to account for the ongoing
process; the comments he wrote in the section 'Communications'
remain lucid counterpoints, enlightening about the ways in which
America was brought to Europe. After a relatively smooth start, Ford
lost control and from the April issue onwards, the table of contents
was redesigned in favour of the American component; the review was
less and less 'international' and more and more 'made in the USA'.
Gertrude Stein, John Dos Passos, William Carlos Williams, George
Antheil, Djuna Barnes, Robert McAlmon, Man Ray, and of course
Ernest Hemingway and Ezra Pound are among the American authors
whose works were published in the *transatlantic review*. Emblematically – if not ironically – Gertrude Stein's volume *The Making of
Americans*, was first serialised in the *transatlantic*, starting from the
April issue.

It was Pound who encouraged Ford to hire Hemingway as his
assistant; and it was always Pound who supported Hemingway's
editorial choices by monitoring each issue and by sending letters to
blast or bless the published authors. Not surprisingly, most of the
blessings were in favour of his younger countrymen and women:

Cher F.
April number good. Especially Hem. and Djuna. Want more of them and of
McAlmon and Mary Butts.
May number not so good.

So and so: Nix. (British Contributors. Ed.) Blank. Not Sufficient. (British Contributor)
Dash. Oh Gawd. This village Idyll stuff (British Contributor)
The chap on Palestrina, Cingria, quite intelligent.
H.Z.K.T. = Times Lit. Sup. Rubbish…
The So and So is regular ole magazines stuff. (British Contributor)
[…]
Best action you have in McAlmon, Hemingway, Mary B., Djuna, Cingria, K. Jewett.
Will come back and manage you at close range before you bring out any more numbers.
Yours
Old Glory. (*TRev* I [June 1924] 481)

Ford published Pound's comments in full, blanking only the names of the various British victims but quietly commenting that similar letters revealed 'the proper Protectionist Spirit of the tough old Yankee inheritance, the contributors unfavourably referred to being uniformly British'.[10] As a matter of fact, more than protecting the 'old Yankee inheritance' Pound was here advocating the *new* American 'Risorgimento' which would 'make the Italian Renaissance look like a tempest in a teapot'.[11] Even as he was promoting their work, Ford seemed to younger writers like Pound and Hemingway too compromised by the past. While Pound always respected Ford as a writer and an intellectual, in *A Moveable Feast*, Hemingway offers an unpleasant portrait of Ford: he presents the older writer as someone who is out of place, no longer in harmony with the setting he is inhabiting, a faded 'gentleman' patronising without understanding what is really going on.

In their battle in favour of the new American literature, Pound and Hemingway could rely upon a solid partner: John Quinn, a wealthy American lawyer, patron of the arts and a financial backer of Ford's review. Thus, even though it was meant to be 'transatlantic' (it was conceived in Paris and distributed also in London and in New York), the review was predominantly American, in the editorial staff as well as in the financing. Ironically, Hemingway's take-over was finally accomplished in August 1924, while Ford was travelling to New York to meet Quinn;[12] he was on a pilgrimage to get additional financial support to keep the review running. Unfortunately, Quinn was already quite ill and died soon after Ford's visit, a sad event which accelerated the closing of Ford's editorial enterprise. Even though Hemingway himself tried hard to find new supporters, the last issue of the *transatlantic* was published in December 1924. In later writings, Ford suggested that the American business side of the review perhaps accounted for the commercial failure;[13] similarly, he unjustly insinuated that Hemingway himself was not blameless:

> When I went to New York, I confided that review to him. I gave him strict injunction as to whom not to print and above all whom not to cut.
>
> The last mortal enemy he made for me died yesterday. Hemingway had cut his article and all those of my most cherished and awful contributors down to a line or two apiece. In return he had printed all his wildest friends in extenso. So that uncapitalised review died. I don't say that it died of Hemingway. I still knew he must somehow be disciplined. (*IWN* 250)

At the same time, Ford couldn't but acknowledge that his review was reflecting the reality of the time, insisting on the dominance of the American literary and artistic community in post-war Paris and, of course, on Hemingway's 'patriotic coercion':

> The Middle West was seething with literary impetus. It is no exaggeration to say that 80% of the manuscripts in English that I received came from west of Altoona and 40% of them were of such a level of excellence that one might just as well close one's eyes and take one at random as try to choose between them. (*IWN* 338)
>
> Thus through no volition of my own but I daresay partly through the patriotic coercion of Mr Hemingway the Review was Middle Western as to a little more than half and a little less than one third French. The remaining sixth, mostly consisting of chronicles, came from the Eastern States, New York and England. (*IWN* 340)

It was a new age and it was a new American age, as the overwhelming presence of American writers in the pages of the *transatlantic review* confirms.

It is well known that World War I was a social and political watershed; and, as Wyndham Lewis underlined, it was a watershed also affecting culture and the arts before and after the event;[14] the twentieth century was born between the pre- and the post-war periods. However, when in Paris, Ford still looked 'pre World War One in appearance'[15] and continued to believe in the healing powers of literature and the arts. His editorials bore witness to his prewar artistic credo and to his idea that an International Republic of Letters could still civilise society. Henry James is the writer that he chose as a model for all artists because he embedded all traditions at once: he was the American who came to Europe, shared Flaubert's poetics, admired Turgenev, and sealed all lessons into universal masterpieces. True. What Ford was still missing, though, was the fact that the Grand Tour mentality was no longer part of the new century; it started to change in the last decades of the nineteenth century

In the 1920s, the idea of the Grand Tour had finally been replaced by that of *expatriation*, a self-imposed exile which brought many wandering Yankees to Europe and especially to Paris. Ford was himself an expatriate in Paris; however, contrary to the younger Americans, he went to Paris not to fight for himself as a writer, but to pursue his life-long artistic dream. As a World War One veteran, Ford could no longer cope with post-war London:

> We who returned [...] were like wanderers coming back to our own shores to find our settlements occupied by a vindicative and savage tribe [. . . .] The world was changed and our places were taken by strangers [. . . .]
> London had become a terribly sad place. The people I had known and liked before the war seemed to have fallen alike under a course. (*IWN* 65, 82)

Since 1919, London, dominated by 'young men [...] charming and well mannered' and no longer by the 'Men of 1914' fuelling the city of the Great Vortex, was perceived by Ford more and more as an Enemy Nation:

> I never had much sense of nationality. Wherever there were creative thinkers was my country. A country without artists in word, in colours, in stone, in instrumental sounds – such a country would be forever an Enemy Nation. On the other hand every artist of whatever race was my fellow countryman – and the compatriot of every other artist. The world divided itself for me in those who were artists and those who were merely the stuff to fill graveyards. (*IWN* 74, 75)

In the same memoir Ford also confessed that if one was a working novelist, one could not afford to be out of touch with the Paris literary and artistic scene, France being 'the second fatherland of every human being [....] It is only in France that you will find the Arts of Peace esteemed above science and warfare'. That said, Paris was the elected city, the sun 'that was alive to the Arts', the place from which one could fight against 'the age of mistaken nationalism and of an equally mistaken and artificial internationalism'.[16] It was the ideal capital for Ford's ideal Republic of Letters: 'Our Second Country right; our Second Country wrong; but right or wrong our Second Country. This because of Toutes les glories de la France' (Poli 39-40). The young Americans who went to Paris soon after World War I were not moved by the same reasons.

In the writing of the American expatriates, moving to Paris was often reinterpreted through two recurring metaphors: it was either a 'pilgrimage' or a 'colonisation'. Both metaphors pertain to the American puritan tradition and are associated to the conquest of a new territory, the promised 'city upon the hill'. Henry James himself used the term 'pilgrim' to refer to his own condition as an American expatriate; however, his pilgrimage is similar to Ford's and is always associated to an ideal vision of both the art and the artist. It is in Sylvia Beach's memoir *Shakespeare & Company*, that a new idea of 'pilgrimage' is revealed; in the chapter dedicated to 'Pilgrims from America', she introduces the spirit of their coming to Europe in the early post-war period. If the Pilgrim Fathers had gone to America in search of a promised land in which to establish a better society, the new American pilgrims of the early twentieth century landed in Paris to fight for their Risorgimento. They established a noisy colony and made sure everybody noted it. In his volume *Exile Returns*, Malcolm Cowley compared such a journey to a pilgrimage to the Holy Land, a metaphor which well represented what the *ville lumière* became for him and his generation: it was from Paris that the members of the new colony grew confident of their value and potential; it was from there that they started to spread their wings.[17] Returning from a journey to Paris, F. Scott Fitzgerald wrote to his friend Edmund Wilson:

> What an over-estimated place Europe is! [...] God damn the continent of Europe [. . . .] It is of merely antiquarian interest [. . . .] France makes me sick. Its silly pose as the thing the world has to save [. . . .] They're thru and done [. . . .] Culture follows money and all the refinements of aestheticism can't stave off its change of seat [. . . .] We will be the Romans in the next generation as the English are now.[18]

Coolidge was right: the business of America was business.

As Alide Cagidemetrio wrote, it is in Paris that the young Americans discovered their 'Americaness'; not only did they develop a new approach to old Europe (as Fitzgerald's letter shows, France – therefore Europe – no longer was the 'second country' right or wrong), but they also renegotiated their own identity and bloomed as American writers.[19] While America was rapidly marching towards its new 'normalcy', the wandering Yankees started to fictionalise

America; by so doing, they also created its new mythology. In turn, Europeans discovered America through the novels of Hemingway, Dos Passos, Fitzgerald and others; only, in the interwar period, Europeans mostly concentrated on the positive side of the 'Roaring Twenties'. The America of Americans was not only the land of jazz, commodities and new golden opportunities, but also the land of bootleggers, speakeasies, the red scare and political repressions; the America of Europeans was the land of Gatsby's fabulous parties and of Henry Ford's new cars. Thus, whereas Europeans began to dream about America as their own Holy Land, Americans turned the real America into a fictional setting to stage their own existential (or political) quest. In both cases, America was observed from a distance and was translated into 'images' situated in the authors' mind. Ironically, Americans grew even 'more American' precisely because they were far from home, as Henry Miller wrote in his 1934 novel, *Tropic of Cancer*:

> It was high time we were leaving. The city looked different in the early morning light. The last thing we talked about, as we stood there waiting for the train to pull out, was Idaho. The three of us were Americans. We came from different places, each of us, but we had something in common – a whole lot, I might say. We were getting sentimental, as Americans do when it comes time to part. We were getting quite foolish about the cows and sheep and the big open spaces where men are men and all that crap. If a boat had swung along instead of the train we'd have hopped aboard and said good-bye to it all [. . . .] It's best to keep America just like that, always in the background, a sort of picture post card which you look at in a weak moment. Like that, you imagine it's always there waiting for you, unchanged, unspoiled, a big patriotic open space with cows and sheep and tenderhearted men ready to bugger everything in sight, man, woman or beast. It doesn't exists, America. It's a name you give to an abstract idea.[20]

Such an abstract idea was planted and watered also (if not mostly) from Europe, nourished by 'a whole Horde of Montparnasse from anywhere between North Dakota and Missouri', as Ford wrote in the early 1930s.[21] They did not bring a process of internationalisation to Europe, they began to Americanise it. In the 1920s they settled in Paris situating themselves in its territory on the basis of their social status: symbolically, the penniless, the bohemians 'colonised' the Left Bank of the Seine; the socialites and well-to-do colonised the luxurious hotels on the Right Bank. Emblematically, the two American writers who led the American Risorgimento stayed on different Banks and embedded two different though lasting typologies of Americans and therefore of Americas. Hemingway lived on the Left Bank, unveiled the misery of the lost generation in Europe and became the spokesperson of all wandering Yankees; Fitzgerald lived on the Right Bank, took frequent trips to the Côte d'Azur, and with Zelda nourished the myth of the Beautiful and Damned. The geography of the Left and the Right Banks recalls that of the West and the East Egg in Fitzgerald's *The Great Gatsby*: in both cases, Americans are separated by a line of water which seems to suggest that it is better for them not to meet but to glance at each other from the distance. If or when they meet, they often clash and the encounter risks turning into tragedy, as in *Gatsby*; and what glitters at a distance looks empty in close proximity, as in *Fiesta*. Similarly Europeans who went to America in the interwar period were soon to discover the real world under the opalescent surface.

It is important to recall that Ford's *transatlantic* was published in 1924, because the American expatriates arrived in Europe in different waves, and each of them belonged to a different moment in 'the making' of Americans. The different implications of the time of expatriation are noted by American writers themselves, and especially by Hemingway and Fitzgerald. The two writers agree in cutting a line between those who arrived before or after 1925-6. In 1928, looking at his countrymen in Paris, Fitzgerald stated that the French capital city was inhabited by 'American Neanderthals', certainly a different 'species' from the would-be 'Romans in the next generation'. Hemingway himself offered a sociological analysis and distinguished two different eras of expatriation: 'the early "serious" period, dominated by real experiment, and the wild era after 1926 composed largely of Americans in flight from "repressive" America'.[22] Europe became an outpost for 'wild' Americans escaping a 'normalised' America, while America consolidated in the Europeans' mind as the golden land, at least until the Wall Street Crash of 1929, which brought everybody back to reality. By that date, the American Risorgimento was over, its mission fully accomplished:

> [...] what is clear is that these writers were part of a vast transformation not just in artistic history but in the very balance of cultural power, a change that was only half-sensed at the time [....]
> The American Risorgimento became simply one part of a yet larger transformation, part of a Western cosmopolitanisation of the arts [....]
> By the decade's end, American literature was acknowledged as a modern world literature. Its acceptance was perhaps signalled by the award of the

Noble prize for Literature to Sinclair Lewis in 1930, the first American to be honoured. But by 1930, though, everything had changed. The Depression had come, the bank drafts stopped, the exiles returned, to discover their writing had won its own American audience. The transatlantic experiment in writing, as in painting, dance and music, had actually succeeded. American writing was no longer a sub-branch of English literature. It was an active component of a far larger international experiment, acknowledged abroad and increasingly at home. That, in the end, is why the twenties episode remains so influential, and so important.[23]

Ford's *transatlantic review* was part of the American Risorgimento, therefore it was part of the larger 'transformation, part of a Western cosmopolitanisation of the arts.' And it was inscribed in the 'early serious period' of this change. Even Ford, who tried to resist and counterbalance the forceful invasion of the wandering Yankees and who continued to publish old and new glories from various lands (among others, Conrad, Cassou and Valéry) couldn't but acknowledge it. It took him about a decade, but in *It Was the Nightingale* he even mythologized the American expatriates in Paris and underlined the importance of that setting – and implicitly of his review – for the establishment of 'the young American literature of today':

Those were exciting days in Paris. The young American literature that today forms the most important phase of the literary world anywhere was getting itself born there [. . . .] Young America from the limitless prairies leapt, released on Paris [. . . .] The noise of their advancing drowned all sounds [. . . .] I might have been described as – by comparison – a nice, quiet gentleman for an elderly tea-party. (*Reader* 248-9)

Thus, MacShane's claim no longer sounds hyperbolic because the *transatlantic review was* a bringer of America to Europe. Certainly, 'those were exciting days in Paris', and quite certainly part of Ford's 'excitement' came from his collaboration with Ernest Hemingway, his troublesome Yankee assistant editor. Established by an English-born writer with German and Italian antecedents and having a European understanding of literature and the arts, the *transatlantic review* did not foster an International Republic of Letters. Instead, it became 'a rag-time affair where a great many things did go astray' (MacShane 160). In a few weeks, the review became the ship taking the wandering Yankees to Europe. They mutinied *en masse* against Ford-Consul Sharpless, their 'nice, quiet gentleman for an elderly tea-party', and took control; guided by Hemingway-Pinkerton they colonised their century. It was 'America forever' or, at least, for several decades, until new shock waves began to come from the Far East. Butterfly was striking back.

NOTES

1   Ford, *No Enemy*, ed. Paul Skinner, Manchester: Carcanet, 2002, p. 106.
2   Bernard J. Poli, *Ford Madox Ford and the 'Transatlantic Review'*, Syracuse, NY: Syracuse University Press, 1967, pp. 37-9.
3   Ernest Hemingway, *A Moveable Feast*. The Restored Edition, Foreword by Patrick Hemingway, Edited with an Introduction by Sean Hemingway, New York: Scribner, 2009, p. 49.
4   Frank MacShane, *The Life and Work of Ford Madox Ford*, London: Routledge & Kegan Paul, 1965 – henceforth 'MacShane'; p. 164.
5   Malcolm Bradbury, *Dangerous Pilgrimages. Transatlantic Mythologies and the Novel*, New York: Viking, 1995, p. 321.
6   Originally inspired by an American short-story (John Luther Long's 'Madame Butterfly', 1898), Puccini's opera premiered at La Scala Theatre, Milan, on 17 February 1904. It was a fiasco and was very poorly received by critics and audience alike. Puccini edited it and the new performance (Brescia, 28 May 1904) was a great success, as it has been ever since.
7   *Madama Butterfly*. Music by Giacomo Puccini; *Libretto* Giuseppe Giacosa, Luigi Illica, Act I, Scene I.
8   In Italy, during the Fascist years, to study and translate American authors was not simply a literary act, but it also became an act of resistance against a regime which was suffocating anything conceived outside the national borders, and especially overseas. Accounts of that can be found in F. Pivano, *Mostri degli Anni Venti*, Milan: La Tartaruga Edizioni, Baldini & Castoldi, 2002, pp. 37ff.
9   Bradbury, *Dangerous Pilgrimages*, p. 340.
10 *Ibid.*
11 Ezra Pound, quoted in Bradbury, *Dangerous Pilgrimages*, p. 338.
12 'Hemingway took over for him [Ford] and I remember the period very well as we had been left you might say "pending". He was guest of honour and acclaimed at a dinner of leading authors, to which I was invited to accompany him as a representative of the Review. I think he added lustre to the Review or maybe it did to him', Marjorie Reid, Ford's secretary (Poli 103).
13 'I all the time was wondering what was the matter with the American business side of the *Review* [. . . .] I had not any accounts of the American sales of the review; neither, apparently, had Mr Quinn....': Ford, *It Was the Nightingale*, London: William Heinemann, 1934 – henceforth *IWN*; p. 353.
14 '[T]he war is such a tremendous landmark that locally it imposes itself on our computation of time like the birth of Christ. We say 'pre-war' and 'post-war', rather as we say 'B.C.' or 'A.D. [...] You will be astonished to find how like art is to war, I mean 'modernist art'. They talk a lot about how a war just finished effects art. But you will learn here how a war about to start can do the same

thing'; Wyndham Lewis, *Blasting and Bombardiering*, London: Eyre and
Spottiswoode, 1937, pp. 1, 4.

15 See Herbert Gorman, 'Ford Madox Ford: the Personal Side', *Princeton University Library Chronicle*, 9 (April 1948), 119-22.

16 T. S. Eliot letter to Ford Madox Ford, *TRev* I [Jan. 1924] 95.

17 Malcolm Cowley, *Exile's Return. A Literary Odyssey of the 1920's* [1934], New York: The Viking Press, 1951.

18 Bradbury, *Dangerous Pilgrimages*, p. 312.

19 Alide Cagidemetrio, *Una strada nel bosco. Scrittura e coscienza in Djuna Barnes*, Vicenza: Neri Pozza, 1979.

20 Henry Miller, *Tropic of Cancer*, Introduction by Karl Shapiro, Preface by Anaïs Nin, New York: Grove Weidenfeld, 1961, pp. 207-8.

21 *The Ford Madox Ford Reader*, ed. Sondra J. Stang, Manchester: Carcanet, 1986 – henceforth *Reader*; p. 249.

22 Bradbury, *Dangerous Pilgrimages*, p. 329.

23 *Ibid.*, pp. 335-9.

CUTTING REMARKS:
WHAT WENT MISSING
FROM *THE GOOD SOLDIER*?

Martin Stannard

Having already given three papers on editing *The Good Soldier*, two of which were published,[1] I was hesitant about offering a fourth. The third, for the Society of Textual Scholarship's New York conference in 1995,[2] was an extrapolation of the 'Rules of Engagement' section at the end of my Norton Critical Edition (1995; hereafter 'Stannard'). What was there to add? Then I remembered something which had nagged me for years: the manuscript (MS) sections which Ford had deleted and the ways in which their inclusion might have rendered the text even more self-consciously proto-postmodern than it now appears. As I had been unable to include this text *because* Ford was responsible for excluding it, I had merely recorded it in the 'Manuscript Development and Textual Variants' section of my edition, and there it had lain buried for thirteen years. Alongside these passages we might place other intriguing MS and typescript (TS) variants: additions to the MS by Ford; MS words, even lines, omitted by the typist; perpetuated mistranscriptions by the typist; and 'house style' corrections to punctuation. As I deal with the last category in the edition, I won't discuss it here but, in brief, one of the things that 'went missing' (along with the original title and author's name) was Ford's careful correction of TS punctuation and the use of short, ungrammatical sentences. As this seemed to spoil the self-reflexive, 'conversational' tone of the novel, I generally restored the punctuation of the TS.

Let me begin by outlining the textual transmission of *The Good Soldier*. It was dictated by Ford to three amanuenses: Brigit Patmore, H. D. [Hilda Doolittle], and Richard Aldington. The MS in Cornell is not, in fact, an autograph manuscript entirely, containing several sections of TS, sometimes apparently typed by Ford (there are signs of spontaneous composition) or dictated by him to a typist. The whole has been corrected twice by Ford, once in ink and once in pencil. It is thus a complex palimpsest which confirms Ford's claims in the 1927 'Dedicatory Letter to Stella Ford [Bowen]' that he both put a great deal of work 'into the construction of the book, [...] the intricate tangle of references and cross-references', and that he 'wrote it with comparative rapidity' (Stannard 5). It contradicts, however, part of what he said in his 1928 publicity release for the second American edition: 'I had almost every word of it in my head, and I dictated it very quickly.'[3] Although he dictated it quickly, he certainly did not have 'every word of it in [his] head'. The MS reveals over thirty disruptions of composition, Ford often going back over original MS dictation and revising it so heavily that sections had to be replaced by TS, thousands of careful tiny corrections, and some larger ones, before the palimpsest was ready to be typed.

After typing the whole thing, the opening 42 pages of it went off to Wyndham Lewis's *Blast*, where it appeared in the magazine's first issue dated 20 June, 1914. Cornell holds this TS in ribbon copy and a complete TS consisting of ribbon copy for the first four pages, carbon copy for the rest of the first 42 pages, and ribbon copy for the rest, suggesting that Ford re-typed those early pages to smarten up a rather battered TS, and submitted it to John Lane after correcting it in ink. *When* he submitted it, or rather when the novel was finished, I've discussed in 'Intention and Execution' but in my view it was after the outbreak of war in August 1914, and not before it, as Ford stated. There was then a delay, the book not appearing until March 1915, simultaneously published by John Lane in New York and London, apparently using sheets printed in America. If, however, we collate these two texts (identical save for the reversal of two lines on the title page) with the earlier MS and TS states, it becomes clear both that a house style has been imposed and that there were numerous substantive proof corrections, probably by Ford. I therefore took the first UK and US edition as my copy-text, generally altering the punctuation to conform to that of the TS, because the first edition appears to have been the last one overseen by the author.

Ultimately, then, we have something of an editor's nightmare: a MS in three hands with Ford's corrections and including TS insertions which clearly replace parts (now lost) of the original MS; a TS of the whole novel with Ford's corrections, the punctuation of which is radically different from that of the published text; another, shorter, *Blast* TS and the printed *Blast* text (which has its own variants); and the John Lane published text which alters substantive readings in the complete TS. How I tried to resolve these difficulties I have explained in the edition. There was no space there, however, to discuss those categories of variant mentioned earlier: additions by Ford, MS lines omitted by the typist, and perpetuated mistranscriptions by the typist. I'll deal with these in reverse order, ending with the most intriguing variants: the longer sections of the MS that Ford himself deleted.

Perpetuated mistranscriptions are simply that: the typist mis-reads the handwriting of a MS and this 'error' is transmitted through all subsequent states. These variants present a particular problem for an editor taking the last edition overseen by the author as copy-text. Should s/he 'correct' them, restoring the MS reading which clearly seems to represent the author's original intention? Or should s/he ignore them if, as here, the author oversaw subsequent states? In general, I decided to ignore them on the grounds that Ford implicitly approved the changes even though he might not have been conscious that they *were* changes. On a few occasions, however, I did intervene and restore. Why?

One instance is purely technical and concerns the place names 'Bramshaw Tellragh' and 'Mudford', as they appear in the MS. In the TS, 'Bramshaw Tellragh' alters to 'Branshaw Tellragh' then to 'Bran-shaw Teleragh' in the first edition, where 'Mudford' becomes 'Mumford'. I followed the MS spelling because, in the case of 'Bramshaw', the compositor seems to have taken the first mistran-scription as standard and set up 'Branshaw' thereafter, while simply mis-setting 'Mudford' as 'Mumford' throughout, despite the fact that the typist transcribed it correctly.[4] Ford probably left the corruptions because it would have been too expensive to alter them: a financial rather than an editorial decision.

Other cases for restoration arise when a perpetuated mistranscription results in a more obscure, or less subtle, reading. One example centres on 'mad' and 'main'. The MS reads:

> It must have rattled poor Florence pretty considerably. For you see, the main idea – the only mad idea of her heart that was otherwise cold – was to get to Fordingbridge and be a county lady in the home of her ancestors.[5]

TS alters 'mad' here to 'main' so I restored 'mad' as rendering more vivid sense in opposition to 'that was otherwise cold'. Similarly, but more complicatedly, the MS later reads:

> And he [Ashburnham] was beginning to perceive dimly that, whereas his own
> traditions were entirely collective, his wife was a sheer individualist. His own
> ideal – the feudal theory of an over-lord doing his best by his dependents, the
> dependents meanwhile doing their best for the over-lord – this theory was
> entirely foreign to Leonora's nature. [6]

In the TS, 'His own ideal' is mistranscribed as 'His own indeed' making the sentence somewhat awkward with 'his own' apparently referring us back to 'traditions'. Clearly recognizing this, someone, presumably Ford at proof stage, has altered 'indeed' to 'theory'. As we have three different words in the same place here, I restored the original 'ideal' thus removing the repetition of 'theory' and reclaiming Ford's more precise original word suggesting ideology.

Two last instances simply, in my view, restore sense. Describing Ashburnham's delinquent behaviour with 'La Dolciquita', MS reads:

> He was too drunk to recognise her, and she sat in his armchair, knitting and
> holding smelling salts to his nose – […].

TS alters 'his nose' to 'her nose' and this is how it is printed. Although one could argue that she might have needed smelling salts when confronted by this spectacle, she is on the other hand not a woman given to the vapours and remains unperturbed throughout. It is more likely that he is the one who requires reviving, being 'pretty far gone with alcoholic poisoning'.[7]

In my last example for this section, TS changes MS's 'nurse' to 'purse', and it is printed as 'purser'. The original MS sentence reads:

> For I daresay all this may sound romantic but it is tiring, tiring, tiring to
> have been in the midst of it; […] to have chosen the cabins, to have
> consulted the nurse and the stewards as to diet for the quiescent patient who
> did nothing but announce her belief in an omniscient deity.[8]

I felt justified in opting for 'nurse' here because one does not consult a purser, let alone a purse, about diets. Again it seems that Ford noticed the anomaly of 'purse' and hastily made a correction at proof stage without checking back to the MS. His MS word was surely better because the ideas of nursing, being nursed, having or not having 'a heart', loving as selflessly caring for another as opposed to rapacious lust or the desire to control, seem crucial to the novel's complicated sub-text. Pursers, on the other hand, could not be regarded as one of its substantial motifs.

The next set of examples comes from what textual editors call 'eye-slip': those occasions when the scribe's, or in this case the typist's, eye wanders, losing words and sometimes whole phrases. Eye-slip might be considered as a specific case of perpetuated mistranscription. Typically this happens when the same word appears in two nearby lines, often towards the beginning or end of a line, and the eye slips down to the second word, losing the text between. Where this occurs, I have restored the lost words in square brackets to signify that, although this is not an 'authorised' reading in the sense that Ford authorised the text without the words, they did form part of the original conception and might well have been included had their omission been drawn to his attention or the MS been accurately typed. This is important because even single lost words can dramatically affect our reading, especially when their absence does not render the text absurd.

The first edition, for example, when Maisie Maidan's letter to Leonora is presented, reads:

> 'And I heard Edward call me a poor little rat to the American lady. He always called me a little rat in private'.

This follows the TS but the typist has added an 'a' before the second 'little rat'. The MS reads:

> 'And I heard Edward call me a poor little rat to the American lady. He always called me little rat in private.'

This might seem an issue of near-monumental inconsequence but I would argue that it is, in fact, a significant, and unfortunate, change for the worse because the addition of that second 'a' completely changes the sense of Ashburnham's phrase from one of affectionate derogation to one of harsh dismissal. As Ford well knew, Flaubert's sister, Caroline, signed her fond letters to him 'little rat'.[9] Maisie, for all her simplicity, is surely sensitive here to the dismissive nature of Ashburnham's description of her to the American lady, contrasting it painfully with the intimacy of his private pet-name. Indeed, Maisie says as much. The private address she '"did not mind. But if he called me it to her, I think he does not love me any more"' (55). By losing that second 'a', a certain irony and disappointment leak out through subtle linguistic inflection.

Similarly, the compound adjective 'well-behaved' has been lost in the sentence describing Maisie's attitude to her fellow guests in the hotel dining room when she first encounters Ashburnham:

> But, of course, she was taking a line of her own in which I at any rate – and no one else in the room [...] – counted as any more than so many clean, [well-behaved] bull terriers.[10]

And later, 'my' has disappeared from:

> For Florence, if you please, gaining in time a more composed view of [my] nature and overcome by her habits of garrulity, arrived at a frame of mind in which she found it almost necessary to tell me all about it.[11]

The concluding 'it' here refers to her affair with Ashburnham. In the first quotation, the addition of 'well-behaved' develops the novel's continuous reflection on the tension between passion and good form. Human animals in a polite environment are not only like 'clean' bull-terriers, they are also, like dogs again, *trained* to be well-behaved, an issue that will come up later in a lost reference to Nancy's social 'training'. In the second example, without the 'my', Florence's 'composed view of nature' makes little sense; with it, we understand that Florence is assessing *Dowell's* nature, quite a different proposition, in order to take advantage of it while simultaneously becoming irritated by his meek good form and the impossibility of saying anything of her affair.

Longer eye-slip errors result in a loss of Dowell's own garrulousness, and thus damage to the hesitant conversational tone, and rhetoric, of his narrative. Here is a selection as printed in my edition with the missing sections again in square brackets:

1)   Yet even that can't have been enough time to get the tremendously long conversations [she must have had with Leonora – conversations] full of worldly wisdom that Leonora has reported to me since their deaths.[12]

2)   There were guncases and collar cases, and shirt cases, and letter cases [and cases each containing four bottles of scent] and cases each containing four bottles of medicine; and hat cases and helmet cases.[13]

3)   And the wrist was at its best in a black or dog-skin glove and there was always
        a gold circlet [round it – a gold circlet] with a little chain supporting a very
        small golden key to a dispatch box.[14]

4)   Those were troublesome times in Ireland, I understand. At any rate Colonel
        Powys had tenants on the brain – his own tenants having shot at him with
        shot-guns. And in conversations with [Edward – and in much longer
        conversations with] Edward's land-steward [–] he got it into his head that
        Edward managed his estates with a mad generosity towards his tenants.[15]

5)   She hadn't made any fuss; her eyes were quite dry and glassy. Even when she
        was mad Nancy could behave herself. [She was well trained.][16]

6)   At one moment she was all for [self-sacrifice; at the next she was all for]
        revenge.[17]

7)   And she repeated to Edward in every possible tone that the girl did not love
        him; that the girl detested him for his brutality, his overbearingness, his
        drinking habits. [She pointed out more than a dozen good reasons why the girl
        should not love him.] She pointed out [...].[18]

In all of these one might argue that losing the bracketed words has
improved the text by reducing verbosity. In each, however, one can
also argue that the text is impoverished without them. In the first, we
lose that characteristic Dowellian rhetorical sub-clause, going back
over a statement and revising it slightly as though trying to make
better sense of what he has just said. In the second, we lose a sense of
Ashburnham's more feminine, decadent self when those four bottles
of scent disappear. The third example is even more intriguing because
in the MS we had a much more emphatic sense of the positioning of
the gold circlet round the (dog-skin) glove, thus providing a sharper
focus on the wrist, glove, and chain over it and suggesting again that
perennial tension between a polite exterior and an animal interior.
There is (or was) even a hint of sado-masochism in the image, of
Leonora not only as medieval chatelaine but also as a dominatrix who
enjoys the pain she causes. She holds the key to the money and the
secrets, and Ashburnham is partly attracted to, partly repulsed and
frightened by, her power over him. Example 4 simply offers more
detail but it is important detail because, in adding the fact that Colonel
Powys also consulted Ashburnham, the original does not imply, as the
printed text does, that Powys is going behind his back. Example 5 is
the one mentioned earlier. In the MS, Nancy does not simply behave
herself in public because she chooses to, she behaves herself because

she has been trained to do so like a 'clean bull-terrier', and so ingrained is this English etiquette that she complies with it even when insane. It has become not merely something learned but its own spontaneous discourse. Examples 6 and 7 demonstrate how eye-slip can radically alter the construction of character. In the first, Leonora is simply vengeful in the printed text. In the MS she veers between vengefulness and altruism and is presented much more as someone suffering as all the others do from a 'divided personality'. The seventh example has the opposite effect, losing Ford's original emphasis on the negative side of her personality: the cruelty, masquerading as truth and virtue, of her rational destruction of Ashburnham's (and Nancy's) innocent passion.

In my edition, and in the essay mentioned earlier, '*The Good Soldier*: Editorial Problems', I discussed one crucial 'addition'. On MS p. 180 (reproduced on p. 178 of the edition) Ford made a large marginal insertion to consolidate the use of the date 4 August 1914 as the spine of the novel's chronology. This has now been discussed *ad nauseam* and I won't bother readers with it here. But there is another addition by Ford which, although it is another famous one, is worth revisiting in the light of what has been said so far. At the very end of the novel both the MS and the TS read:

> He just looked up to the roof of the stable, as if he were looking to Heaven and he remarked:
>   'Girl, I will wait for you there.'

The printed text, presumably following Ford's proof correction, reads:

> He just looked up to the roof of the stable, as if he were looking to Heaven, and whispered something that I did not catch.[19]

I could not alter this back to the original because it is clearly a substantive proof correction and, although it might have been pressed on Ford by John Lane in order to deflect attention from Ashburnham's undying love for a minor, it might equally have been Ford's decision to render the whole affair ambiguous. In any case, it can be argued that the correction improves the text for this reason and that, taken generally, Ford's emendations are designed to blur motivation, to shift the characters just slightly out of focus, as they would have been in Dowell's bemused vision. As I say in the edition, Ford's:

whole concept of Ashburnham altered from that of rake and wastrel to that of tragic sentimentalist. Ford also seems to have toyed with the idea of making the novel more a study of Edward's schizophrenia – his 'nervous affection [...] [which] can be cured by a counter dread', his 'dual personality' – but subdued the theme. Leonora was originally more chilly and sardonic, with good reason to fear her husband's excesses, Nancy more self-aware in her craving for Edward, Dowell more passionate, Florence even less innocent, and Jimmie more sympathetic. As the revisions progress, one senses Ford's concern to etherealise his characters, to befog any clear-cut motivation, to displace authority for information from the narrator to his characters. Much of this is purely technical: Ford's sitting down as he said in his 'Dedicatory Letter', 'to show what [he] could do' as an impressionist writer. It also allows the focus of the novel to shift from what is known to what is unknown and to suggest those epic, abstract patterns of coherence which appear only in parodic form in the savage narrative present: chivalry, courtly love, the just war, the Universal (Catholic) Church – all the values of feudal society which the Reformation unstitched (184-5).

There is nothing here that I would wish now to revise but, looking at his larger deletions again, I find myself thinking that the form of the book might have been even more pertinent to its discussion of self-consciousness had Ford been able to keep passages 1-7 above, and had he not struck out passages 8-17 below.

Here, at last, we come to Ford's larger deletions which, of all the things that 'went missing' are perhaps the most intriguing, Again, I shall simply list them first:

8) [I have asked novelists about these things, but they don't seem able to tell you much. They say it comes.
    I don't know that I particularly want to write a novel; but I do know that I want what I write to be read by at least one sympathetic soul, or by all souls that are in sympathy throughout the world. How many are they? A million? A hundred million? Or isn't there one?
    Here again one has just no means of knowing – none! But, I suppose, if I want to write something that will be read by one sympathetic soul I must want to write a novel – I don't see how to get away from that.]
    I don't know how it is best to put this thing down – whether it would be better to try and tell the story from the beginning, as if it were a story; or whether to tell it from this distance of time, as it reached me from the lips of Leonora or from those of Edward himself.[20]

9) And that poor devil beside me was in an agony. Absolute, hopeless, dumb agony such as passes the mind of man to imagine. [But all this is rather wandering round sort of stuff. Only it's the way it comes into my head [.] I

must try to be more direct. I will put down very shortly the essential facts about Florence & myself & then we can get on to the first meeting of all us four at Nauheim.

Or no, I will go straight to Nauheim. I don't know how to tell this story.][21]

10) From the Englischer Hof, starting on the sidewalk, it was ninety-seven paces and the same four hundred and twenty, but turning lefthanded this time. [From the end of the tennis courts to Florence's seat after she had been at Nauheim a week was exactly five hundred steps; from the same place to a seat higher up the hill – she was allowed so much to extend her walk during the second week – was just seven hundred & fifty. From the same place to the steps of the Casino, by the path Dr Bittelmann told us to take during the fourth week was exactly seven hundred and fifty.][22]

11) And of course she entertained me with her conversation. It was, as I have said, wonderful what she could make conversation out of. [- the husband of the lady who sold the so very expensive violets in the kiosk at the bottom of the street that comes from the station; the expression on the face of the wife of the Czar of Russia as she drove from Friedberg where her girlhood had been spent; the quality of the rubber on the tyres of a cab we took a drive in. Anything in the world she could talk about. So I would walk with her as far as the bath ...] She walked very lightly, and her hair was very nicely done, and she dressed beautifully and very expensively.[23]

12) It was like a chap in the middle of the eruption of a volcano, saying that he might just manage to bolt into the tumult and set fire to a haystack. Madness? Predestination? Who the devil knows?

[I can't for the life of me make up my mind how to tell this part.][24]

13) I think the modern civilised habit – the modern English habit of taking everyone for granted is a good deal to blame for this. I have observed this matter long enough to know the queer, subtle thing that it is; to know how the faculty, for what it is worth, never lets you down. [Of course there is the regular introduction with a character – as it were the sort of character you get with a cook or a housemaid. You are introduced to Mr & Mrs So-&-So of Clopton [?] Hough. And it is suggested to you that these are quite good Lancashire people. It may be cotton; or it may be land. But you may be quite certain that if your friend Mrs Fuller introduces you to the So-& sos that in that case the cotton will be of the very best Bolton sheeting – meaning I suppose that the factory is in a second or third generation; for I do not really understand these things I only know that in the case of Mrs Fuller her tact is so certain that the So-& sos must be all right & that Clopton [?] Hough is the sort of place to which it is a privilege to be invited for a week. That is the introduction with a character. And then the taking for granted begins at once. You will all four take it for granted that you like your beef [MS p. 62 begins here with apparently another whole page, original MS p. 58, having been scrapped after 'beef'] also take for granted that you change your shirt three times a day ...][25]

14)   You meet a man or a woman and, [from the look in his eyes, from the part of
       the throat from which his voice comes; from her method of sitting down in a
       deck-chair; from the fact that she offers you a certain type of novel which she
       has done reading when you are sitting with nothing in your lap after lunch -]
       from tiny and intimate sounds, from the slightest of movements, you know at
       once whether you are concerned with good people or with those who won't
       do.[26]

15)   The matter was one [of what in France is called détournement de mineur; it
       was, in consequence a criminal offence] of a divorce-case, of course, and she
       wanted to avoid publicity as much as Edward did, […].[27]

16)   He had made however the mistake of not telling Leonora where he was going,
       so that, having seen him go to his room to fetch the code for the telegram, and
       seeing, two hours later, Maisie Maidan come out of his room, Leonora
       imagined that the two hours she had spent [in agony (for she really imagined
       that Ashburnham was going to let her in again for all sorts of past misdeeds,
       she really thought that once more they would have to let Bramshaw Teleragh,
       pawn the plate, sell another picture by Gainsborough and scrape on for
       another ten years at the ends of the earth) so she imagined that the two hours
       she had spent] in silent agony Edward had spent with Maisie Maidan in his
       arms.[28]

17)   She made tentative efforts at remonstrating with him. Her father, whom she
       saw now and then, said that Edward [gave himself too much side] was much
       too generous to his tenants.[29]

In example 8 we have something rather extraordinary. Had this appeared in a novel of 1995 rather than 1915, critics might have
applauded its self-reflexivity as postmodern. We find ourselves reading a novel in which the central character / narrator does not want to
write a novel but finds himself trapped in one. The distinction between
fact and fiction collapses. The narrator is discussing fictional narrative
technique in a text which is supposedly a spontaneous oral account.
Similarly, in no. 9 we gain a much stronger sense of Dowell's
hesitancy about how best to *tell* this story, and that he feels he might
not be able to tell it at all.

Example 10 is interesting in the wake of the *nouveau roman*. In
Robbe-Grillet's work, this obsessive attention to detail, parodying
realism and naturalism, leads nowhere, is fundamentally absurd. Here
it stresses Dowell's neurosis. His manic attention to the precise number of steps suggests both his intense concentration on, and care for,
Florence's supposedly delicate health (he is, after all, walking alongside his wife, a woman whom he believes might die at any moment),

and his own alienation, reducing the painful moment to numbers. And it is, of course, doubly painful for him on reflection as he tries both to recapture his anxiety about Florence's medical condition and then to work out how, exactly, amid this statistical plotting of her movements, she managed to escape his gaze for long enough to pursue her affair with Ashburnham. In no. 11 we see another aspect of this as he revisits his conversations with his wife, or rather her monologues. In retrospect, Florence's gay stream of observations transforms from what at the time he thought to be an intimate exchange deriving from the desire to entertain him, into a screen thrown up to prevent his penetration, to stop talk, real talk about real things, with a kind of white noise.

Examples 12-15 develop this further. In no. 12 we return to the uncertainty about narrative strategy but this time the missing text emphasises Dowell's pain in attempting to relate a story in which he appears as cuckold, betrayed by his best friend. Dowell can't quite renege here on his infatuation with Ashburnham, and the anxiety about narrative form becomes closely linked to the anxieties of intimacy. In no. 13, for example, we return to a kind of postmodern self-reflexivity. Dowell is ostensibly discussing social introductions. 'Character' here is initially used in the antique sense of a 'reference' for a job, and he parallels this with social introductions guaranteeing the *bona fide* credentials of polite strangers to whom one is introduced. On this level we gain a much stronger sense of him as an American bemused by all this European flim-flam. More importantly, though, he is implicitly talking about 'characters' in fiction and the way a realist narrator introduces them and guarantees the parameters of their psyche. Good or evil, they are knowable in such novels. Good or evil, they are unknowable in the real world and in the impressionist novel. Those absolute moral categories disintegrate. The social encounters of Bad Nauheim become stranger than realist fiction as the two come to reflect each other, to intersect, to become indistinguishable and equally delusory. Is he, Dowell wants to know, real or a character in a fiction? The fact that he is both, pinpoints his agony.

There is, however, more to this agony than a sense of epistemological collapse. For the novel, in describing others' nervous breakdowns is also, unconsciously, describing Dowell's. His struggle for sanity, to be outside the scenario, regarding it rationally in retrospect, as a narrator, is futile. On the simplest (most complicated) level, his 'story' changes as he records it because more information becomes available as he progresses. But, even if this had not been the case, even if the body of supposed 'data' had been stable from the outset, all his concerns would have gone straight to his own centre of self or non-self. In examples 14 and 15 we see Ford blurring Ashburnham's bad behaviour but in a sense this means that Dowell is also blurring it, airbrushing things he cannot confront. For ultimately, this is perhaps not so much a novel or autobiography about Ashburnham's and Dowell's relations with women and vice versa. It is about Dowell's (unspoken) love for Ashburnham and with the European culture of good form he represents. It is a tale told not by an idiot but by an intelligent American besotted with Ashburnham's stylish sang-froid, and his stylishness generally: his clothes, his complexion, his luggage and those discreet bottles of scent. This is not necessarily to say that Dowell has erotic, or even suppressed erotic, feelings towards his friend. But it is to say that he loved him passionately because he was everything Dowell, despite his wealth, could never be. He was, or had seemed to be, the narrator of his own story rather than a Prufrockian figure like Dowell. Ashburnham was meant, was born, to be Prince Hamlet – or so it had seemed. How could it have been that he was merely human or, worse, inhuman in his treatment of women: a rapist, a paedophile, an adulterer. How could he have cuckolded his best friend, used him, made him a laughing stock to Florence, Leonora, and God knows how many others? Dowell has to, and fails to, find answers to these questions. And so, oddly, he writes a love story without realising it: not about Ashburnham's infatuations or Leonora's passion for the institution of marriage, not about Florence's possessive lust or Nancy's idealised hero-worship, but about the love of an American for Europe.

NOTES

1   'Intention and Execution: Manuscripts and the Problems of Copy-Text in Ford Madox Ford's *The Good Soldier*', *Scenes of Change: Studies in Cultural Transition*, ed. Carla Dente and Jane Everson, Pisa: Edizione ETS, 1996, pp. 93-107; '*The Good Soldier*: Editorial Problems', *Ford*

Madox Ford's Modernity, ed. Robert Hampson and Max Saunders, Amsterdam: Rodopi, 2003, pp. 137-48.

2 'Editing Ford Madox Ford's *The Good Soldier*: A New Methodology for the Production of a Single Text'.

3 Publicity release, Boni & Liveright, 6 April, 1928 [Janice Biala collection, New York]; quoted Stannard, p. 180.

4 Stannard, 'Manuscript Development and Textual Variants' – henceforth 'MDATV', p. 197, 21, first entry and p. 208, 97, third and fifth entries.

5 *Ibid.*, MDATV, p. 204, 64, last entry.

6 *Ibid.*, MDATV, p. 208, 98, last entry.

7 *Ibid.*, MDATV, p. 209, 108, third entry.

8 *Ibid.*, MDATV, p. 214, 149, fourth entry.

9 *Ibid.*, MDATV, pp. 202-3, 55, fourth entry.

10 *Ibid.*, MDATV, p. 199, 27, third entry.

11 *Ibid.*, MDATV, p. 205, 70, fifth entry.

12 *Ibid.*, MDATV, p. 196, 13.

13 *Ibid.*, MDATV, p. 198, 24, last entry.

14 *Ibid.*, MDATV, p. 199, 28, fourth entry.

15 *Ibid.*, MDATV, p. 207, 97, first entry.

16 *Ibid.*, MDATV, p. 215, 150, third entry.

17 *Ibid.*, MDATV, p. 215, 153, first entry.

18 *Ibid.*, MDATV, p. 215, 155, first entry.

19 *Ibid.*, MDATV, p. 216, 162, second entry.

20 *Ibid.*, MDATV, p. 196, 15, third entry.

21 *Ibid.*, MDATV, p. 197, 21, second entry.

22 *Ibid.*, MDATV, p. 197, 22, second entry.

23 *Ibid.*, MDATV, p. 198, 22, third entry.

24 *Ibid.*, MDATV, p. 198, 27, first entry.

25 *Ibid.*, MDATV, p. 199, 31, fourth entry.

26 *Ibid.*, MDATV, p. 199, 31, seventh entry.

27 *Ibid.*, MDATV, p. 202, 49.

28 *Ibid.*, MDATV, p. 202, 50, fourth entry.

29 *Ibid.*, MDATV, p. 207, 96, second entry.

'A CARICATURE OF HIS OWN VOICE': FORD AND SELF-EDITING IN *PARADE'S END*

Isabelle Brasme

Besides and beyond the immediate meaning of selecting and preparing texts for publication, editing denotes more largely the activity of reassessing a work and altering it to suit a particular design. While Ford performed as editor for his own, and others', works, I wish to focus here on the way in which his vocation as a literary editor also forms an intrinsic part of his novelistic aesthetics. It seems to me significant that Ford edited the *transatlantic review* at the very moment when he was working on the beginning of *Parade's End*, and even had parts of *Some Do Not . . .* published in the magazine. Ford's interest in editing, altering, and refining a text, may indeed also be considered as a literary agenda for his novelistic work. Reading *Parade's End*, while bearing in mind the contemporaneous activities of Ford as editor, brings a new and fertile perspective to the various processes of alteration and suppression that are everywhere to be found in *Parade's End*.

My purpose here is not to discuss the literal processes of revision at work in the various manuscripts of *Parade's End*: these will be addressed in the forthcoming annotated critical edition of *Parade's End* by Max Saunders, Joseph Wiesenfarth, Sara Haslam and Paul Skinner. No doubt this publication will bring a new dimension to the question of self-editing in *Parade's End*. Likewise, I do not address the minor revisions between the version of *Some Do Not . . .* published in the *transatlantic review* and the Duckworth edition. Rather, my focus here is to examine the process of editing as a literary paradigm and as an aesthetic agenda on the part of Ford.

We shall first see in what way the specific use of punctuation alerts us to a text that is shown as undergoing a constant and open process of self-editing. We shall also observe that this stance is shared to some degree by the characters, through their practice of Englishness. Moreover, through the constant rewriting of their stances and statements, both the characters and the writer adopt a position akin to that of a film editor. Finally, it should prove interesting to observe how the final volume of the tetralogy acts as a major addendum to the work and constitutes a sweeping gesture of a re-editing of the whole.

Self-editing as a major aesthetic stance of the text

Ford's text keeps signalling the potentiality of stating something and simultaneously amending it. There is a constant vibration between the elaboration of an initial text, and the re-editing of this text.

This is first made apparent in the novels' titles. Titles serve as the initial interface between the reader and the literary work; as such, they are the object of much attention in the editing process – and often of controversy between author and editor. 'Some Do Not . . .' is perhaps the most interesting title in this respect, in that it relates the text's constant process of self-correction to that of the characters, which we shall observe later. The phrase forming the title of the first novel, 'Some do not', occurs several times in the novel itself, and is opposed several times to its positive counterpart, 'some do'. The two faces – the temptation of an uncensored, un-amended story – 'some do' –, and its suppressed, decent version – 'some do not' – are thus given to exist simultaneously in the mind of the reader.

Another major element in this and in another title of the tetralogy's, is the specific use of punctuation: the suspension dots in *Some Do Not . . .*, and the dash in *A Man Could Stand Up –*. Such punctuation is not commonly found in titles; before we have even opened the book, we are thus made aware that a highly specific use of punctuation will be at work in the novels. These punctuation marks also bespeak Ford's keen interest in an accurate and significant use of the typographic means at his disposal.

Both the suspension dots and the dashes also function as instruments for editing a first version, a first layer of text. One may open *Parade's End* at any page and be certain to find an impressive number of suspension dots. The text appears literally as holed out, if not hollowed out, by this proliferation of dots. This perforated text may evoke visually the shelled landscapes of Northern France at war. The suspension dots and dashes signal blanks that have been intentionally carved into the text. Besides the bombed landscape of France, this process is also reminiscent of another consequence of war: that of censorship, in which Ford was directly involved during World War I. Censorship constitutes a specific modality of editing, in that it involves reading a text with a view to erase or rephrase its politically questionable content. War censorship *is* mentioned in *Parade's End* – we learn that Tietjens censors his soldiers' letters.

However, censorship is not limited to the context of war in *Parade's End*, nor is it endowed only with a patriotic and political dimension. Throughout the tetralogy, it seems as though an eraser has left gaps in a text that was initially written, or at least intended, as a complete whole; but this whole is never delivered to us.

The dots that pervade conversations and stream-of-consciousness passages act as traces of the characters' suppressed thoughts, of the pauses they make as they are talking or thinking to censor their own speech before putting it into words. This is where the constant process of self-editing of the text echoes that of the characters. Indeed, just as the narration seems permeated with marks of correction and revisions, so do the characters' conversations and inner speeches.

One particular use of the dash symbol illustrates a discrepancy between the soldiers' and the officers' speeches – or more largely, between lower and upper middle classes. The common soldier and the gentleman at war have different ways of swearing. Where the common soldiers say 'bleeding', or more often, 'bleedin'', the upper ranks say – or rather, do NOT say – 'bloody'; as a matter of fact, the word in the text is almost completely suppressed through the censoring dash: the reader is left with 'b—y', and has to guess the word half obliterated by the dash. The dashes do appear visually as a gesture of crossing-out on the part of both the characters and the author.

Editing out one's behaviour: an inherent mark of the English gentleman

Editing out one's behaviour and one's speech constitutes indeed an inherent mark of the English gentleman such as he is described in *Parade's End*.

The quality of being English – which in the novels is usually made equivalent to that of being a gentleman – is hardly ever defined directly in *Parade's End*: instead, it is delineated through a series of suppressions.

Tietjens thus identifies Colonel Levin as non-English because of his inability to check his speech. He remarks to him: 'You betray your non-Anglo-Saxon origin by being so vocal'.[1] Further on, he comments: 'You'll excuse my having been emotional so far. You aren't English, so it won't have embarrassed you' (*NMP* 458). The Englishman thus keeps *editing out* his speech and action. This is perhaps best brought to light in *A Man Could Stand Up* – through one of Tietjens' musings: 'Gentlemen don't earn money. Gentlemen, as a matter of fact, don't do anything. They exist. Perfuming the air like Madonna lilies' (*MCSU* 589). The gentleman is thus essentially characterized by what he chooses *not* to do.

It is indeed through what a gentleman edits out of his behaviour that he is revealed as one. Tietjens and his brother are thus first and foremost described through what they suppress: when they are first shown together in the narration, they are each described as 'completely expressionless' (*SDN* 201). Expressionlessness does not mean here a sheer absence of expression, but rather a voluntary suppression of what one may choose to express. This is best exemplified by Mark's attitude in the final volume of *Parade's End*: Mark in *The Last Post* embodies the resistance of Englishness to change and to foreign influence; this resistance is achieved through obstinate silence. Mark considers his muteness as a deliberate elision of speech (notwithstanding his doctors believing his aphasia is the result of a stroke). Paradoxically, though, *The Last Post* is also the volume in which Mark's inner voice is most present. The contrast between the fluency of Mark's thoughts in *The Last Post* and his actual muteness figures all the more the forceful work of suppression that he exerts over himself.

These corrections and suppressions are not mere subtraction; on the contrary, they generate an added meaning. This emphasis on the characters' and the text's perpetual self-corrections contributes substantially to the dynamism of the work: the markers of editing highlight the perpetual shifts both in the characters' thoughts, and in the text's own aesthetic project.

Film editing

The dual nature of editing as cutting out and editing as adding in is perhaps made most present in the analogy between the narration's structure and film editing.

The process of cutting out parts of a story is explicitly mentioned by the characters. Christopher and Valentine, who may in some respect be considered as the two quintessential instances of Englishness and gentleman- (or woman-)liness in the novel, explicitly articulate their wish to edit out their own story. Towards the end of the first volume, Tietjens asks Valentine to be his mistress, and she accepts; later that day, however, they finally decide *not* to become lovers, and wish they could edit out the moment when they considered what would have amounted to a free, uncensored expression of their feelings. Here is their conversation on this occasion:

> She said:
> 'If we *could* wash out this afternoon. . . . It would make it easier to bear.' [. . .]
> 'Yes, you *can*,' he said. 'You cut out from this afternoon, just before 4.58 it was when I said that to you and you consented . . . [. . . .] To now. . . . Cut it out; and join time up. . . . It can be done. (*SDN* 284-5)

Tietjens' fantasy of cutting out a moment and joining time up resembles very much the process of *film* editing, where the director cuts unwanted bits of filming, and reconnects the reels, leaving out the unwanted parts.

In this respect, Tietjens and Valentine may be considered as wishful doubles of the novelist Ford. Attempting aesthetic experiments, then cutting out what proves to be unsatisfactory, is something Ford is constantly and openly performing in *Parade's End*.

Interestingly, though, in the situation of the characters as in that of the writer, both would-be editors finally decide to leave their story as it is: Valentine considers editing her story, but in the end refuses to leave this moment out, unfortunate though it may have been: 'But I wouldn't cut it out . . . It was the first spoken sign' (*SDN* 285). Similarly, while Ford makes amendments to the writing, he is nonetheless careful to leave traces of the initial text. The markers of editing are left within the text as a way to draw our attention to various coexisting versions of the story. The temptation of cutting things out is made obvious, but is not carried to its full conclusion, so that we are not left with a clean and smoothly emended final version.

Besides, film editing is obviously not merely a negative gesture of leaving things out: it also involves reorganizing film cuts in a different order. Editing in the cinematic sense is of course akin to the way in which Ford builds the narration in *Parade's End*: Ford cuts up the linear story and rearranges the sections into a different order, sometimes leaving whole parts out of the final result. This process is most obvious in the ellipses between the novels, or between the main parts within each of the novels; it is central to the practice of literary impressionism and has been perhaps best brought to light by the narrator of *The Good Soldier*, in this oft-quoted passage:

> When one discusses an affair – a long, sad affair – one goes back, one goes
> forward. One remembers points that one has forgotten and one explains them all
> the more minutely since one recognizes that one has forgotten to mention them in
> proper places and that one may have given, by omitting them, a false impression.[2]

This process is everywhere at work in *Parade's End*. Ford's narration aims at rendering this process of omission, of flashback, and of belated emendation. Editing thus involves here both cutting out and adding in elements.

Moreover, by rearranging them into different patterns and setting them in varying contexts, Ford imbues the initial occurrences with a renewed richness of meaning.

Variation-within-repetition
Another mode through which the text appears to be re-edited in the course of the writing is the phenomenon of variation-within-repetition. The text is continually quoting itself, albeit with slight and not-so-slight variations. While one may wonder at first whether these are not involuntary misquotations of the text by itself, they are however too numerous – and we owe Ford's intelligence too much respect – not to be considered as programmatic.

For instance, in *A Man Could Stand Up –*, Campion writes a report and then pauses to reflect on the situation. Going back to his report after a while, he reads again the last sentences that he has previously written; except they are now altered. When his report is first quoted, it ends with 'conclusion of hostilities'; when it is mentioned again after his digression, the last words have become 'termination of hostilities' (*MCSU* 468-9). Nothing in the narration indicates that Campion has intentionally altered his text. This is but one of many instances of this phenomenon in *Parade's End*; one may wonder if these discreet shifts are not there as subtle hints to the text's perpetual movement of auto-correction.

Even when the text is repeated exactly, the context in which the repetition takes place invites us to reconsider the first occurrence in the light of the latter. This phenomenon is made explicit at the end of *Some Do Not . . .*, when Tietjens recalls words that he has uttered several years previously, in the first pages of the novel, and before the war broke out.

> *'I stand for monogamy and chastity. And for no talking about it. Of course if a*
> *man who's a man wants to have a woman he has her. And again no talking about*

> *it. . . .'.* His voice – his own voice – came to him as if from the other end of a
> long-distance telephone. A damn long-distance one! Ten years. . . . (*SDN* 281)

The rendering of the same sentence in italics in the second instance, paired with the analogy of the telephone, highlights the discrepancy between the two occurrences of the same sentence. Because the context and Tietjens' own positions have shifted, because the war has made him reconsider his moral tenets, he now hears his past discourse as 'a caricature of his own voice': 'His own voice, a caricature of his own voice, seemed to come to him: "Gentlemen don't . . ."' (*SDN* 138). The iteration of the 'own', which Tietjens seems to use as if to convince himself of the continuity between his previous tenets and his present state of mind, in effect emphasizes the alterity between his past and present selves. One may wonder whether, through the many processes of iteration and rewriting, Ford did not consider his own text at times as 'a caricature of his own voice'.

The problem lies of course in knowing which of the various versions should impose itself as the right one. While at the front, Tietjens tries to put his relations with Sylvia and Valentine into writing:

> He said to himself that he must put, in exact language, as if he were making a
> report for the use of garrison headquarters, the exact story of himself in his
> relation to his wife. . . . And to Miss Wannop, of course. 'Better put it into
> writing,' he said. (*NMP* 345)

Tietjens suggests again a double of the novelist. However, he keeps correcting his so-called 'exact report'. This is how he narrates his leave-taking with Valentine:

> So I touched the brim of my cap and said: So long! . . . Or perhaps I did not even
> say *so long*. Or she. . . I don't remember. I remember the thoughts I thought and
> the thoughts I gave her credit for thinking. But perhaps she did not think them.
> There is no knowing. (*NMP* 347)

Tietjens thus finally renounces the pretence of knowing and deciding which version is correct. This position is also shared by the narration. Every layer of text is added to the others until they form a palimpsest where no layer is to be given more importance or credit than the others: the text does not settle on a final, definite version whence the previous layers should be expunged. This indecision, however, need not be perceived as negative: on the contrary, while the wish for a

stable meaning needs to be abandoned, this is more than made up for
by the added depths and the enriched meaning that results. Ford may
appear here as experimenting with an aesthetic of the trace – what
endows *Parade's End* with such fascination is precisely what is half
there, and half erased, or half altered as the novel unfolds. Ford offers
a work whose ideological and aesthetic orientations he is consciously
and conspicuously reconsidering in the very course of the writing.

The Last Post as a major gesture of self-editing

The final volume of the tetralogy, *The Last Post*, may appear as the
largest and most significant gesture of self-editing on the part of Ford.
The process of self-editing is here effected on the scale of the whole
tetralogy.

The oft-debated question of the inclusion of the fourth volume
within *Parade's End*, a question equivocated by Ford himself, sustains
the notion of a text whose overall design is continually re-examined,
amended, and eventually left in suspense. The heterogeneous character of *The Last Post* within the tetralogy deepens the impression of
Ford's refusal to smooth out the asperities left by his deliberate shifts
in writing. This in my view contributes to make *The Last Post*
inseparable from the rest of *Parade's End*.

The fourth novel as a whole may indeed appear as a profound
gesture of radical editing of the aesthetic, epistemological and
philosophical project of the whole tetralogy. I propose to examine a
few of the modalities of amendment effected by *The Last Post*.

Mark Tietjens probably offers the most striking re-writing of
the main plot in *Parade's End*. Throughout the novels and up to the
very finale of *The Last Post*, Mark is convinced that his father has
committed suicide on hearing the rumour that his son Christopher is
having an affair with Valentine: Mark's opinion is that his father had
an affair with Mrs. Wannop and that Valentine is his child, and that
the resulting incestuous affair between Christopher and Valentine
drove him to despair. In the very last pages of *The Last Post*, however,
Mark, experiencing an epiphany of sorts, realizes his father did not
commit suicide, and deduces thereby that no incest was perpetrated
either. Another major indecision characterizing the plot in *Parade's
End* is the question of the paternity of Sylvia's son. Here as well,
Mark gains the conviction on seeing Sylvia's son that he is also Christopher's, and therefore not an illegitimate heir to Groby. Through a
series of sweeping statements, Mark quite clearly rewrites the prev-

ious versions to the main strings of the plot: 'The worst of it rolled up together. No suicide. No incest. No by-blow at Groby' (*LP* 832). Once again, one may observe that the plot is eventually reduced to what it is *not*.

The characters are also all profoundly re-evaluated in the fourth novel. Despite hitherto appearing as the main protagonist in *Parade's End*, Christopher Tietjens is hardly present in the final volume, except overhead on a plane; when he does end up making a brief appearance in the very last pages, he is shown very much diminished. The last sentence referring to him in the novel likens him to a contrite, 'dejected bulldog' (*LP* 835). Conversely, Marie-Léonie, who is hardly mentioned in the first three novels, occupies the forefront in the last volume.

A similar reversal occurs when we consider the novels' two main feminine figures: Valentine, who has been represented through-out the first three novels as a paragon of feminine activity and as the embodiment of a new, positive concept of femininity, shuts herself up in her room and appears to regress towards constant bickering. On the other end of the spectrum, Sylvia, who was often presented as Valentine's negative double, is made much more sympathetic in the final volume: she finally relents in her animosity against Tietjens and Valentine, and is even heard to sob.

Another major amendment to the tetralogy that is brought about by the last volume concerns the respective values ascribed to the trivial and to the sublime, to the material and to the ideal. Throughout the first three volumes, Tietjens and Valentine have been presented as above the obsession for the material that is evinced by most of the other characters; and this stance was made to appear as the more positive. This detachment from material things was made most evident at the end of *A Man Could Stand Up –* when Tietjens got rid of all his furniture and Valentine happily embraced his decision: '[The rooms] did not look sordid and forlorn. They looked frugal. And glorious!' (*MCSU* 651). In the final volume, however, Tietjens has become an antique dealer, in consequence of which their house is cluttered with a variety of furniture for sale. Valentine is engrossed in material considerations, from the obsession for the bed in which she insists sleeping and giving birth to her child, down to purchasing new *cache-corsets*. Strikingly, though, this shift is not made to be felt as utterly negative. Marie-Léonie, who has come to occupy the forefront of the narration along with her husband, espouses most fervently the sheer thingness of life; and she is certainly not presented without sympathy.

The Last Post thus highlights and stages most clearly the text's reflexivity and its constant instability between various conflicting versions – of the way to build a narrative, of the characters' values, of the text's possible ideological and aesthetic meaning, and of its consequent positioning within the canons of its time.

Conclusion

The radical *addendum* to *Parade's End* that constitutes *The Last Post* contributes largely in my view to the fascination exerted by the work as a whole. The text's reflexivity and movement of self-questioning and self-correction, while it is at work throughout the four novels, is asserted as the major direction of the final volume; retrospectively, it comes to shed a new perspective on the whole work. It invites us to become in turn editors of our own reading: we are required to consider *Parade's End* anew, in the light of a text that is continually, and creatively, crossing parts of itself out and rewriting an ever-updated version, while allowing traces of the previous text to show underneath. *The Last Post* sounds to some extent as Ford's deliberate 'caricature of his own voice': it may appear as though Ford was intentionally forcing the discrepancy to deepen our uncertainty about the whole. Through this lighter-hearted volume, Ford points out his will not to take his own aesthetic choices for granted, but to keep them continually in progress.

NOTES

1   *No More Parades* (henceforth *NMP*) in Ford Madox Ford, *Parade's End*, Harmondsworth: Penguin, 1982, p. 454. Page numbers are given in parentheses in the body of the text with the abbreviation for the volume title. Abbreviations for the other volumes in the tetralogy shall stand as such: *SDN* for *Some Do Not . . .*, *MCSU* for *A Man Could Stand Up –*, and *LP* for *The Last Post*.
2   Ford Madox Ford, *The Good Soldier*, ed. Martin Stannard, New York: Norton, 1995, p. 120.

EDITING FORD MADOX FORD'S POETRY

Ashley Chantler

This essay considers some of the issues that impact on an editor of Ford's poetry, but also on an editor of any student-focused poetry collection and on tutors who want their students to be sensitive to more than the meaning of the words on the page, to be aware of and hopefully excited by the complexity of literary history. I use as an example the work that is commonly known as *Antwerp*, which exists in several states.

The earliest extant version is an undated typescript, with revisions in Ford's hand, titled 'October 1914', which is held in the Ford archive at Cornell University. This would almost certainly have been based on an autograph manuscript (AMS): having analysed much of Ford's pre-publication material, it seems that Ford usually composed poetry by hand. Judging by the scrawls, he would often write rather quickly, then either write out the poem again or type it up. Robert Lowell recounts how Ford 'wrote poetry with his left hand – casually and even contemptuously',[1] and in the preface of the 1913 *Collected Poems*, Ford states:

> the writing of verse hardly appears to me to be a matter of work: it is a process, as far as I am concerned, too uncontrollable. From time to time words in verse form have come into my head and I have written them down, quite powerlessly and without much interest, under the stress of certain emotions. And, as for knowing whether one or the other is good, bad or indifferent, I simply cannot begin to trust myself to make a selection.[2]

In the early days of his poetry career, Ford would not even type up a copy for printers to work from: the printers who produced *The Questions at the Well* (1893), for example, worked from a neatly written manuscript, some of whose poems had gone through three or four drafts.

Around the time of the 'October 1914' typescript, Richard Aldington was acting as Ford's secretary/amanuensis:

Ford claimed that writer's cramp made it impossible for him to write himself,
and he certainly wrote a detestable hand. But I think he enjoyed dictation
[. . . .] During the months I worked with him I believe he turned out 6000 to
8000 words a week. Which didn't prevent his writing poetry. I well remember
his reading us the first draft of his best poem, *On Heaven*, and later on, the
poem about Antwerp and some shorter poems inspired by the delicate intense
work of H. D.[3]

This supports the theory of a (now lost) manuscript written by Ford
rather than dictated. Who produced the 'October 1914' typescript is
not known, but the spelling errors and idiosyncratic suspension dots
suggest it was Ford. The typescript opens thus (square brackets
contain text deleted in pen; curly brackets contain handwritten
corrections or revisions):

Gloom!
An[d] October like November;
August a hundred thousand hours,
And all September,
A hundred thousand, dragging, sunlit days,
And half October like a thousand years....
And doom!

That then was Antwerp......
                    In the name of God,
How could they do it?
[Those were the bravest men that ever lived;]
Those sorts of souls that dived
Into the dirty caverns of mines;
{They} hived
In whitened hovels under ragged poplars
{L}umbering to work {over} the gr{e}asy mud{, over} the greasy sod....
That man there, with the appearance of a clod,
Is the bravest man that a fat, gross priest of God
Ever shrived....

    It is not for me to sing him an anthem;

The second surviving text is 'In October 1914', published in the
Outlook (24 Oct. 1914), which was probably based on a typescript that
is no longer extant. It opens:

GLOOM!
An October like November;
August a hundred thousand hours,
And all September,
A hundred thousand, dragging sunlit days,

> And half October like a thousand years . .
> And doom!
> That then was Antwerp. . .
>   In the name of God,
> How could they do it?
> Those souls that usually dived
> Into the dirty caverns of mines;
> Who usually hived
> In whitened hovels; under ragged poplars;
> Who dragged muddy shovels, over the grassy mud,
> Lumbering to work over the greasy sods. . .
> Those men there, with the appearances of clods
> Were the bravest men that a usually listless priest of God
> Ever shrived. . .
> And it is not for us to make them an anthem.[4]

There are two obvious, substantive variants between this and 'October 1914'. For publication, Ford tones down the 'fat, gross priest of God', making him 'usually listless'. It is not known whether Ford initiated the revision or made it at the insistence of *Outlook* or another third party (Aldington, perhaps, or Violet Hunt). There are possible parallels with Thomas Hardy revising for periodical publication:

> When Thomas Hardy's novels were first published in periodicals, the texts were considerably changed at the urging of editors. Sometimes the alterations were verbal, as the change from 'lewd' to 'gross,' 'loose' to 'wicked,' and 'bawdy' to 'sinful' in *Far from the Madding Crowd*; sometimes they were more substantial, as the omission of the seduction scene from *Tess of the D'Urbervilles* and the substitution of a mock marriage.[5]

Hardy, however, when he 'got his manuscripts ready for book publication [...] restored nearly everything that the magazine editors had made him change';[6] Ford did not revert to 'fat, gross priest', but kept 'usually listless' in all subsequent versions of the poem.

The other substantive variant is the broadening of the poem: 'That man there' becomes 'Those men there' (l. 17); and 'it is not for me to sing him an anthem' is now: 'it is not for us to make them an anthem' (l. 20). The revision was perhaps made for simple aesthetic, phenomenological reasons: it makes the opening stanza more affecting, arguably more shocking; and by avoiding the 'clod', 'sod', 'God' rhyme, the unshriven men are associated more strongly with the earth, the priest alone with God. But there might also be a political reason for including the reader with 'us', which will be returned to later in this essay.

Regarding accidentals, the two suspension dots after 'years' (l. 6) seem initially to be a printer's error; after 'Antwerp' (l. 8) and 'shrived' (l. 19) there are the conventional three. The semi-colons in line 14 are also curious: Ford tended to favour commas, so one would expect him to render the line: 'In whitened hovels, under ragged poplars'. Whether the semi-colons, particularly the first one, a rather unFordian caesura, indicate the intrusion of a third party (typist or printer), it is not possible to say, but Ford kept them in all subsequent versions. Interestingly, in the 1915 pamphlet version, there are two suspension dots after 'years', three after 'Antwerp' and 'shrived'. A coincidence? It is unlikely.

In January 1915, Harold Monro's Poetry Bookshop published *Antwerp*, a pamphlet illustrated by Wyndham Lewis.[7] Judging by similarities between this and the *Outlook* version, the copy-text was the same typescript on which the *Outlook* version was based, assuming Ford did not just give Monro a copy of the 24 October 1914 *Outlook*. Due to lack of material relating to the Poetry Bookshop version, we do not know if the new title was Ford's idea. It is more striking, more resonant, and indeed more political, but it loses the allusion to Heinrich Heine's 'In October 1849' (sometimes given as 'October 1849'), which, like Ford's poem, is a meditation on war, violence, heroism, and poets and musicians making an 'anthem'.[8] Reviewing the pamphlet in *Poetry: A Magazine of Verse*, Harriet Monroe's assistant editor, Alice Corbin Henderson, wrote:

> Mr. Hueffer's poem [has] an arrangement of forked diagonals, and a soldier represented by the sharp onward thrust of lines. Yet what a relief these are after the perpetual pretty-girl covers of our books and magazines! Unfortunately it is not possible to reproduce the very appropriate head-piece for the middle section of Mr. Hueffer's poem – a poem of great beauty which I wish it were possible to quote in full. I think I have had more lasting enjoyment from this poem than from any that I have seen on the war.[9]

A review in the *New Witness* notes:

> After an orgy of such irresponsible balderdash as was crowded into the pages of 'Blast,' Mr. Hueffer steadies himself and, even among the same angular decorations, contrives to appeal to the deep sentiment, the most universal altruistic sentiment perhaps that we are at present capable of – the human faith that is common to all, the admiration of bravery.[10]

Antwerp was reprinted without Lewis's illustrations in Monroe and Henderson's *The New Poetry: An Anthology* (1917). In his review of the anthology, T. S. Eliot declares that 'Mr. Hueffer is well illustrated by the only good poem I have met with on the subject of the war'.[11] It is not known whether his opinion was influenced by the Poetry Bookshop pamphlet, but the wording of the statement suggests that it is possible.

A stemma illustrating the probable genealogy of the poem to 1917 could be presented thus:

Putative AMS
[not extant]
|
'October 1914' TS; undated
(Cornell University)
|
'In October 1914' Putative TS
[not extant]
/\
'In October 1914' (*Outlook*, 1914); *Antwerp* (Poetry Bookshop, 1915)
|
The New Poetry: An Anthology (1917)

For publication in *On Heaven and Poems Written On Active Service* (1918), the copy-text seems to have been the lost 'In October 1914' typescript, or the Poetry Bookshop pamphlet: the final line of part I in both the pamphlet and *On Heaven* is, 'In the name of God, how could they do it?', whereas in *Outlook* the comma is missing. Ford did, however, make one substantive revision. Part IV of the Poetry Bookshop version concludes:

> But the thought of the gloom and the rain
> And the ugly coated figure, standing beside a drain,
> Shall eat itself into your brain:
> And you will say of all heroes: "They fought like the
>   Belgians!"
> And you will say: "He wrought like a Belgian his fate
>   out of gloom,"
> And you will say: "He bought like a Belgian
> His doom."
> And that shall be an honourable name;
> "Belgian" shall be an honourable word,
> As honourable as the fame of the sword,
> As honourable as the mention of the many-chorded lyre,
> And his old coat shall seem as beautiful as the fabrics
>   woven in Tyre.

In *On Heaven*, part IV ends:

> But the thought of the gloom and the rain
> And the ugly coated figure, standing beside a drain,
> Shall eat itself into your brain.
> And that shall be an honourable word;
> "Belgian" shall be an honourable word,
> As honourable as the fame of the sword,
> As honourable as the mention of the many-
>   chorded lyre,
> And his old coat shall seem as beautiful as the
>   fabrics woven in Tyre. (*OH* 22)

By 1918, Ford did not have to be so impassioned, or try so hard to influence reader-response. In the Norton Critical Edition of *The Good Soldier*, Martin Stannard notes that 'Dowell expresses loathing of Belgium, in keeping with Conrad's attack on its rapacious imperialism in *Heart of Darkness* (1899, 1902)':

> There are several substantive variants between [the 'printer's copy'] and [the first English edition], among which are three abusive remarks about Belgium. [...] All are canceled, presumably at proof stage. Belgium, often criticized for her rapacious imperialism, suddenly became on August 4, 1914, the focus of British sympathies. Posters read: 'Remember Belgium. Enlist To-Day.'[12]

The German invasion of Belgium and 'the dramatic appeal from King Albert for assistance [...] led to an almost solid phalanx of national unity in favor of a war which most people seem to have thought would be brief, glorious, and victorious',[13] but there were, of course, objectors and sceptics, and in the autumn of 1914 a poet no doubt still had to work, or at least assume he better work, to make his readers, people like Dowell and Conrad, empathise with Belgians. (Parliamentary Recruiting Committee posters followed the meeting on 3 September 1914 of the 'publications subdepartment'; by early January 1915, over a million are supposed to have been printed.[14]) In *I Have This to Say* (1926), Violet Hunt gives an anecdote about Frieda Lawrence:

> Mrs. Lawrence was in and gave us tea. It was the first time I had seen her. She appeared a handsome, golden-haired, tall woman with a magnificent figure, like a Teutonic goddess. Most charming herself. But it was the autumn of 1914 and reports had come through and we were spilling over with emotion, obviously anti-German in tendency. Joseph Leopold had just written *Antwerp*, which was being recited all over the place. To get the copy for it he had gone

EDITING FORD MADOX FORD'S POETRY

> every night after dinner to Charing Cross and hung over the barrier by the
> arrival platform, watching the fugitive population . . . the dead-faced, black-
> robed women with their feather beds, their children and their little all pressed
> to their bosoms . . . in the wild lights of the station. And the thought that some
> relative of this lady had been the one to drive the troops of fugitives along the
> road in front of the cannon – that detail was all that had come through, then,
> was too much for me. One tiny word of reproach forced from an over-charged
> heart provoked the supreme phrase of contempt magnificently delivered in a
> foreign accent, not till then betrayed:
> 'Dirty Belgians! Who cares for them!'[15]

It might be expected, or at least unsurprising, that 'a Silesian aristocrat', daughter of Baron Friedrich von Richthofen, 'a professsional
soldier',[16] might utter such a statement,[17] but it is not that far removed
in its prejudice from sentimentalist Dowell's (and presumably Ford's)
opinion, in the novel's pre-publication material, of Belgian railway
timetabling: 'It is a mean, dirty trick, typical of the Belgians'.[18]

We can return, then, to the issue of Ford broadening the poem
when revising it for publication in *Outlook*, changing 'it is not for me
to sing him an anthem' to: 'it is not for us to make them an anthem' (l.
20). The reason for doing so might be slightly more complicated than
a simple aesthetic, phenomenological one: by drawing the reader into
the poem through the use of 'us', the Belgians are drawn closer, so the
response to them is more personal, the empathy (not sympathy) more
profound. It can be suggested, therefore, that the revision was, if only
in part, subtly political.

The final version of *Antwerp* published in Ford's lifetime, the
copy-text for which seems to have been the version in *On Heaven*, is
in the 1936 *Collected Poems*. In a 1937 *Poetry* review of the collection, John Peale Bishop states: '*Antwerp* remains one of the
distinguished poems of our time.'[19] It is likely that his first reading
was of the 1915 pamphlet.

A key question for an editor is which version of the work to use
as copy-text. It is considered unscholarly to use different copy-texts
throughout a poetry collection, for example, the first published version
for one poem, the last authorised published version for another. An
editor wanting to capture an author's early intentions will give
primacy to pre-publication material. Fredson Bowers, under the
influence of W. W. Greg, the scholar who looms largest over early
twentieth-century textual editing, has argued that when 'an author's
manuscript is preserved, this has paramount authority'.[20] The manuscript is, however, not necessarily sacrosanct. The first edition may be

used to correct 'positive errors in the accidentals of the manuscript'; when there is no manuscript, 'a later edition that contains corrections or revisions that proceeded from the author' will be used as copy-text.[21] In Ford's case, some poems are preserved in manuscript, some not. To give uniformity to the copy-texts, so the reading texts are not a confusion of states, it is necessary, therefore, to go to the published versions.

The reading texts in Carcanet's 1997 *Selected Poems* are the first published versions. This gives the collection scholarly neatness, but as so often with textual editing, it also raises various issues. What should we call Ford's poem about the Belgians and which version should be reproduced if factors beyond copy-text uniformity are considered: 'October 1914', 'In October 1914' or *Antwerp* (1915, 1918 or 1936)?

Antwerp is *Antwerp* in the same way that *The Good Soldier* is *The Good Solider*, not *The Saddest Story*, whatever Ford's early intentions and the publication of the novel's opening in *Blast* (1914), and the copy-text should be the Poetry Bookshop version, with, if possible, the original illustrations. What we might call the poem's public life proper began with the pamphlet, not the *Outlook* version. It was this that was reviewed in the *New Witness* and by Henderson in *Poetry*; that influenced Monroe and Henderson to include it in *The New Poetry*; that perhaps influenced Eliot's statement in his review; and it is this version that has kept the poem alive in articles and essays after Ford's death.

The influence of the public life of a work on an editor's decisions should not be underestimated. G. Thomas Tanselle, for example, has written:

> When Keats in his sonnet of Chapman's Homer wrote of 'stout Cortez,' rather than Balboa, staring at the Pacific with eagle eyes, he created what has become the classic instance of a factual error in a work of imaginative literature. Yet few readers have been bothered by the error or felt that it detracts from the power of the sonnet, and editors have not regarded it as a crux calling for emendation.[22]

The example raises a number of important editorial issues. 'If "Cortez" need not be or should not be corrected, the reason is not simply that factual inaccuracies are necessarily irrelevant to the artistic success of poems; the reason must instead focus on why it is either impractical or unwise to make a change in this particular case.'

Tanselle goes on to raise questions that cover four areas: the aesthetic, the reader, the author, and the poem's public history. Regarding the last, he asks: 'does the long familiarity of the "Cortez" reading have any bearing on the editor's feeling that a change cannot now be contemplated?'[23] After a rigorous promotion of authorial intention, Tanselle concludes: '"Cortez" must remain, not because author's accidents do not matter, but because it – accident or not in origin – became, as Keats wrote, an inextricable part of the work.'[24] Changing 'Cortez' would create a version of the poem that contradicts the canonical version's place in the history of literature.

In Ford studies, *Antwerp* is 'canonical'. Giving primacy to 'In October 1914' could be seen as an act of 'textual primitivism', to appropriate Jack Stillinger's term of criticism for the editorial approach of the Cornell *Wordsworth* series, which prioritised pre-publication material. Regarding 'I Wandered Lonely as a Cloud', for example, the reader is given a poem with a stanza missing, so not the version for which Wordsworth is famous, the published, public, reviewed, anthologised, much-quoted version. Furthermore, Words-worth's revisions are 'relegated to the apparatus', which are long and complicated, and anyone wishing to reconstruct later versions must do so by 'a process inconvenient to the trained scholar and, realistically considered, out of the question for the student and general reader'.[25]

One of the things Stillinger is concerned about is the influence the Cornell series is likely to have on other, affordable editions. He fears that these will publish Cornell's reading texts, so help to rein-force the effacement of the 'later' Wordsworth. 'In October 1914' could efface the more important *Antwerp*, as has happened already with a recent translation and in an essay.[26] In Carcanet's *Selected Poems*, the poem is titled 'In October 1914 [Antwerp]'. This rightly acknowledges the later poem, but by publishing the *Outlook* version Lewis's illustrations are missing. Also, the lack of a note explaining the impassioned, rather over-the-top lines about 'honourable' Belgians means that students might not think about why Ford needed to be impassioned, so not fully appreciate the relationship between author, reader and historical context. Overall, they might be rather baffled as to why the poem is a major work in Ford's *oeuvre*.

Even the most exciting recent developments in textual criticism, the recognition of the importance of the 'bibliographic code' – the 'body language' of books – has failed to make much of a dent in the traditions of classroom text publication. Among the most compelling presentations of this

approach are works by Marta Werner, Nicholas Frankel, and George
Bornstein, showing spectacularly that bibliography, book history and textual
criticism enrich interpretive criticism. Nevertheless, anthologies of poetry, in
particular, seem dedicated to the notion that poems exist essentially apart from
their originating contexts or material appearances; for, by presenting all
poems in a homogenized type font, they deny each poem's body language.[27]

Publishers should of course be praised for producing affordable,
accessible editions of both canonical and non-canonical authors, but
their general avoidance of illustrations and textual apparatus is problematic. As noted above, Alice Corbin Henderson commented first on
the pamphlet's Vorticist cover, which was 'a relief […]' after the
perpetual pretty-girl covers of our books and magazines', and the *New
Witness* reviewer on *Blast* and the 'angular decorations'. *Antwerp*
exists in relation to *Blast*, Vorticism and other 'books and magazines'.
Its 'bibliographic code', its 'body language', affected, and will still
affect, reader-response, as indeed does, and will, 'homogenized' 'body
language'. Lewis's illustrations and one or two footnotes (which
would add very little to the cost of production) would help students
place the poem at a particular time in cultural history and appreciate
its significance and ongoing critical history.

It would, of course, be possible to use as copy-text the *Outlook*
version and incorporate into it Lewis's illustrations, but as Hans Zeller
has said: 'As long as the editor sees his function as that of a historian,
he has a wide range of freedom in the selection of the version for the
edited text, but this version he must reproduce without contamination'.[28] Zeller's approach to editing is connected to what Peter
Shillingsburg has called the 'historical orientation' in editorial practice, and 'the historical orientation frowns on the mixture of
historically discrete texts'.[29] To mix 'historically discrete texts' is to
produce eclectic texts which mix history, to create a text that never
before existed, which arguably hinders an understanding of the past
and past responses to those texts. But as Bowers has observed, by
trying to be completely objective and printing separate versions, the
documentary editor tends not to supply textual apparatus containing
speculations about corruptions and errors. Worse still is when only a
single version is supplied with no apparatus concerning variants.[30]

The issue of 'contamination' is an important one, especially in
relation to line-breaks and helping students see beyond the words on
the page, complicating their views of 'the author' and his/her
intentions. Critics of Zeller's historical, documentary approach, such

as Bowers and Tanselle, tend to be concerned with reclaiming authorial intention. For them, the author is the original source of the work and should, therefore, be respected, even if the resulting text is an eclectic one. Theories such as Zeller's, which deny the author the primary place in the editor's concerns, are linked to New Historicism and cultural materialism. As Louis A. Montrose has written: 'the newer historical criticism is *new* in its refusal of unproblematized distinctions between "literature" and "history," between "text" and "context"; new in resisting a prevalent tendency to posit and privilege a unified and autonomous individual – whether an Author or a Work – to be set against a social or literary background'.[31] In New Historicism, the author is not seen as god-like, the creator and controller of sacred words, he is just one part of a network:

> The fact is that the works of an artist are produced, at various times and places, and by many different people, in a variety of different textual constitutions (some better than others). Each of these texts is the locus of a process of artistic production and consumption involving the originary author, other people (his audience[s], his publisher, etc.), and certain social institutions.[32]

Poems can be 'contaminated' by homogenised type size and style, standardised presentation, and journals' and publishers' page formats. The pages of *Outlook*, for example, were split into two columns, which meant that the printers had to break a long line in a poem; they also put spaces before colons and after opening (and some closing) double quotation marks:

> And you will say of all heroes : " They fought like the
>   Belgians ! "
> And you will say : " He wrought like a Belgian his fate
>   out of gloom,"
> And you will say : " He bought like a Belgian
> His doom."

These lines are presented in *Selected Poems* thus:

> And you will say of all heroes: 'They fought like the Belgians!'
> And you will say: 'He wrought like a Belgian his fate out of gloom,'
> And you will say: 'He bought like a Belgian his doom.'

They are no doubt closer to the missing typescript, but reproducing the *Outlook* version, with a brief footnote explaining the unauthored presentation, would hopefully get students thinking about more than just the meaning of the lines, about the poem as 'the locus of a process of artistic production and consumption'.

Ideally, then, publishers of poetry collections aimed predominantly at students should allow for some textual apparatus, and in some instances illustrations, and copy-texts should be reproduced as exactly as possible, to prompt discussions about 'the author', authorial intention and the authorised; the text and the work; and the private and public life of literature. The scholarly convention of having uniform copy-texts might then have to be ignored, but so be it: it can lead to 'textual primitivism' and the most important version of a work being erased.

NOTES

1   Robert Lowell, 'On Two Poets', *New York Review of Books*, 6:8 (12 May 1966), 3.

2   Ford, Preface, *Collected Poems*, London: Max Goschen, [1913], p. 9.

3   Richard Aldington, 'Homage to Ford Madox Ford: A Symposium', *New Directions*, 7 (1942), 457.

4   Ford, 'In October 1914', *Outlook*, 34 (24 Oct. 1914), 523.

5   James Thorpe, *Principles of Textual Criticism*, San Marino, California: Huntington Library, 1972, p. 17.

6   *Ibid.*, p. 17.

7   Ll. 2-28, with introduced errors, were published under the title 'Gloom!' in Guido Bruno's *Greenwich Village* (15 Aug. 1915), 91; for further information, see Stephen Rogers, 'Ford's Contribution(s) to Guido Bruno's New York Magazines', *Ford Madox Ford Society Newsletter*, 14 (14 Feb. 2008), 17.

8   Ford, *Antwerp*, London: The Poetry Bookshop, 1915, [p. 1]. Throughout his writing on poetry, Ford praises Heine; in *The March of Literature*, London: George Allen and Unwin, 1939, for example, he states: 'Heine, perhaps the most exquisite of all the world's lyrists since the Greeks, perhaps the greatest of all the world's realistic-bitter romantics, perhaps, at least for his Paris days, the most tragic of deserted literary figures' (pp. 635-6).

9   'A. C. H.', *Poetry: A Magazine of Verse*, 6:3 (June 1915), 153-4.

10 Anon, 'Antwerp. A Poem', *New Witness*, 5 (7 Jan. 1917), 108.

11 'T. S. E.', 'Reflections on Contemporary Poetry', *Egoist*, 4:10 (Nov. 1917), 151.

12 Ford, *The Good Soldier*, ed. Martin Stannard, New York and London: Norton, 1995, pp. 33n9, 187.

13 Roy Douglas, 'Voluntary Enlistment in the first World War and the Work of the Parliamentary Recruiting Committee', *Journal of Modern History*, 42:4 (Dec. 1970), 565.

14 *Ibid.*, p. 568.
15 Violet Hunt, *I Have This to Say: The Story of My Flurried Years*, New York: Boni and Liveright, 1926, p. 259.
16 Richard Aldington, *Portrait of a Genius, But . . .*, London: Four Square, 1963, p. 107.
17 According to Frieda Lawrence, in a 15 January 1955 letter: 'I never said: those "dirty Belgians," I never felt like that!'; quoted in Thomas C. Moser, *The Life in the Fiction of Ford Madox Ford*, Princeton: Princeton University Press, 1980, p. 332, n. 11; see also Arthur Mizener, *The Saddest Story: A Biography of Ford Madox Ford*, London: The Bodley Head, 1972, pp. 281-2.
18 *The Good Soldier*, ed. Stannard, p. 38n1.
19 John Peale Bishop, 'The Poems of Ford Madox Ford', *Poetry*, 50:6 (Sep. 1937), 341.
20 Fredson Bowers, 'Some Principles for Scholarly Editions of Nineteenth-Century American Authors', *Studies in Bibliography*, 17 (1964), 226.
21 *Ibid.*, pp. 226, 223.
22 G. Thomas Tanselle, 'External Fact as an Editorial Problem', *Studies in Bibliography*, 32 (1979), 1.
23 *Ibid.*, p. 2.
24 *Ibid.*, p. 46.
25 Jack Stillinger, 'Textual Primitivism and the Editing of Wordsworth', *Studies in Romanticism*, 28:1 (Spring 1989), 19.
26 Cristoforo Schweeger (trans.), 'Im Oktober 1914', *Vater und Sohn: Franz Hüffer und Ford Madox Ford (Hüffer)*, ed. Jörg W. Rademacher, Münster: Lit Verlag, 2003, pp. 93-7; Jörg W. Rademacher, 'Images of the First World War: Ford's "In October 1914" Read in the Context of Contemporary German Writers', *Ford Madox Ford's Literary Contacts*, ed. Paul Skinner, Amsterdam and New York: Rodopi, 2007, pp. 179-88.
27 Peter L. Shillingsburg, 'Practical Editions of Literary Texts', *Variants*, 4 (2005), 31-2.
28 Hans Zeller, 'A New Approach to the Constitution of Literary Texts', *Studies in Bibliography*, 28 (1975), 245.
29 Peter Shillingsburg, *Scholarly Editing in the Computer Age: Theory and Practice*, Athens, Georgia: University of Georgia Press, 1986, pp. 19-20.
30 Fredson Bowers, 'The Editor and the Question of Value: Another View', *Text*, 4 (1984), 49, 53, 59-63.
31 Louis A. Montrose, 'Professing the Renaissance: The Poetics and Politics of Culture', *The New Historicism*, ed. H. Aram Veeser, New York: Routledge, 1989, p. 18.
32 Jerome J. McGann, *The Beauty of Inflections: Literary Investigations in Historical Method and Theory*, Oxford: Clarendon Press, 1998, p. 119.

CONTRIBUTORS

JOHN ATTRIDGE is a Lecturer in English at the University of New South Wales. His essays on Ford and Conrad have appeared in *Modernism/Modernity*, the *Times Literary Supplement* and *English Literary History*, as well as *Ford Madox Ford: Literary Networks and Cultural Transformations* (IFMFS 7). He is currently completing a book on literary impressionism and the rise of professional society in Britain.

ISABELLE BRASME completed her doctorate on 'Ford Madox Ford's *Parade's End*: Towards an aesthetics of crisis' at the Université Paris 7 – Paris Diderot in 2008. She is now a lecturer in British Literature at the Université de Nîmes. Her interests lie in modernism, transitions and the processes (or lack thereof) of canonization.

ASHLEY CHANTLER is Senior Lecturer in English at the University of Chester. He is the Series Editor of Continuum's *Character Studies*; the author of *Heart of Darkness: Character Studies* (Continuum, 2008) and co-editor of *Translation Practices: Through Language to Culture* (Rodopi, 2009), *Studying English Literature* (Continuum, 2010) and *Literature and Authenticity, 1780-1900* (Ashgate, forthcoming). He is currently working on Ford's poetry.

ANDRZEJ GASIOREK is a Reader in Twentieth-Century Literature at the University of Birmingham. He is the author of *Realism and After: Postwar British Fiction* (1995), *Wyndham Lewis and Modernism* (2004), *J. G. Ballard* (2005) and co-editor (with Edward Comentale) of *T. E. Hulme and the Question of Modernism* (2006) and (with Daniel Moore) of *Ford Madox Ford: Literary Networks and Cultural Transformations* (IFMFS 7). He edits (with Deborah Parsons and Michael Valdez Moses) the electronic journal *Modernist Cultures*.

SIMON GRIMBLE is a Lecturer in English Studies at Durham University, having previously held a temporary lectureship in English literature and intellectual history at Cambridge University. He is the author of *Landscape, Writing and 'the Condition of England': Ruskin to Modernism* (Edwin Mellen Press, 2004) and has edited an annotated collection of contemporary accounts of the life and work of John Ruskin (Pickering & Chatto, 2005). He is currently working on a study of the relation of prominent Victorian and early twentieth-century writers to their publics.

JASON HARDING is Reader in English Studies at Durham University and a Visiting Research Fellow at the Institute of English Studies, University of London. He is the author of *The Criterion: Cultural Politics and Periodical Networks in Interwar Britain* (Oxford University Press, 2002), co-editor (with Giovanni Cianci) of *T. S. Eliot and the Concept of Tradition* (Cambridge University Press, 2007) and editor of *T. S. Eliot in Context* (Cambridge University Press, forthcoming). He is currently part of a three-year AHRC funded project to produce standard editions of *T. S. Eliot's Complete Prose*.

PHILIP HORNE is Professor of English Literature at University College London. He is the author of *Henry James and Revision* (Oxford University Press, 1990) and the editor of James's *The Tragic Muse* (Penguin, 1995), *Henry James: A Life in Letters* (Penguin, 1999), Charles Dickens's *Oliver Twist* (Penguin Classics, 2002) and James's *The Portrait of a Lady* (Penguin, forthcoming). He is currently Series Editor of the Penguin Classics Henry James. He writes regularly on film and literature for newspapers and magazines.

NICK HUBBLE is Lecturer in Modern and Contemporary Literature at Brunel University. His monograph *Mass-Observation and Everyday Life* (Palgrave Macmillan, 2006) provides a cultural history and critical exposition of the social research organization founded in 1937. He has also published articles on Ford (in IFMFS 5 &7), Pat Barker, William Empson, B. S. Johnson, George Orwell, Salman Rushdie and Christopher Priest. Most recently, he has contributed a chapter to Kristin Bluemel's *Intermodernism* (Edinburgh University Press, 2010).

GEORGE HYDE was until his retirement Professor of English and Comparative Literature at Kyoto Women's University and a Senior Research Fellow at the University of East Anglia. His publications include full-length studies of the novels of Vladimir Nabokov (Marion Boyars, 1977) and D. H. Lawrence (Macmillan, 1990), translations of

Vladimir Mayakovsky's *How Are Verses Made?* and *A Cloud in Trousers* (Bristol Press, 1990) and Krzysztof Miklaszewski's *Encounters with Tadeusz Kantor* (Routledge, 2002).

ELENA LAMBERTI teaches American and Canadian Literature at the University of Bologna. She is the author of *Marshall McLuhan: tra letteratura, arte e media* (Bruno Mondadori, 2000) and *Interpreting/Translating European Modernism: A Comparative Approach* (Compositori, 2001), and the co-editor (with Vita Fortunati) of a volume of Ford's essays translated into Italian, *Il senso critico: saggi di Ford Madox Ford* (Alinea, 2001), and a collection of critical essays on him, *Ford Madox Ford and The Republic of Letters* (CLUEB, 2002). She also co-edited with Vita Fortunati *Memories and Representations of War in Europe: The Case of WW1 and WW2* (Rodopi, 2009) and is currently completing two volumes for the University of Toronto Press.

GENE M. MOORE teaches English and American literature at the Universiteit van Amsterdam. His major publications include a comparative study of Marcel Proust and Robert Musil, *Conrad's Cities*, *Conrad on Film*, the *Oxford Reader's Companion to Conrad*, *Faulkner's Indians* and a casebook on *Heart of Darkness*. He has also co-edited the final two volumes of *The Collected Letters of Joseph Conrad* and the Cambridge edition of Conrad's *Suspense*. Current projects include essays on Edith Wharton and William Faulkner and a book to be called *Conrad and the Margins of Empire*.

ELIZABETH O'CONNOR is a doctoral candidate at Fordham University in New York. Her dissertation investigates the interaction of urban female characters with commodity culture in works by Joyce, Rhys and Kate O'Brien. She has published a book chapter on *fin de siècle* little magazines and contributed to *Woolf Studies Annual*.

SEAMUS O'MALLEY is a doctoral student at the Graduate Center of the City University of New York (CUNY). He received his B.A. from New York University and his M.A. from Hunter College, New York. He is currently finishing a dissertation on modernism and historiography in the works of Ford, Conrad and Rebecca West.

RICHARD PRICE is Head of Modern British Collections at the British Library. He is the author of the Whitbread-shortlisted poems *Lucky Day* (Carcanet, 2005) and, more recently, *Greenfields* (Carcanet, 2007) and *Rays* (Carcanet, 2009). He is the editor (with James McGonigal) of *The Star you Steer By: Basil Bunting and British Modernism* (Rodopi, 2000) and (with David Miller) *British Poetry Magazines 1914-2000* (British Library, 2006).

PETER ROBINSON is Professor of English and American Literature at Reading University. He has published over thirty books of poetry, translations, aphorisms, and literary criticism including *The Greener Meadow: Selected Poems of Luciano Erba* (Princeton University Press, 2007), for which he was awarded the John Florio Prize, *The Look of Goodbye: Poems 2001-2006* (Shearsman, 2008), *Poetry & Translation: The Art of the Impossible* (Liverpool University Press, 2009), *Spirits of the Stair: Selected Aphorisms* (Shearsman, 2009) and a limited edition with artworks by Sally Castle, *English Nettles and Other Reading Poems* (Two Rivers Press, 2010).

STEPHEN ROGERS is a researcher working on the Modernist Magazines Project at the University of Sussex. He has written on Austin Osman Spare's *Form* (1916) and *The Golden Hind* (1922-4), and the poetry magazine *The Decachord* (1924-31) for *The Oxford Critical and Cultural History of Modernist Magazines, Vol. I: Great Britain and Ireland, 1880-1955* (Oxford University Press, 2009) and on Guido Bruno, Vachel Lindsay and literary magazines in Greenwich Village for *The Oxford Critical and Cultural History of Modernist Magazines, Vol. II: North America, 1880-1960* (Oxford University Press, 2010). He is currently editing *Some Poems by Harold Monro* for the Greville Press.

MAX SAUNDERS is Professor of English at King's College London. He is the author of *Ford Madox Ford: A Dual Life*, 2 volumes (Oxford University Press, 1996), the editor of Ford's *Selected Poems, War Prose*, and (with Richard Stang) *Critical Essays* (Carcanet, 1997, 1999, 2002), and has published essays on Life-writing, Impressionism and on many nineteenth and twentieth-century authors. His most recent book is *Self-Impression: Life-Writing, Autobiografiction, and the Forms of Modern Literature* (Oxford University Press, 2010). He is the general editor of International Ford Madox Ford Studies and was chairman of the Ford Society from 1997 to 2007.

MARTIN STANNARD is Professor of Modern English Literature at the University of Leicester. He has published extensively on Evelyn Waugh, including *The Critical Heritage* (1984), followed by a major biography in two volumes (1986 and 1992). His *Muriel Spark: The Biography* appeared in 2009 and he has also published on a wide variety of modern authors, on textual criticism, biography, auto-biography, and letters. In 1995, he edited the Norton Critical Edition of Ford's *The Good Soldier*. He is a Fellow of the Royal Society of Literature and a Fellow of the English Association.

NORA TOMLINSON worked for the Open University from 1971, when the first students were admitted. Until her retirement, she was a course tutor, counsellor, and a writing contributor to several course teams. During this time she was awarded a Ph.D. on 'The Achievement of Ford Madox Ford as Editor'. She contributed the introduction to the *English Review* for the online Modernist Journals Project at Brown University.

ABSTRACTS

JOHN ATTRIDGE 'Liberalism and Modernism in the Edwardian Era: New Liberals at Ford's *English Review*'

This chapter fills in some of the detail in our picture of the *English Review*'s politics by identifying a previously unnoticed bloc within its list of contributors, several of whom were associated with a form of Liberal collectivism known to Edwardian observers as New Liberalism. I trace the presence of this group of writers in Ford's magazine and suggest how and why they may have ended up there, focusing particularly on the six essays published there by the rogue economist, anti-imperialist and prominent New Liberal J. A. Hobson. Finally, I propose an oblique and unexpected correlation between the New Liberal political outlook and Ford's own. Although Ford's incorrigible Tory leanings would have made New Liberal political theory hard for him to stomach, his belief in the role played by sentiment and idealism in the public sphere does align him with one aspect of New Liberal thinking.

ISABELLE BRASME '"A caricature of his own voice": Ford and Self-Editing in *Parade's End*'

This chapter argues that Ford's vocation as editor also forms an intrinsic part of his novelistic aesthetics. Ford's interest in editing may also be considered as a literary agenda for his novelistic work, which is particularly apparent in *Parade's End*. Ford thus keeps asserting and then re-evaluating his views on ideology, philosophy and aesthetics. The use of punctuation signals a text that is undergoing a constant and open process of self-editing. This process is shared to some degree by the characters. Moreover, through the rewriting of their stances and statements, both the characters and the writer adopt a position akin to that of a film editor. Finally, the concluding volume of the tetralogy may be considered as a major addendum to the work and a sweeping gesture of re-editing of the whole. This process of doing and undoing contributes to the dynanism of the work.

ASHLEY CHANTLER 'Editing Ford Madox Ford's Poetry'

Using the work that is commonly known as *Antwerp* (1915), this chapter considers some of the issues that impact on an editor of Ford's poetry, but also on editors of student-focused poetry collections. Topics discussed include: the choice and emendation of copy-texts; 'textual primitivism' and the use of early versions as reading texts; assumptions about errors and third-party intrusion; the influence of the imagined reader and historical context on the revising author and the public life of a work on an editor; the importance of reproducing copy-texts as exactly as possible, but including some textual apparatus; and the burden on an editor of the scholarly convention of having uniform copy-texts throughout a collection.

ANDRZEJ GASIOREK 'Editing the *transatlantic review*: Literary Magazines and the Public Sphere'

This chapter explores Ford Madox Ford's aims in editing the *transatlantic review* after the First World War. It suggests that Ford sought to bring together in one journal contemporary writings from various aesthetic traditions and national backgrounds; to encourage communication between writers and artists from different societies; to contribute to the cultural reconstruction of post-war Europe; to publish the most interesting writing of the day, and to establish continuities between pre- and post-war literature and art. Ford was always in favour of artistically innovative writing, but he drew the line at Surrealism and Dada (and specifically the work of Elsa von Freytag-Loringhoven). Ford held that the French literature he admired was being cast to one side by Dada and Surrealism. In contrast to these movements' iconoclastic 'radicalism' Ford sought to maintain continuity with the past, to defend the aesthetic as a category, and to argue that imaginative writing was a key component of a properly functioning public sphere.

SIMON GRIMBLE '"A few inches above the moral atmosphere of these islands": The Perspectives of the *English Review*'

In this chapter, I examine the various perspectives that Ford builds into his written editorial contributions to the *English Review* and think about some of his rather conflicted positions: the public moralist who despises public moralising, the (sometime) anti-Englishness of his *English Review*, the author of ringing editorials who thinks that such editorialising is a defunct mode. In all of this, I will try to locate where this elusive figure is, in fact, speaking from: from some commanding Parnassian or Olympian height or from a ground-level position where he can 'observe only the little things'.

PHILIP HORNE 'Henry James and the *English Review*'

This chapter reviews the relationship between Ford and James, considers the editorial policies of the *English Review* in relation to James's critical attitudes, and examines in this context James's profile in the magazine, both in the editorial matter and in the James stories that appeared there – 'The Jolly Corner', 'The Velvet Glove', 'Mora Montravers' and 'A Round of Visits'. By looking at the details of their publishing history, it argues that 'Mora Montravers' is the only one written specially for the magazine; but reads that story and 'The Velvet Glove' as, in a number of respects, in sympathy with Ford's high editorial intentions.

NICK HUBBLE 'A Music-Hall Double Act: Fordie and Wells's *English Review*'

While the editorial decisions Ford made concerning the *English Review* in the boxes and stalls of local music-halls might seem a world away in seriousness of intent from the performance on the stage, this chapter takes the position that both activities were complementary; with the various turns offering the spectator an insight into the unconscious motivations underlying the ostensible cultural and political purposes of the age. A similar complementary paradigm can be constructed around one of the key personal and working relationships concerned with the *English Review* – that between Ford and Wells. While numerous earnest, not to mention pompous, petty quarrels between the two seem to provide real-life justification for a critical reception that separates them into member of the modernist canon and the straw man of social-realist mimetic fiction, the actual relationship was much more complex as demonstrated by the sheer satirical excess of the two's fictional portraits of each other. By reading elements of Wells's *Tono-Bungay*, *Boon* and *The Bulpington of Blup* against elements of Ford's *The Simple Life Limited* and *The New Humpty-Dumpty*, it is possible to chart the ebb and flow of a relationship that bridged the fault-lines of Edwardian cultural politics. Such a reading illuminates the undoubted significance and influence of the *English Review* but it also highlights the opportunity that was lost because an extraordinary cultural moment could not be held open longer than it was.

GEORGE HYDE 'Lawrence, Ford, Strong Readings, and Weak Nerves'

As editor of the *English Review*, Ford played a major part in introducing the young Lawrence to the reading public. He branded Lawrence a realist, thereby associating him with French writers like Flaubert and Maupassant. Lawrence's appreciation was tempered with dismay at being labelled a 'genius' when he was still finding his way and penniless. Moreover, the doctrine of 'realism' smacked of inacceptable detachment from the fictional world. Lawrence felt that Ford could not help him much more, though by introducing him to Edward Garnett he did him a big favour. Garnett was just the man to help Lawrence with *Sons and Lovers*, and his wife Constance was translating Dostoevsky, whom Lawrence in the end came to see as a great writer. By the mid-20s the 'Ford effect' was a thing of the past.

ELENA LAMBERTI '"Wandering Yankees": The *transatlantic review* or How the Americans Came to Europe'

This essay explores Frank MacShane's definition of the *transatlantic review* as 'essentially the bringer of America to Europe'. Notwith-standing Ford's original intentions (to establish an 'International Republic of Letters'), the *transatlantic review* was not a new *English Review* bringing various traditions together and talent scouting new would-be writers; similarly, it was not an outstanding literary review mirroring what was blooming in Paris at the time; it was the one which bore witness to the dawning Americanisation of the twentieth century. Following Pound's suggestion, Ford took on Hemingway as his assistant editor and Hemingway performed that role by fully embracing the spirit of the 'wandering Yankee' whose praise is sung by Lt. Pinkerton in Puccini's famous opera, *Madama Butterfly*. The American shock waves overwhelmed Ford's editorial strategy to the extent that the *transatlantic review* became the torchbearer of the new American literary and artistic Risorgimento.

GENE M. MOORE 'Ford as Editor in Joseph Conrad's "The Planter of Malata"'

Ford Madox Ford has been criticized for his unflattering portrait of Joseph Conrad as the author Simon Bransdon in *The Simple Life Limited*, but there is no hard evidence of malicious intent on Ford's part, nor of actual offence taken by Conrad. The instances where Conrad is thought to have subjected Ford to similar treatment are also unconvincing. However, the unnamed Editor in Conrad's story 'The Planter of Malata' bears a striking resemblance to Ford in many respects that offer grounds for a reevaluation of the relationship between the two authors and their use of each other as characters.

ELIZABETH O'CONNOR 'Jean Rhys's *Quartet*: A Re-inscription of Ford's *The Good Soldier*'

Ford Madox Ford's influence on Jean Rhys's personal and artistic life has been a source of frequent critical comment. Too often, however, critics emphasize the autobiographical aspects of the works produced after the affair, speculating on the correspondence of fictional characters to real life counterparts, discussing the differences between the various accounts, or debating whose version of events is most authentic, and neglect a full appreciation of the texts themselves. Rather than dwell on the biographical details of Ford and Rhys's 'entanglement', in this chapter I argue that Rhys writes back to Ford in *Quartet* by transforming and centrally responding to *The Good Soldier's* portrayal of the power dynamics of gender, class, and the male gaze. As a key in examining Rhys's intertextuality, I use Ford's and her repeated invocation of the phrase 'playing the game' and analyze how this common theme is used differently by each author.

SEAMUS O'MALLEY 'The Ferociously Odd, Mutually Beneficial Editorial Relationship of Ford and Wyndham Lewis'

Ford Madox Ford published Wyndham Lewis's first literary works in the *English Review* in 1909. These essays – 'The "Pole"', 'Some Innkeepers and Bestre', and 'Les Saltimbanques' – were purportedly travel sketches of Brittany, but in Lewis's young hands they functioned as discourses on narrative itself. Five years later Lewis was editing

Ford's own meditation on narrative, publishing part of *The Good Soldier* in the first issue of *Blast* (1914). The long relationship of the two writer-editors dates back to these instances of mutual editing. Starting from this early exchange, they used each other as literary foils: Ford repeatedly cast Lewis as an exemplar of the modernist upstart, and Lewis included Ford's work in *Blast* to lend a profess-ional legitimacy to his avant-garde project. Ford was keenly aware of this mutual posturing: his colourful description of accepting the younger writer's manuscripts for the *English Review* serves as a dramatization of the transition from one literary era to the next. Ford described the *Blast* segment of *The Good Soldier* as 'a portion of a novel by myself which appears unexciting when I see it in print', a sharp contrast to the 'ferociously odd sensations' produced by Lewis's Vorticist visual and textual experiments. In spite of these stylistic and generational differences, they continued to praise each other's work throughout their careers even as their editorial relationship came to an end.

RICHARD PRICE '"His care for living English": Ford Madox Ford and Basil Bunting'

This chapter looks at the relationship between Basil Bunting and Ford Madox Ford, briefly working together in Paris on the *transatlantic review*, but Ford a life-long influence on Bunting. The poet would later remember Ford's 'willingness to consider everything [...] his care for living English', championing in the 1960s and 1970s Ford's then largely forgotten poetry. Bunting suggests Ford was understood as a particular kind of innovator in his day, with the poem 'The Starling' exemplifying Ford's quietly modernist approach.

PETER ROBINSON '"Written at least as well as prose": Ford, Pound, and Poetry'

The chapter begins by reconsidering Ford's response to Ezra Pound's *Canzoni*, and the contribution it made to modern poetry in English. It explores relations between Ford's poetry and modernism, to whose precepts his poetry only partly adhered. The characteristics of this adherence are related to the role of beloved interlocutors in Ford's writing, and to the association of his ideas with the Flaubertian *mot juste*. Equivocally expressed support for Ford's poetry from poets such as Robert Lowell and Basil Bunting is addressed, and a case is made for the virtues of Ford's improvisational later style, especially in the 'Poems Written on Active Service' and the longer sections of *Buckshee*. The chapter concludes by looking at two readers' reports for Unwin during a failed 1937 proposal to publish a British edition of his *Collected Poems* (1936) and underlines why, despite the difficulties facing publication, such a volume could still benefit readers.

STEPHEN ROGERS 'The *transatlantic review* (1924)'

This chapter attempts to set the history of Ford's involvement with the *transatlantic review* in the context of recent debates about Modernist magazines. The economic basis of the magazine's creation and production is explored at a time when modern consumer culture was being developed. An account is given of the interrelationships that gave the periodical its shifting position between different groupings amid the emergence of modernist aesthetics and the transnational cross-currents that differentiated conflicting responses. The situation of the magazine is generally explored in relation to commercial pressures of the early 1920s. Ford's method of negotiating these factors is discussed – particularly his reflections on the intrusion of advertisements on the content and make-up of periodical literature, along with some of his retrospective attempts to place the magazine in the formation of post-war strategies of self-fashioning.

MARTIN STANNARD 'Cutting Remarks: What Went Missing from *The Good Soldier*'

The MS and TS of *The Good Soldier* reveal numerous interesting deletions and additions which suggest how Ford developed its characters and plot. Other cuts relate to technical presentation. But some lines seem inadvertently to have been cancelled between MS and TS, and something strange happened to the punctuation before the book was printed. This chapter examines these issues and discusses the editorial problems involved in producing a critical edition of *The Good Soldier*.

NORA TOMLINSON 'An old man mad about writing' but hopeless with money: Ford Madox Ford and the Finances of the *English Review*

This chapter examines the finances of the *English Review*. It uses information about backers, sales and advertising to scrutinise income, and looks at payments to contributors, production costs and advertising to assess expenditure. It concludes that one of the major reasons that Ford lost control of the review was his financial mismanagement.

ABBREVIATIONS

The following abbreviations have been used for works cited several times, whether in the text or in the notes. The list is divided into two alphabetical sections: works by Ford and by others. A full list of the abbreviations used in International Ford Madox Ford Studies can be found on the Ford Society website.

(i) Works by Ford

AL   *Ancient Lights* (London: Chapman & Hall, 1911)

Antwerp   *Antwerp* (London: The Poetry Bookshop, 1915)

CA   *The Critical Attitude* (London: Duckworth, 1911)

CE   *Critical Essays*, ed. Max Saunders and Richard Stang (Manchester: Carcanet Press, 2002)

CP1   *Collected Poems* (London: Max Goschen, 1913)

CP2   *Collected Poems* (New York: Oxford University Press, 1936)

CW   *Critical Writings of Ford Madox Ford*, ed. Frank MacShane (Lincoln: University of Nebraska Press, 1964)

EE   *England and the English*, ed. Sara Haslam (Manchester: Carcanet, 2003)

ER   *English Review,* edited by Ford from 1908-1910

GS   *The Good Soldier* (London: John Lane, 1915)

IWN   *It Was the Nightingale* (London: William Heinemann, 1934)

JC   *Joseph Conrad* (London: Duckworth, 1924)

LF   *Letters of Ford Madox Ford*, ed. Richard M. Ludwig (Princeton, NJ: Princeton University Press, 1965)

LP   *Last Post* (London: Duckworth, 1928)

MCSU   *A Man Could Stand Up –* (London: Duckworth, 1926)

ML   *The March of Literature* (London: George Allen & Unwin, 1939)

MS   *Mightier Than the Sword* (London: George Allen & Unwin, 1938)

NC   *The Nature of a Crime*, (with Joseph Conrad) (London: Duckworth, 1924)

NMP   *No More Parades*; in *Parade's End* (Harmondsworth: Penguin, 1982)

OH   *On Heaven and Poems Written on Active Service* (London: John Lane, 1918)

PE   *Parade's End* (one volume edition of all the Tietjens novels: *Some Do Not . . ., No More Parades, A Man Could Stand Up –,* and *Last Post*) (New York: Alfred A. Knopf, 1950)

Reader   Sondra J. Stang (ed.), *The Ford Madox Ford Reader*, with Foreword by Graham Greene (Manchester: Carcanet, 1986)

RY   *Return to Yesterday* (London: Victor Gollancz, 1931)

SDN   *Some Do Not . . .* (London: Duckworth, 1924)

SLL   *The Simple Life Limited* (London: John Lane, 1911)

TR   *Thus to Revisit* (London: Chapman & Hall, 1921)

TRev   *the transatlantic review*, edited by Ford in 1924

VLR   *Vive Le Roy* (Philadelphia: J. B. Lippincott, 1936)

(ii) Works by Others

Bowen   Stella Bowen, *Drawn from Life* (London: Collins, 1941)

Conrad   *The Collected Letters of Joseph Conrad*, ed. Laurence
             Davies *et al.*, 9 vols (Cambridge: Cambridge University
             Press, 1983-2007)

Critical Heritage Frank MacShane, ed., *Ford Madox Ford: The
             Critical Heritage* (London: Routledge, 1972)

CWB   Wyndham Lewis, *The Complete Wild Body*, ed. Bernard
             Lafourcade (Santa Barbara: Black Sparrow Press, 1982)

Edel   *Henry James Letters*, ed. Leon Edel, 4 vols (Cambridge,
             Mass: Harvard University Press, 1974-84)

FCJ   Brita Lindberg-Seyersted, *Ford Madox Ford and His
             Relationship to Stephen Crane and Henry James* (New
             Jersey: Humanities Press International, 1987)

Horne   *Henry James: A Life in Letters*, ed. Philip Horne
             (London: Penguin, 1999)

Hunt   Violet Hunt, *The Flurried Years* (London: Hurst &
             Blackett, [1926])

Judd   Alan Judd, *Ford Madox Ford* (London: Collins, 1990)

Lawrence   *The Letters of D. H. Lawrence*, ed. James T. Boulton *et
             al.*, 8 vols (Cambridge; Cambridge University Press,
             1979-2001)

MacShane   Frank MacShane, *The Life and Work of Ford Madox
             Ford* (London: Routledge & Kegan Paul, 1965)

Mizener   Arthur Mizener, *The Saddest Story: A Biography of Ford Madox Ford* (New York: Harper & Row, 1971; London: The Bodley Head, 1972)

Najder   Zdzisław Najder, *Joseph Conrad: A Life*, tr. Halina Najder (Rochester: Camden House, 2007)

Poli   Bernard J. Poli, *Ford Madox Ford and the* Transatlantic Review (Syracuse, NY: Syracuse University Press, 1967)

P/F   Brita Lindberg-Seyersted (ed.), *Pound/Ford: the Story of a Literary Friendship: the Correspondence between Ezra Pound and Ford Madox Ford and Their Writings About Each Other* (London: Faber & Faber, 1982)

Presence   *The Presence of Ford Madox Ford*, ed. Sondra J. Stang (Philadelphia: University of Pennsylvania Press, 1981)

Q   Jean Rhys, *Quartet* (New York: Norton, 1985)

RA   Wyndham Lewis, *Rude Assignment* (Santa Barbara: Black Sparrow Press, 1984)

Saunders   Max Saunders, *Ford Madox Ford: A Dual Life*, 2 vols (Oxford: Oxford University Press, 1996)

South Lodge
               Douglas Goldring, *South Lodge: Reminiscences of Violet Hunt, Ford Madox Ford and the English Review Circle* (London: Constable, 1943)

Stang and Cochran
               Sondra Stang and Karen Cochran, eds, *The Correspondence of Ford Madox Ford and Stella Bowen* (Bloomington and Indianapolis: Indiana University Press, 1994)

Stannard   *The Good Soldier*, ed. Martin Stannard, Norton Critical Edition (New York and London: W. W. Norton & Company, 1995)

Hybrid Humour

Comedy in Transcultural
Perspectives

Edited by
Graeme Dunphy and Rainer Emig

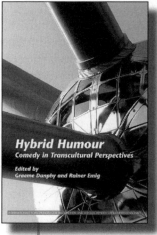

Hybrid Humour
Comedy in Transcultural Perspectives

Edited by
Graeme Dunphy and Rainer Emig

An interdisciplinary and transcultural study of comedy in a pan-European perspective that include East, West, and Southern European examples. These range from humour in Polish poetry via jokes about Italian migrants in English-speaking TV commercials to Turkish comedy, literature and cartoons in Germany, Turkish, Surinamese, Iranian and Moroccan literary humour in the Netherlands, Beur humour in many media in France, and Asian humour in literature, film, and TV series in Great Britain. The volume is prefaced and informed by contemporary postcolonial theories that show humour not as an essential quality of each particular culture or as a common denominator of humanity, but as a complex structure of dialogue, conflict, and sometimes resolution. The volume is of interest for students and scholars of Comparative Literature, Cultural Studies, and Media Studies as well as for students and experts in the cultures and literatures that are covered in the collection of essays. It is relevant for courses on globalisation, migration, and integration.

Amsterdam/New York NY, 2010. 192 pp.
(Internationale Forschungen zur Allgemeinen und Vergleichenden Literaturwissenschaft 130)
Paper € 38,-/ US$ 53,-
E-Book € 38,-/ US$ 53,-
ISBN: 978-90-420-2823-4
ISBN: 978-90-420-2824-1

USA/Canada:
248 East 44th Street, 2nd floor,
New York, NY 10017, USA.
Call Toll-free (US only): T: 1-800-225-3998
F: 1-800-853-3881
All other countries:
Tijnmuiden 7, 1046 AK Amsterdam, The Netherlands
Tel. +31-20-611 48 21 Fax +31-20-447 29 79
Please note that the exchange rate is subject to fluctuations

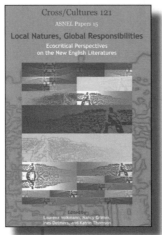

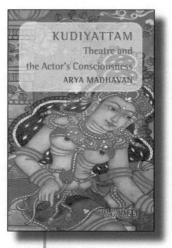